D1237837

WONDER WOMAN
Odyssey

🜂

volume one

DON KRAMER
EDUARDO PANSICA
ALLAN GOLDMAN
DANIEL HDR
Pencillers

MICHAEL BABINSKI
JAY LEISTEN
RUY JOSÉ
SCOTT KOBLISH
MARLO ALQUIZA
WAYNE FAUCHER
EBER FERREIRA
Inkers

ALEX SINCLAIR
Colorist

TRAVIS LANHAM
Letterer

DON KRAMER
Original series cover

ALEX GARNER
Collection cover artist

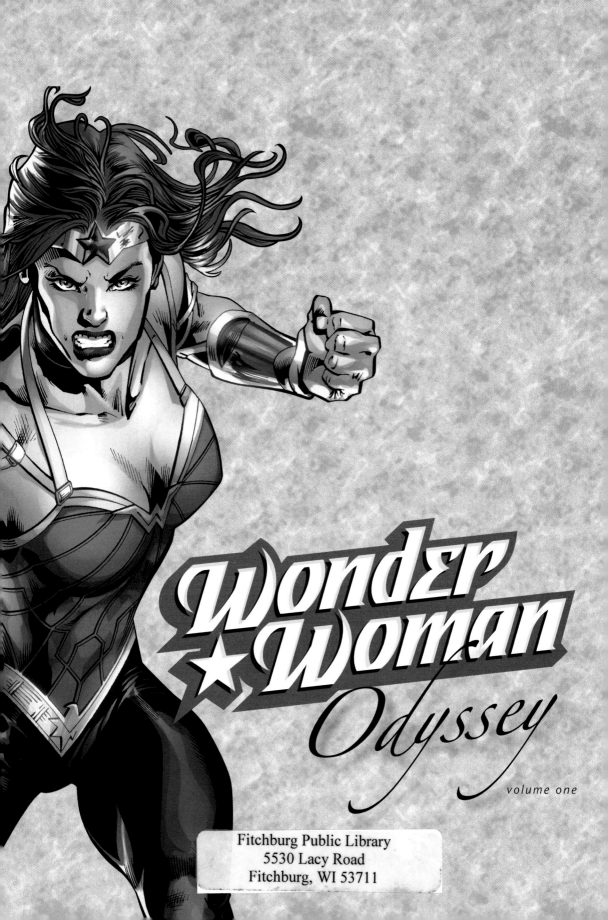

Wonder Woman ★ Woman

Odyssey

volume one

Brian Cunningham Editor-original series
Sean Ryan Associate Editor-original series
Ian Sattler Director, Editorial-Archival Editions
Robbin Brosterman Design Director-Books

Eddie Berganza Executive Editor
Bob Harras VP-Editor in Chief

Diane Nelson President
Dan DiDio and *Jim Lee* Co-Publishers
Geoff Johns Chief Creative Officer
John Rood Executive VP-Sales, Marketing and Business Development
Amy Genkins Senior VP-Business and Legal Affairs
Nairi Gardiner Senior VP-Finance
Jeff Boison VP-Publishing Operations
Mark Chiarello VP-Art Direction and Design
John Cunningham VP-Marketing
Terri Cunningham VP-Talent Relations and Services
Alison Gill Senior VP-Manufacturing and Operations
David Hyde VP-Publicity
Hank Kanalz Senior VP-Digital
Jay Kogan VP-Business and Legal Affairs, Publishing
Jack Mahan VP-Business Affairs, Talent
Nick Napolitano VP-Manufacturing Administration
Ron Perazza VP-Online
Sue Pohja VP-Book Sales
Courtney Simmons Senior VP-Publicity
Bob Wayne Senior VP-Sales

WONDER WOMAN: ODYSSEY VOLUME ONE

DC Comics, 1700 Broadway, New York, NY 10019
A Warner Bros. Entertainment Company
Printed by Quad/Graphics, Versailles, KY, USA. 4/29/11 First printing.
ISBN: 978-1-4012-3077-7
SC ISBN: 978-1-4012-3078-4

SUSTAINABLE FORESTRY INITIATIVE
Certified Chain of Custody
Promoting Sustainable Forest Management
Fiber used in this product line meets the sourcing requirements of the SFI program.
www.sfiprogram.org SGS-SFICOC-0130

Library of Congress Cataloging-in-Publication Data

Straczynski, J. Michael, 1954-
Wonder Woman : odyssey volume one / writer, J. Michael Straczynski ; pencils, Don Kramer.
p. cm.
"Originally published in single magazine form in Wonder Woman #600-606."
ISBN 978-1-4012-3077-7 (hardcover)
1. Graphic novels. I. Kramer, Don. II. Title. III. Title: Odyssey.
PN6728.W6S77 2011
741.5'973--dc22
2011008844

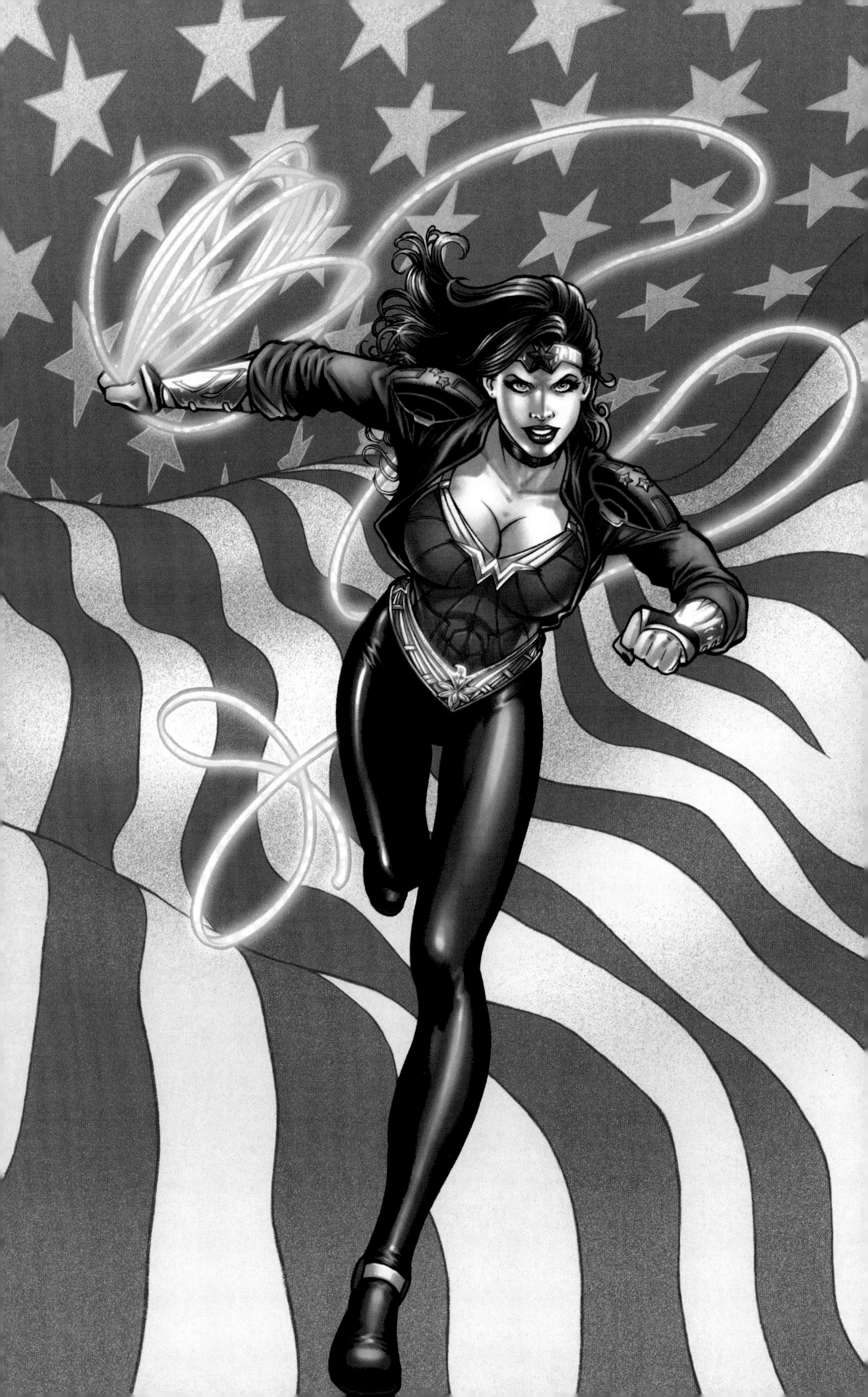

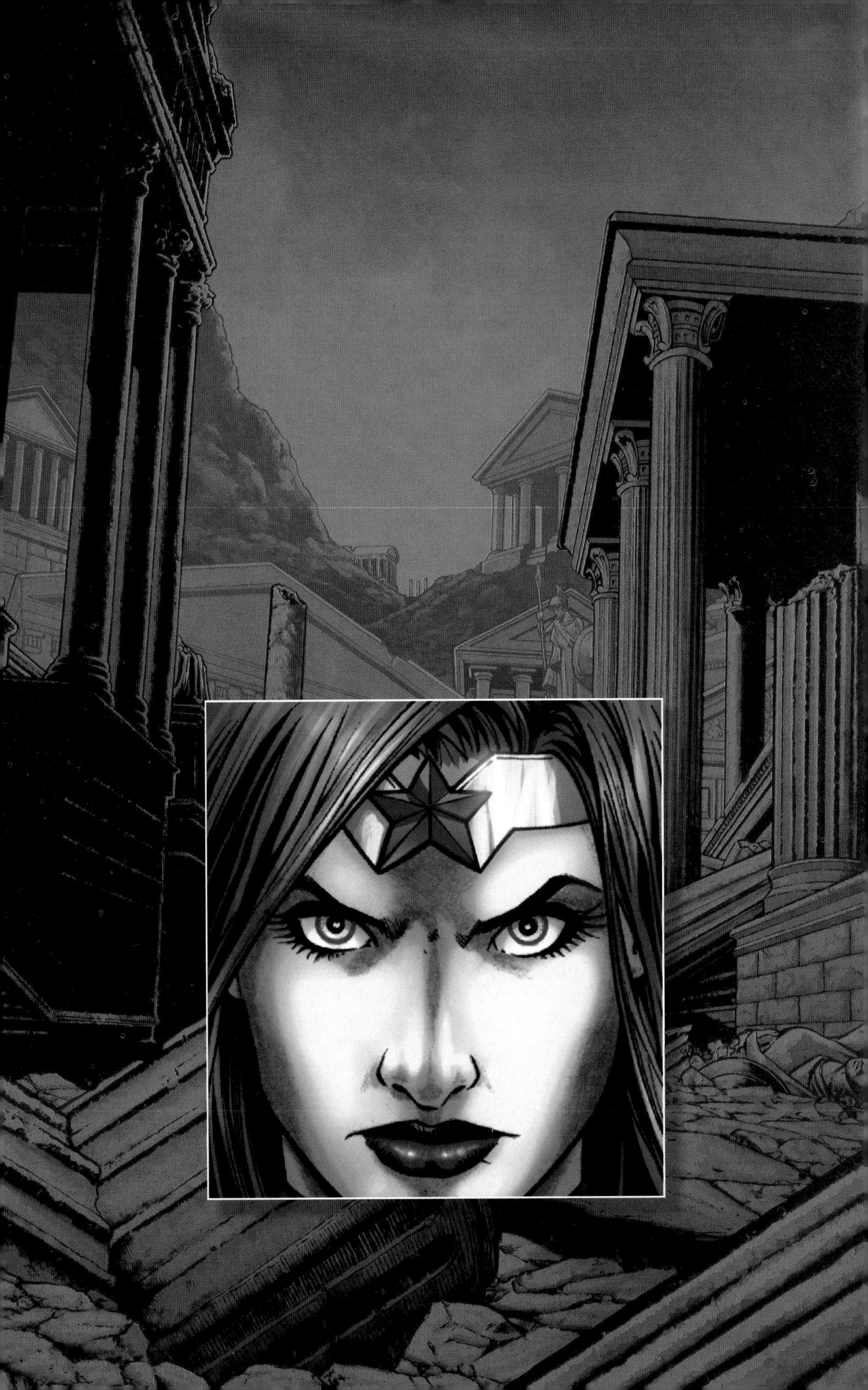

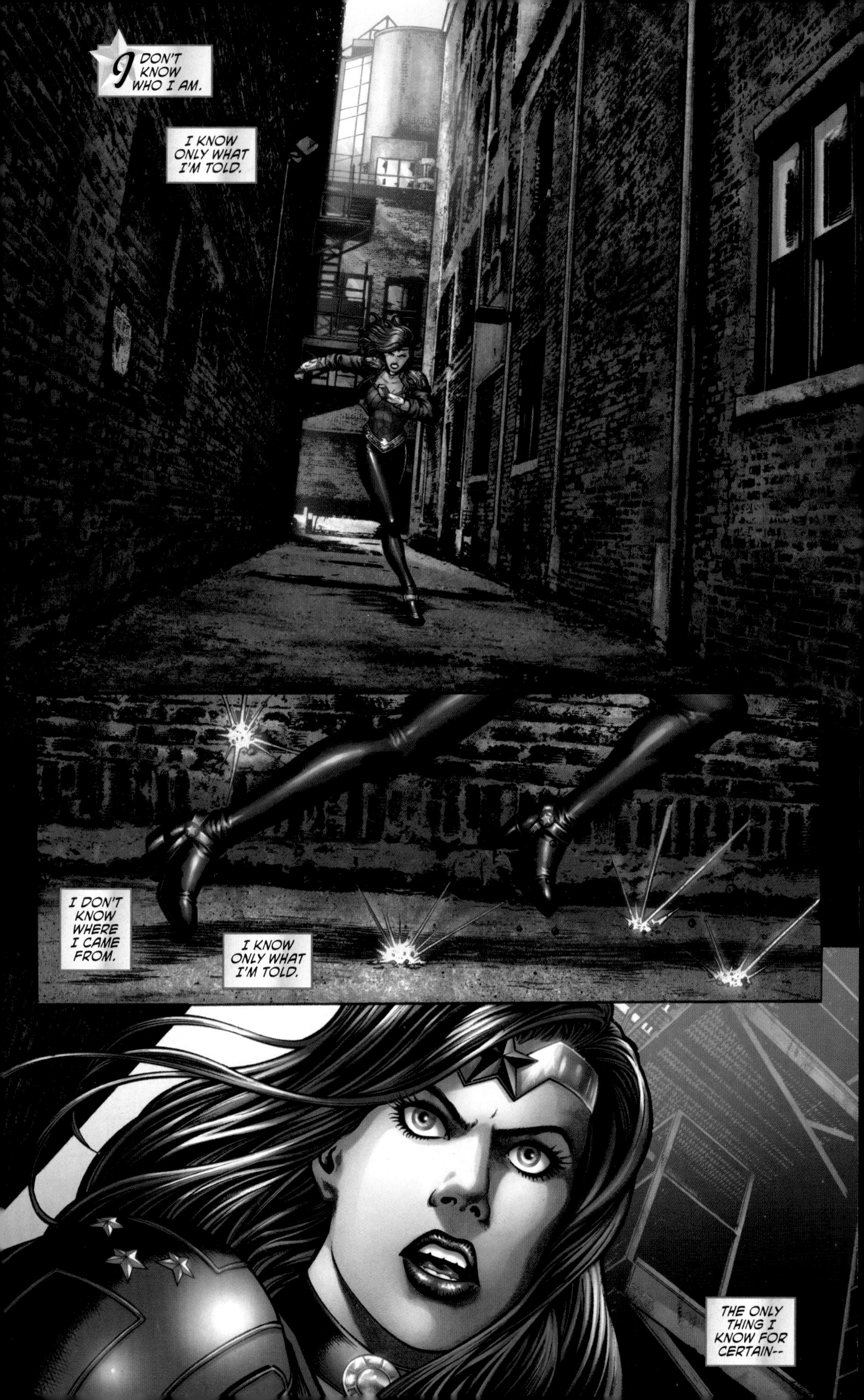
I DON'T KNOW WHO I AM.
I KNOW ONLY WHAT I'M TOLD.
I DON'T KNOW WHERE I CAME FROM.
I KNOW ONLY WHAT I'M TOLD.
THE ONLY THING I KNOW FOR CERTAIN--

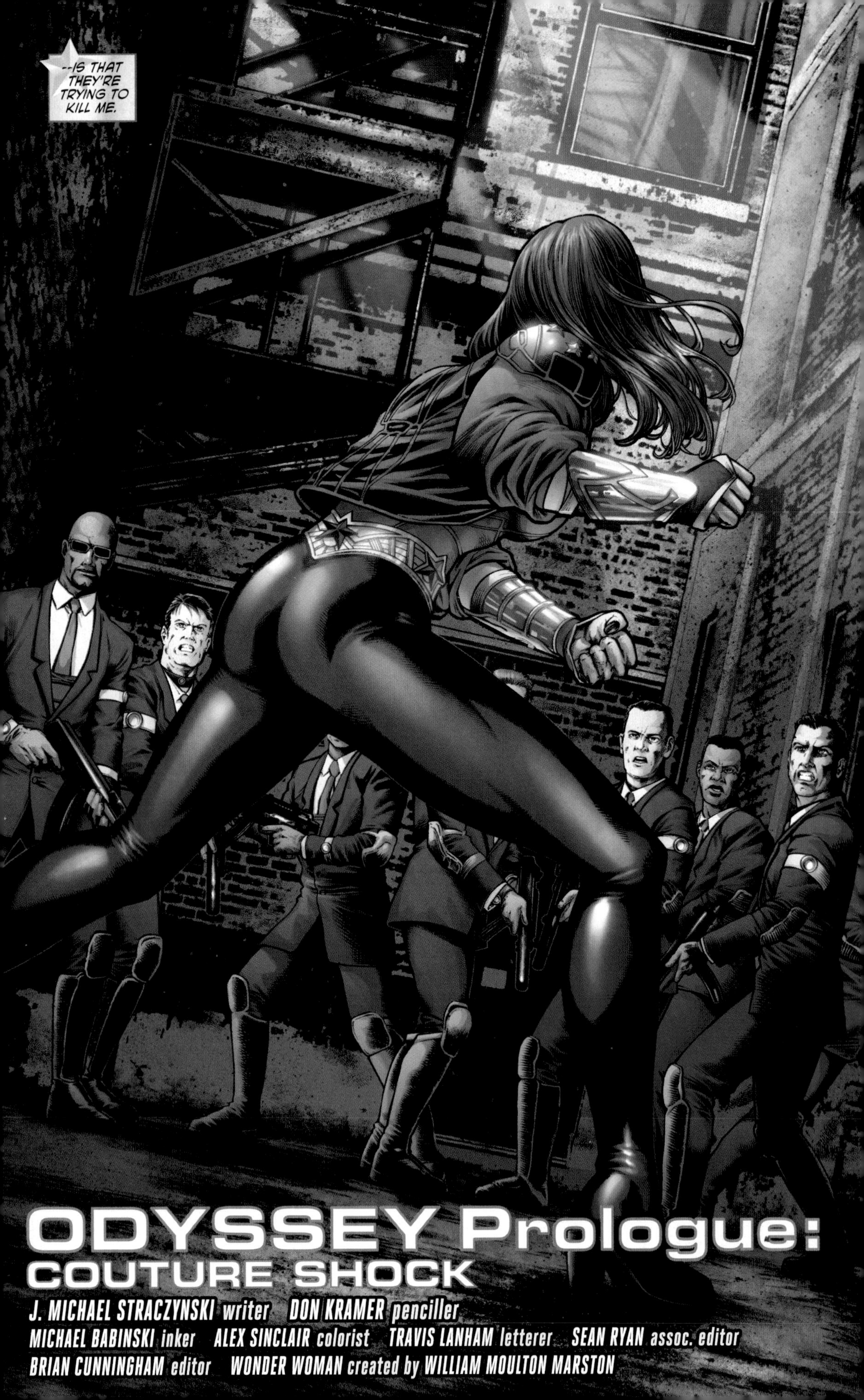
--IS THAT THEY'RE TRYING TO KILL ME.
ODYSSEY Prologue:
COUTURE SHOCK
J. MICHAEL STRACZYNSKI writer DON KRAMER penciller
MICHAEL BABINSKI inker ALEX SINCLAIR colorist TRAVIS LANHAM letterer SEAN RYAN assoc. editor
BRIAN CUNNINGHAM editor WONDER WOMAN created by WILLIAM MOULTON MARSTON

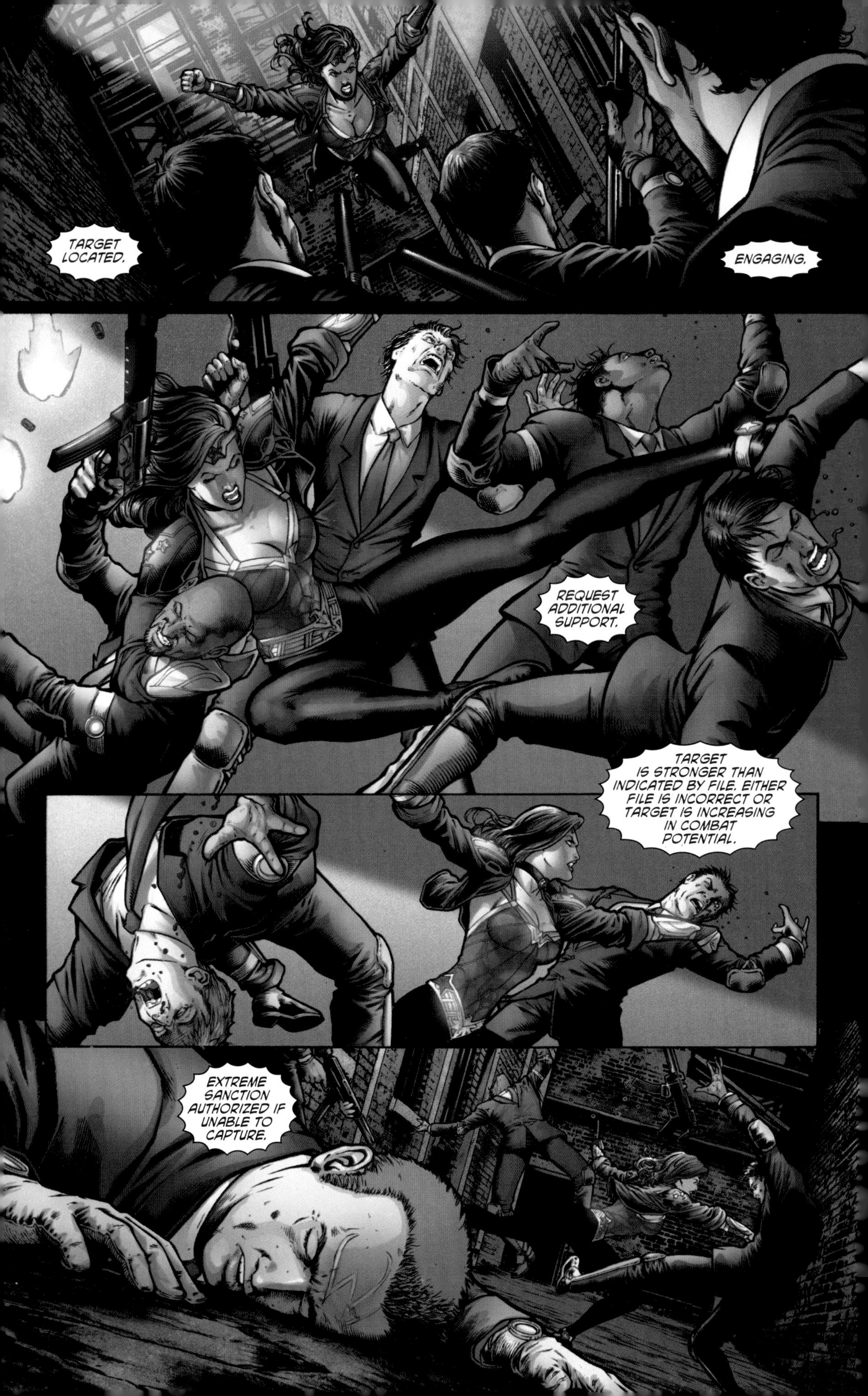
TARGET LOCATED.
ENGAGING.
REQUEST ADDITIONAL SUPPORT.
TARGET IS STRONGER THAN INDICATED BY FILE. EITHER FILE IS INCORRECT OR TARGET IS INCREASING IN COMBAT POTENTIAL.
EXTREME SANCTION AUTHORIZED IF UNABLE TO CAPTURE.

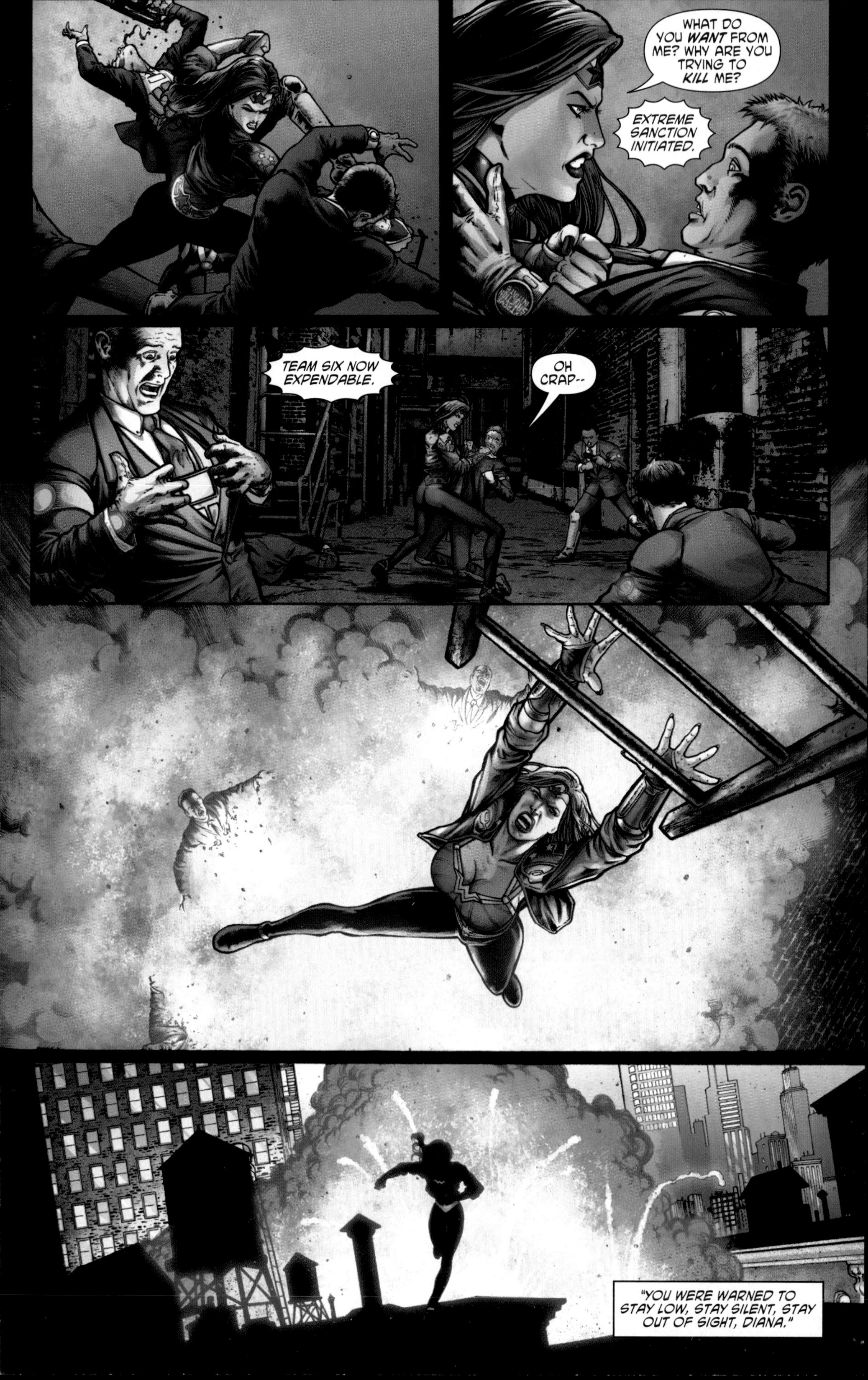
WHAT DO YOU WANT FROM ME? WHY ARE YOU TRYING TO KILL ME?
EXTREME SANCTION INITIATED.
TEAM SIX NOW EXPENDABLE.
OH CRAP--
"YOU WERE WARNED TO STAY LOW, STAY SILENT, STAY OUT OF SIGHT, DIANA."

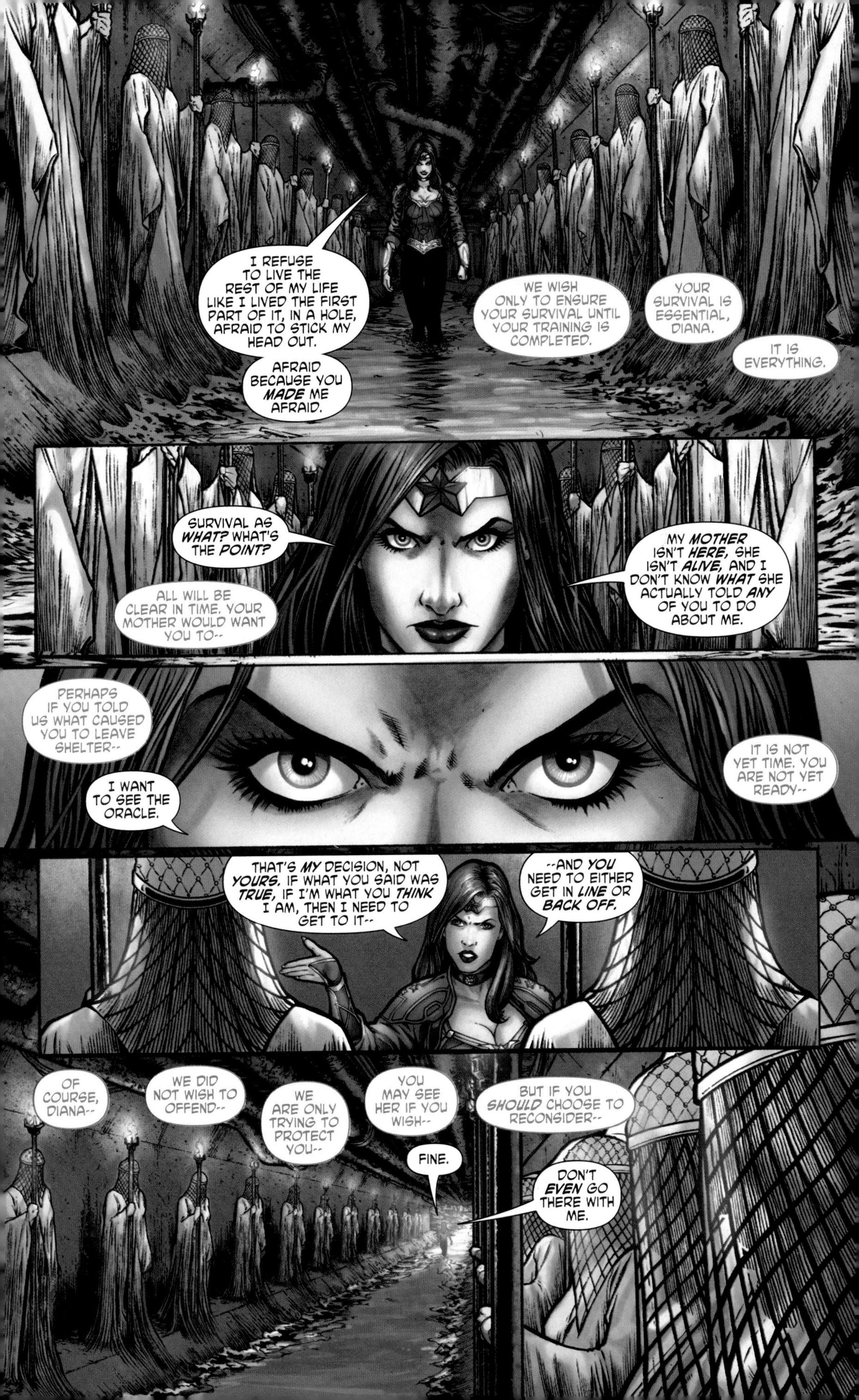
I REFUSE TO LIVE THE REST OF MY LIFE LIKE I LIVED THE FIRST PART OF IT, IN A HOLE, AFRAID TO STICK MY HEAD OUT.
AFRAID BECAUSE YOU *MADE* ME AFRAID.
WE WISH ONLY TO ENSURE YOUR SURVIVAL UNTIL YOUR TRAINING IS COMPLETED.
YOUR SURVIVAL IS ESSENTIAL, DIANA.
IT IS EVERYTHING.
SURVIVAL AS *WHAT?* WHAT'S THE *POINT?*
ALL WILL BE CLEAR IN TIME. YOUR MOTHER WOULD WANT YOU TO--
MY *MOTHER* ISN'T *HERE,* SHE ISN'T *ALIVE,* AND I DON'T KNOW *WHAT* SHE ACTUALLY TOLD *ANY* OF YOU TO DO ABOUT ME.
PERHAPS IF YOU TOLD US WHAT CAUSED YOU TO LEAVE SHELTER--
I WANT TO SEE THE ORACLE.
IT IS NOT YET TIME. YOU ARE NOT YET READY--
THAT'S *MY* DECISION, NOT *YOURS.* IF WHAT YOU SAID WAS *TRUE,* IF I'M WHAT YOU *THINK* I AM, THEN I NEED TO GET TO IT--
--AND *YOU* NEED TO EITHER GET IN *LINE* OR *BACK OFF.*
OF COURSE, DIANA--
WE DID NOT WISH TO OFFEND--
WE ARE ONLY TRYING TO PROTECT YOU--
YOU MAY SEE HER IF YOU WISH--
BUT IF YOU *SHOULD* CHOOSE TO RECONSIDER--
FINE.
DON'T *EVEN* GO THERE WITH ME.

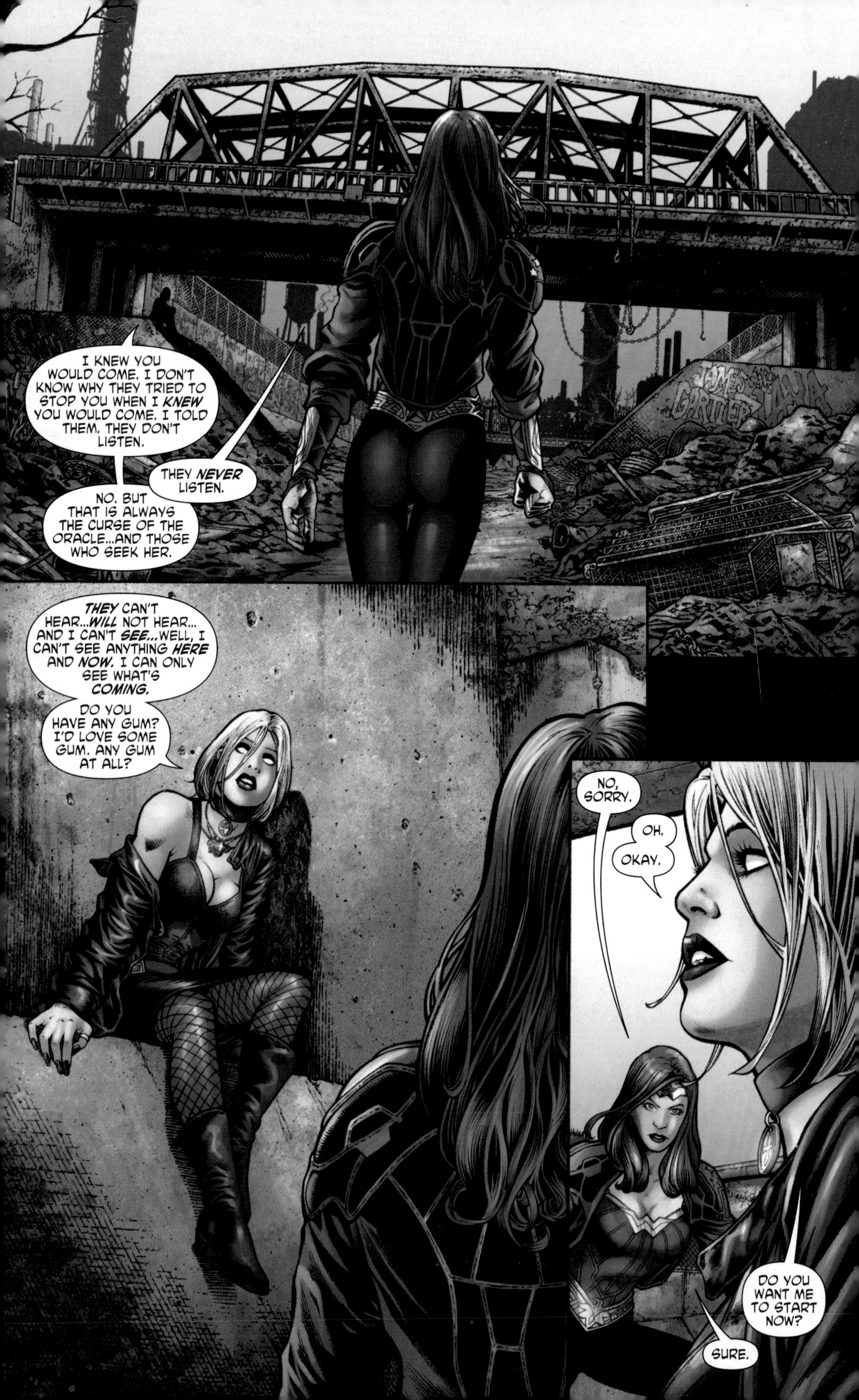
I KNEW YOU WOULD COME. I DON'T KNOW WHY THEY TRIED TO STOP YOU WHEN I *KNEW* YOU WOULD COME. I TOLD THEM. THEY DON'T LISTEN.
THEY *NEVER* LISTEN.
NO. BUT THAT IS ALWAYS THE CURSE OF THE ORACLE...AND THOSE WHO SEEK HER.
THEY CAN'T HEAR...*WILL* NOT HEAR... AND I CAN'T *SEE*...WELL, I CAN'T SEE ANYTHING *HERE* AND *NOW*. I CAN ONLY SEE WHAT'S *COMING*.
DO YOU HAVE ANY GUM? I'D LOVE SOME GUM. ANY GUM AT ALL?
NO, SORRY.
OH.
OKAY.
DO YOU WANT ME TO START NOW?
SURE.

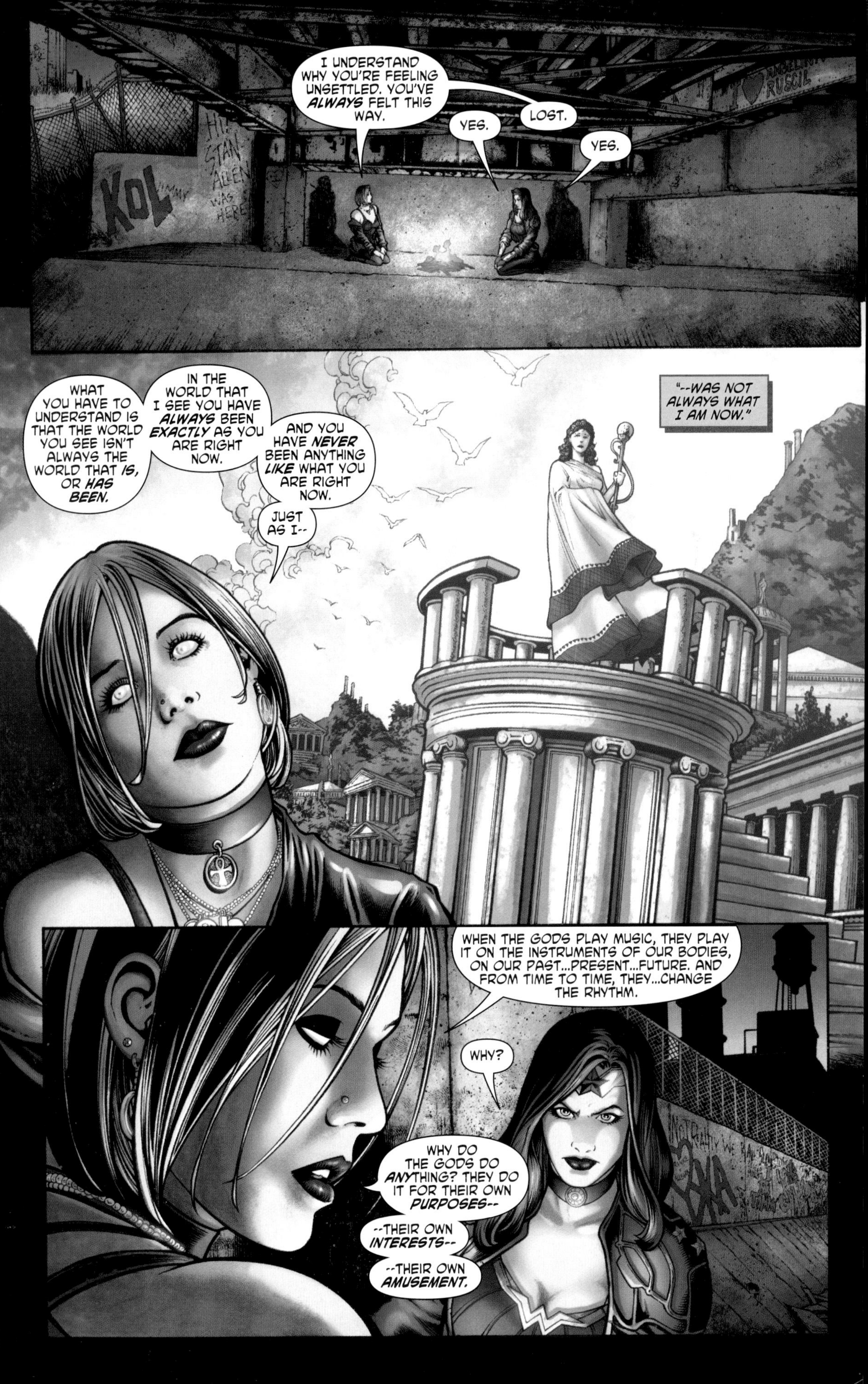
I UNDERSTAND WHY YOU'RE FEELING UNSETTLED. YOU'VE ALWAYS FELT THIS WAY.
LOST.
YES.
YES.
WHAT YOU HAVE TO UNDERSTAND IS THAT THE WORLD YOU SEE ISN'T ALWAYS THE WORLD THAT IS, OR HAS BEEN.
IN THE WORLD THAT I SEE YOU HAVE ALWAYS BEEN EXACTLY AS YOU ARE RIGHT NOW.
AND YOU HAVE NEVER BEEN ANYTHING LIKE WHAT YOU ARE RIGHT NOW.
JUST AS I--
"--WAS NOT ALWAYS WHAT I AM NOW."
WHEN THE GODS PLAY MUSIC, THEY PLAY IT ON THE INSTRUMENTS OF OUR BODIES, ON OUR PAST...PRESENT...FUTURE. AND FROM TIME TO TIME, THEY...CHANGE THE RHYTHM.
WHY?
WHY DO THE GODS DO ANYTHING? THEY DO IT FOR THEIR OWN PURPOSES--
--THEIR OWN INTERESTS--
--THEIR OWN AMUSEMENT.

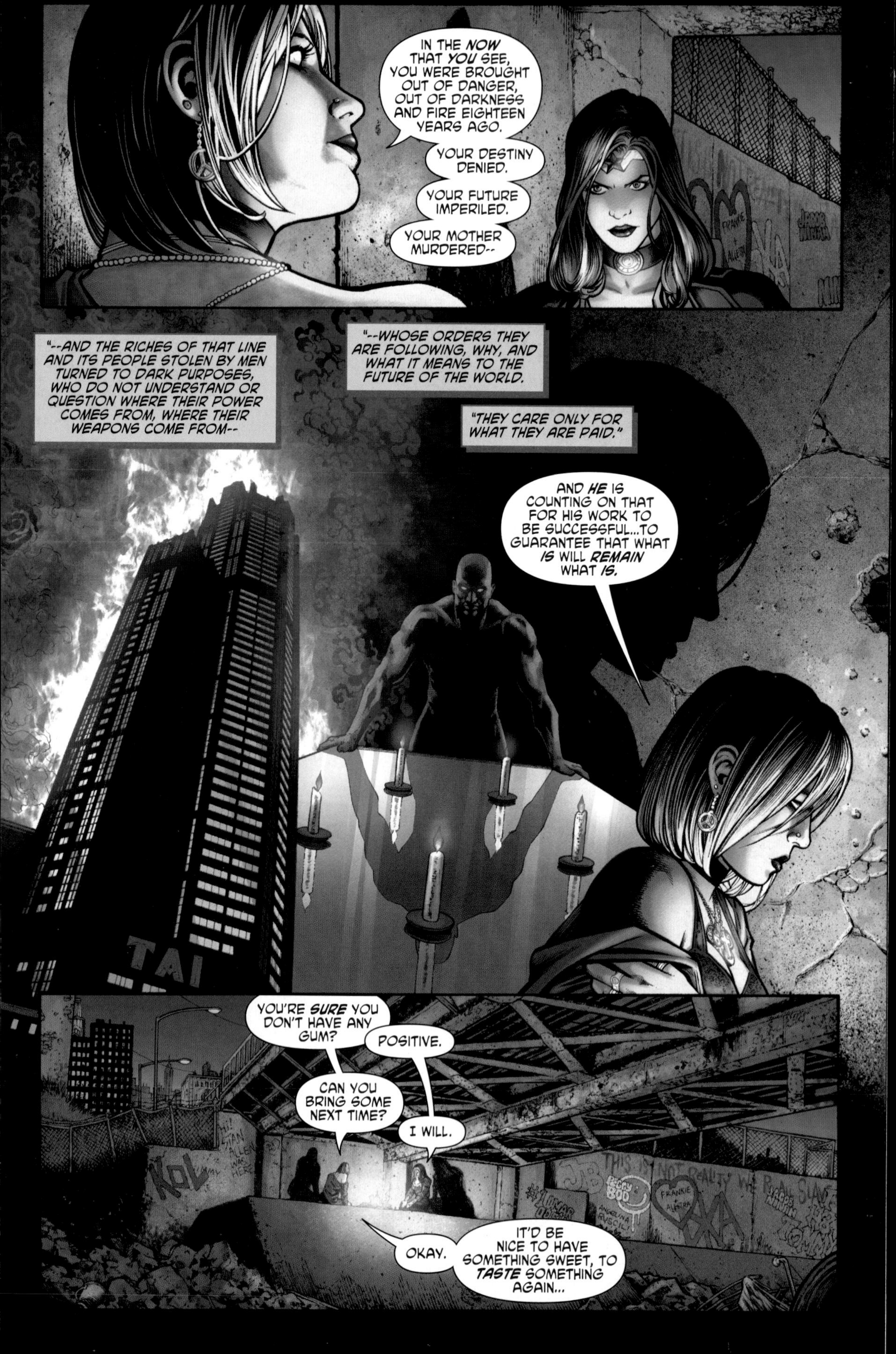
IN THE NOW THAT YOU SEE, YOU WERE BROUGHT OUT OF DANGER, OUT OF DARKNESS AND FIRE EIGHTEEN YEARS AGO.
YOUR DESTINY DENIED.
YOUR FUTURE IMPERILED.
YOUR MOTHER MURDERED--
"--AND THE RICHES OF THAT LINE AND ITS PEOPLE STOLEN BY MEN TURNED TO DARK PURPOSES, WHO DO NOT UNDERSTAND OR QUESTION WHERE THEIR POWER COMES FROM, WHERE THEIR WEAPONS COME FROM--
"--WHOSE ORDERS THEY ARE FOLLOWING, WHY, AND WHAT IT MEANS TO THE FUTURE OF THE WORLD.
"THEY CARE ONLY FOR WHAT THEY ARE PAID."
AND HE IS COUNTING ON THAT FOR HIS WORK TO BE SUCCESSFUL...TO GUARANTEE THAT WHAT IS WILL REMAIN WHAT IS.
TAI
YOU'RE SURE YOU DON'T HAVE ANY GUM?
POSITIVE.
CAN YOU BRING SOME NEXT TIME?
I WILL.
OKAY.
IT'D BE NICE TO HAVE SOMETHING SWEET, TO TASTE SOMETHING AGAIN...

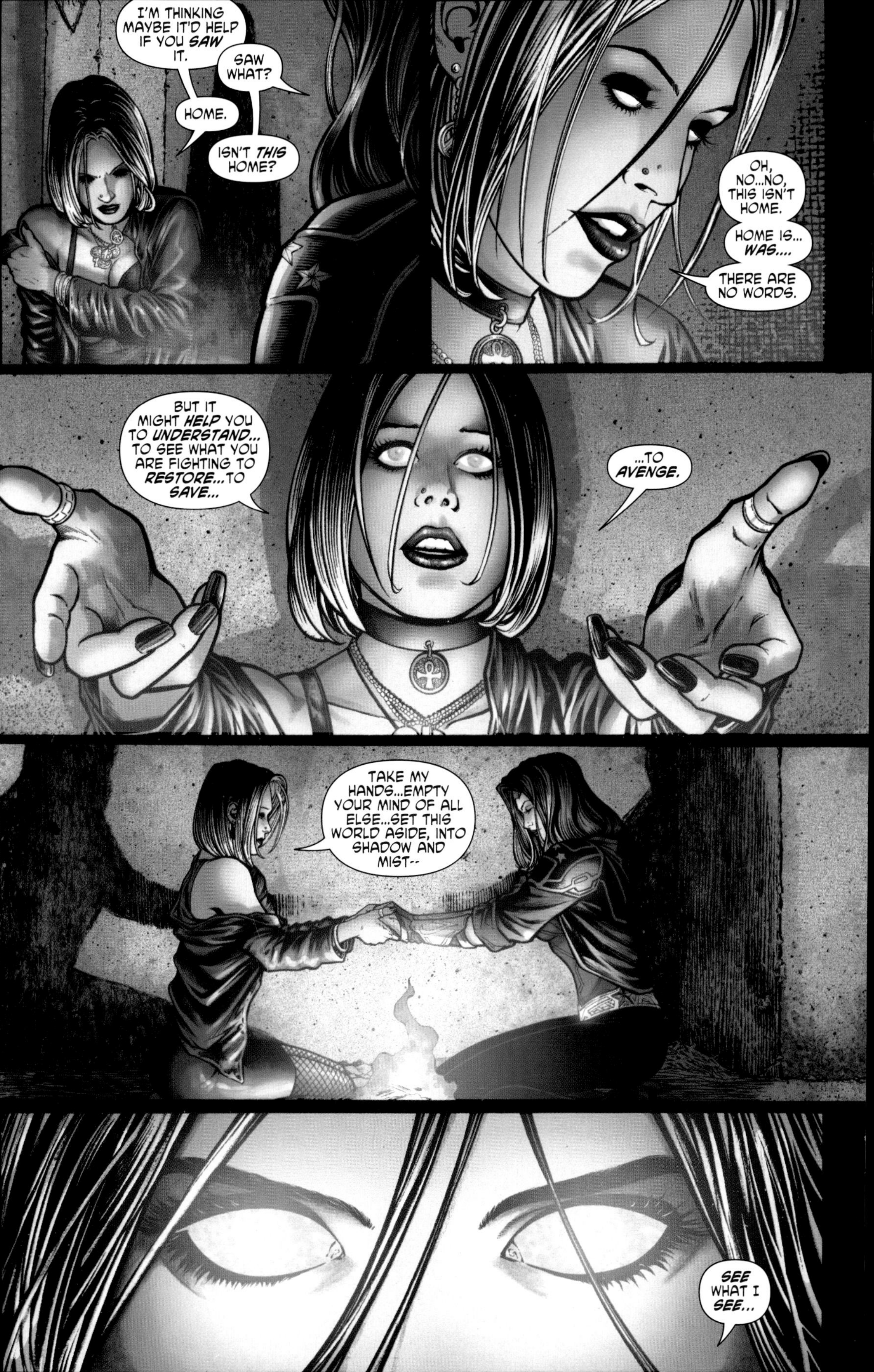
I'M THINKING MAYBE IT'D HELP IF YOU SAW IT.
SAW WHAT?
HOME.
ISN'T THIS HOME?
OH, NO...NO, THIS ISN'T HOME.
HOME IS... WAS....
THERE ARE NO WORDS.
BUT IT MIGHT HELP YOU TO UNDERSTAND... TO SEE WHAT YOU ARE FIGHTING TO RESTORE...TO SAVE...
...TO AVENGE.
TAKE MY HANDS...EMPTY YOUR MIND OF ALL ELSE...SET THIS WORLD ASIDE, INTO SHADOW AND MIST--
SEE WHAT I SEE...

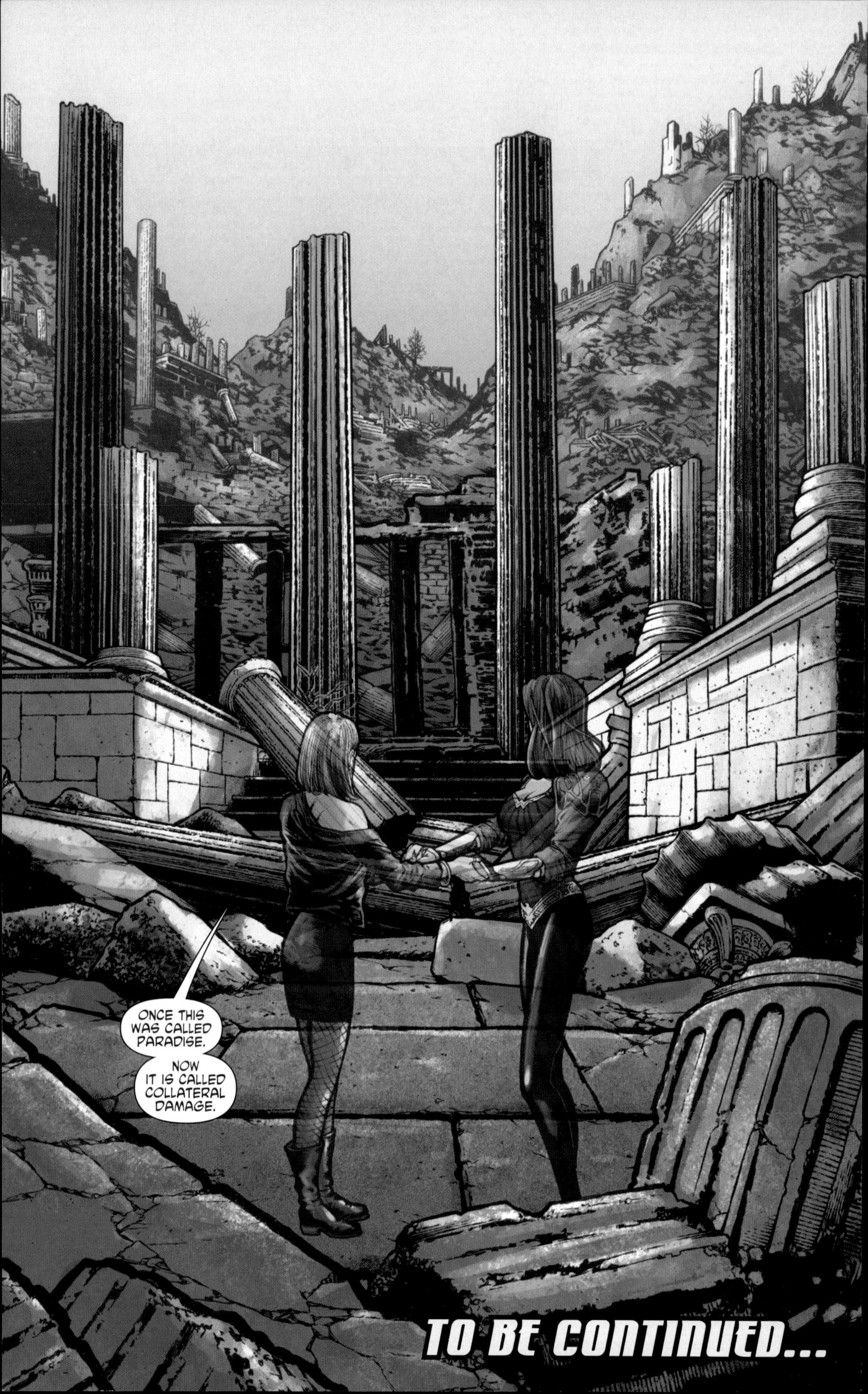
ONCE THIS WAS CALLED PARADISE.
NOW IT IS CALLED COLLATERAL DAMAGE.
TO BE CONTINUED...

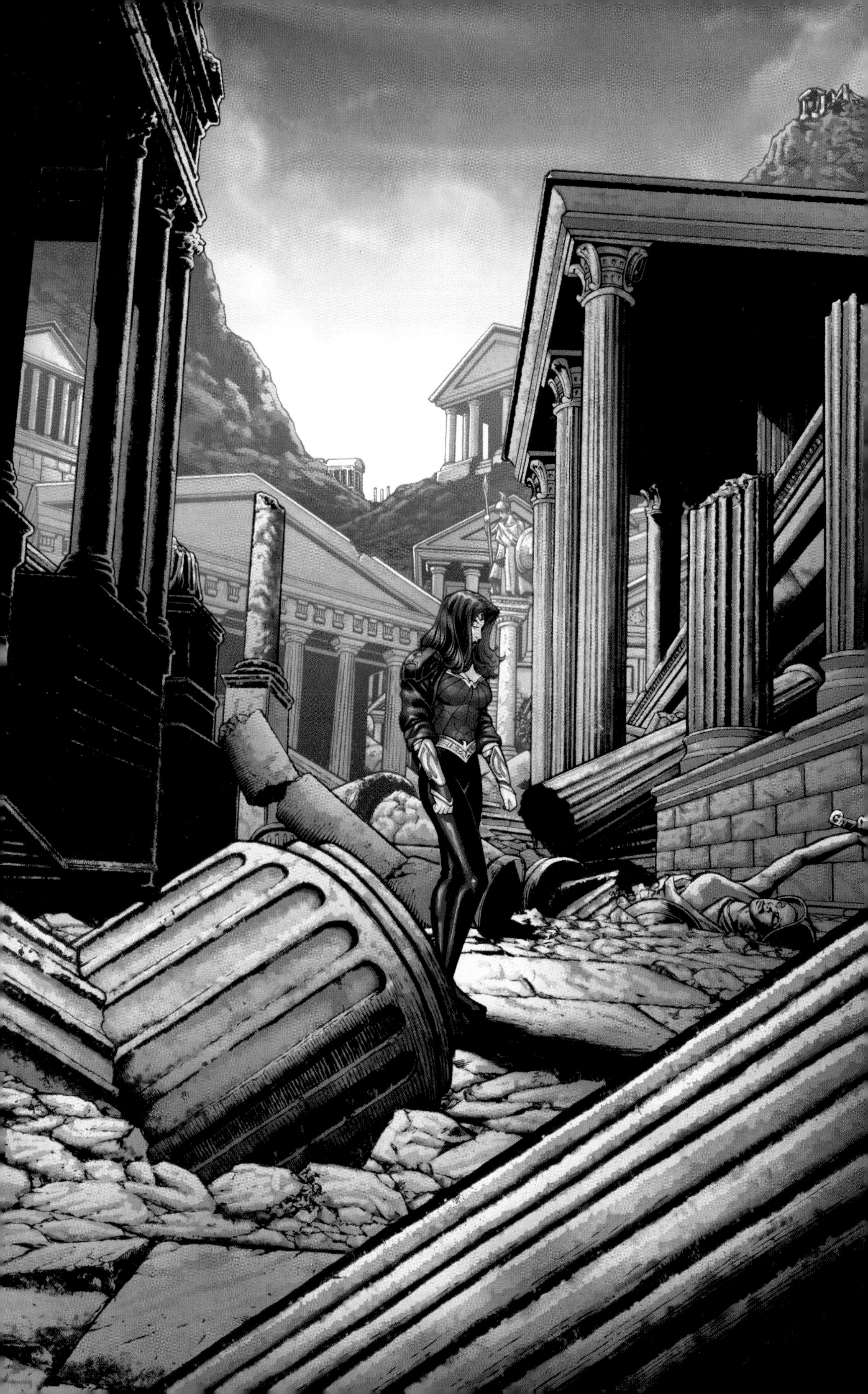

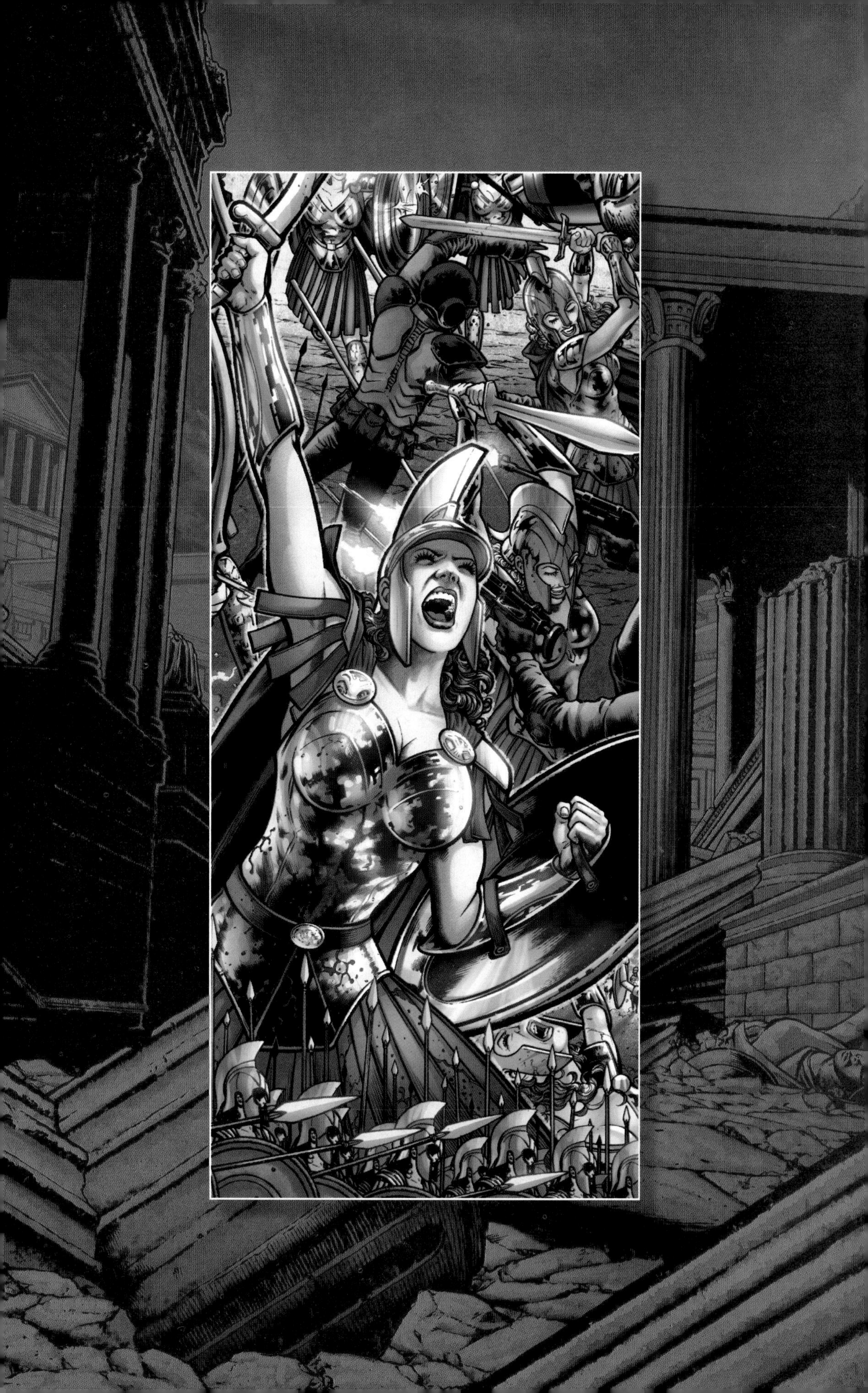

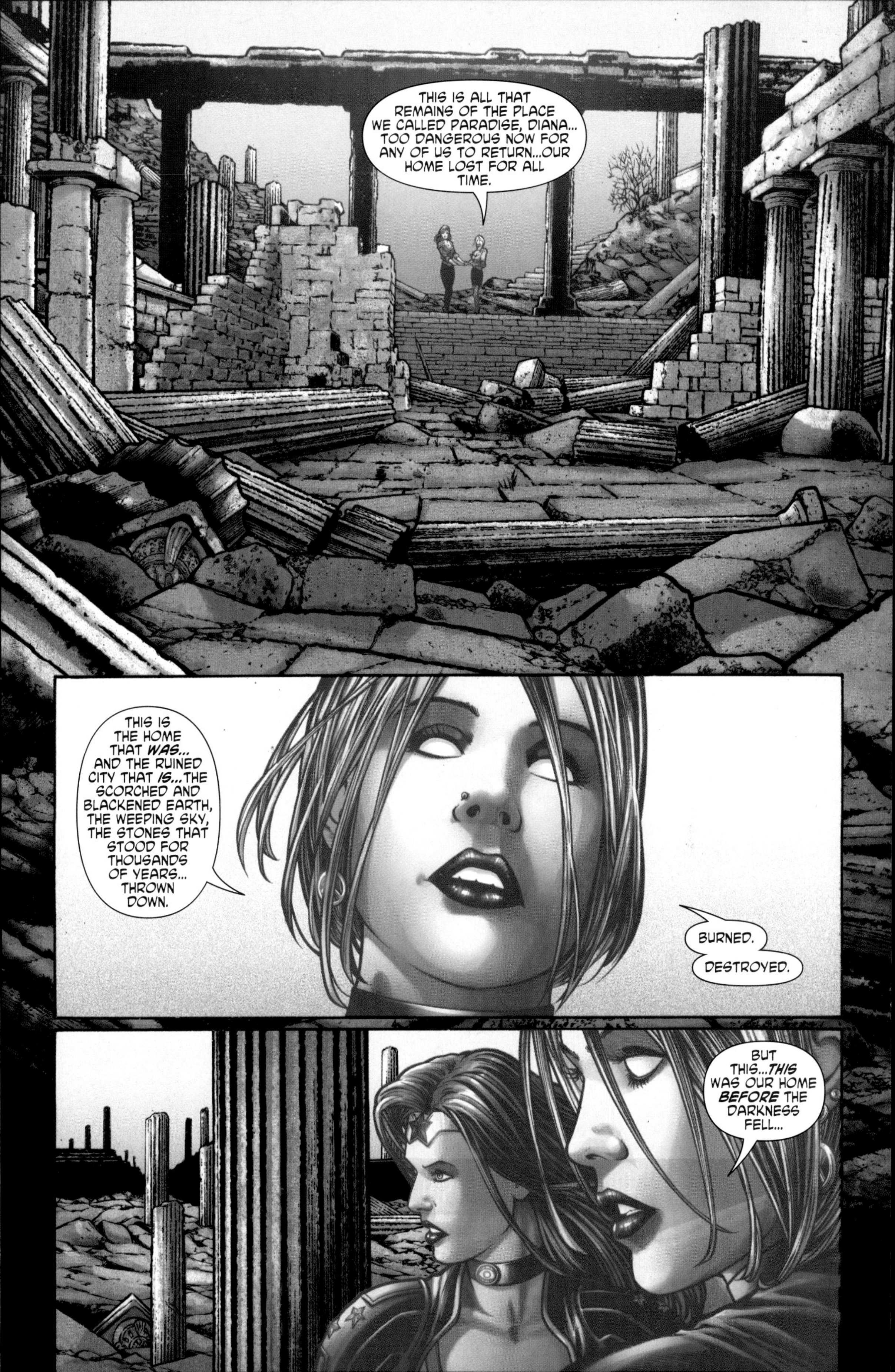
THIS IS ALL THAT REMAINS OF THE PLACE WE CALLED PARADISE, DIANA... TOO DANGEROUS NOW FOR ANY OF US TO RETURN...OUR HOME LOST FOR ALL TIME.
THIS IS THE HOME THAT *WAS*... AND THE RUINED CITY THAT *IS*...THE SCORCHED AND BLACKENED EARTH, THE WEEPING SKY, THE STONES THAT STOOD FOR THOUSANDS OF YEARS... THROWN DOWN.
BURNED.
DESTROYED.
BUT THIS...*THIS* WAS OUR HOME *BEFORE* THE DARKNESS FELL...

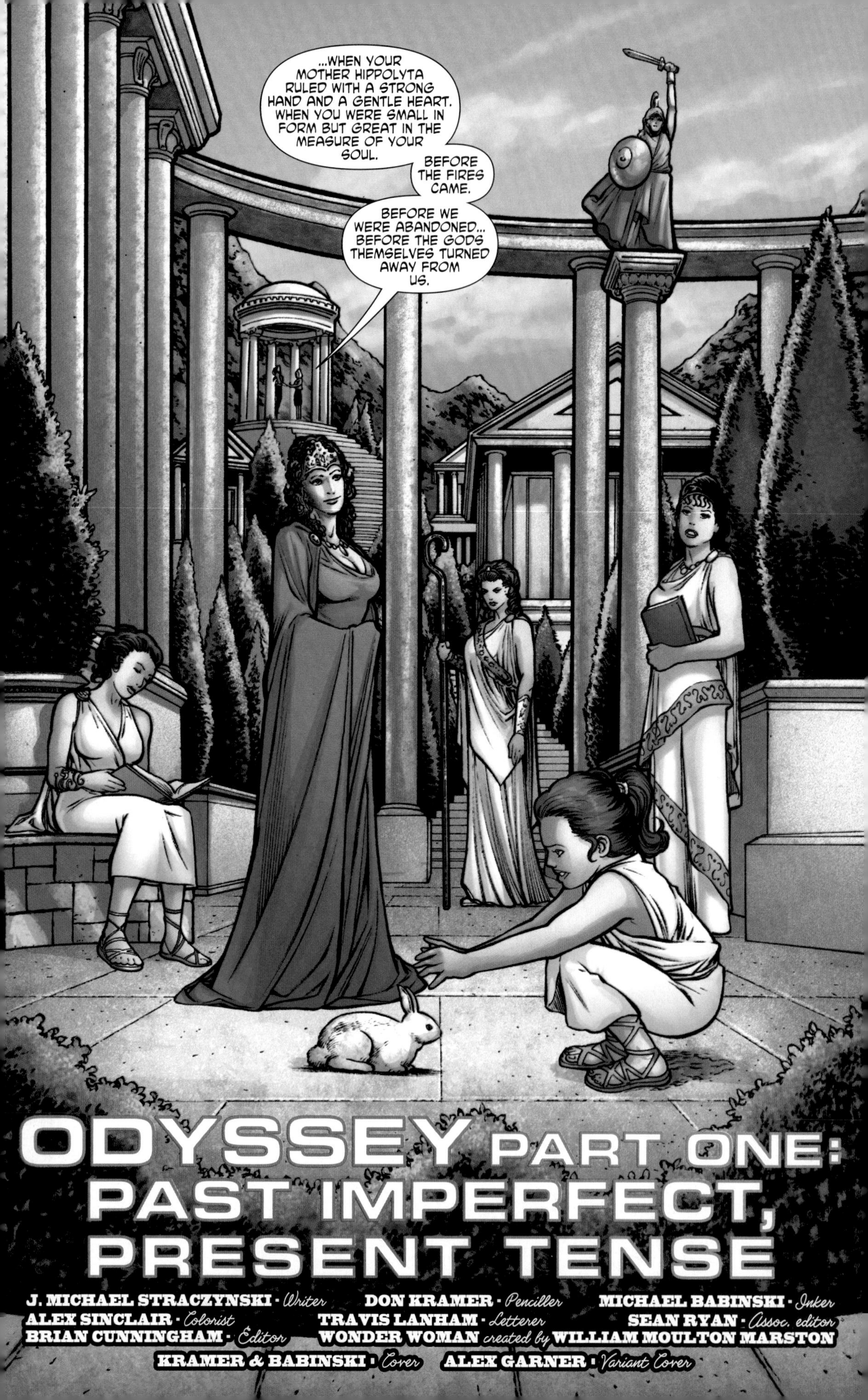
...WHEN YOUR MOTHER HIPPOLYTA RULED WITH A STRONG HAND AND A GENTLE HEART. WHEN YOU WERE SMALL IN FORM BUT GREAT IN THE MEASURE OF YOUR SOUL.
BEFORE THE FIRES CAME.
BEFORE WE WERE ABANDONED... BEFORE THE GODS THEMSELVES TURNED AWAY FROM US.
ODYSSEY PART ONE: PAST IMPERFECT, PRESENT TENSE
J. MICHAEL STRACZYNSKI • Writer
DON KRAMER • Penciller
MICHAEL BABINSKI • Inker
ALEX SINCLAIR • Colorist
TRAVIS LANHAM • Letterer
SEAN RYAN • Assoc. editor
BRIAN CUNNINGHAM • Editor
WONDER WOMAN created by WILLIAM MOULTON MARSTON
KRAMER & BABINSKI • Cover
ALEX GARNER • Variant Cover

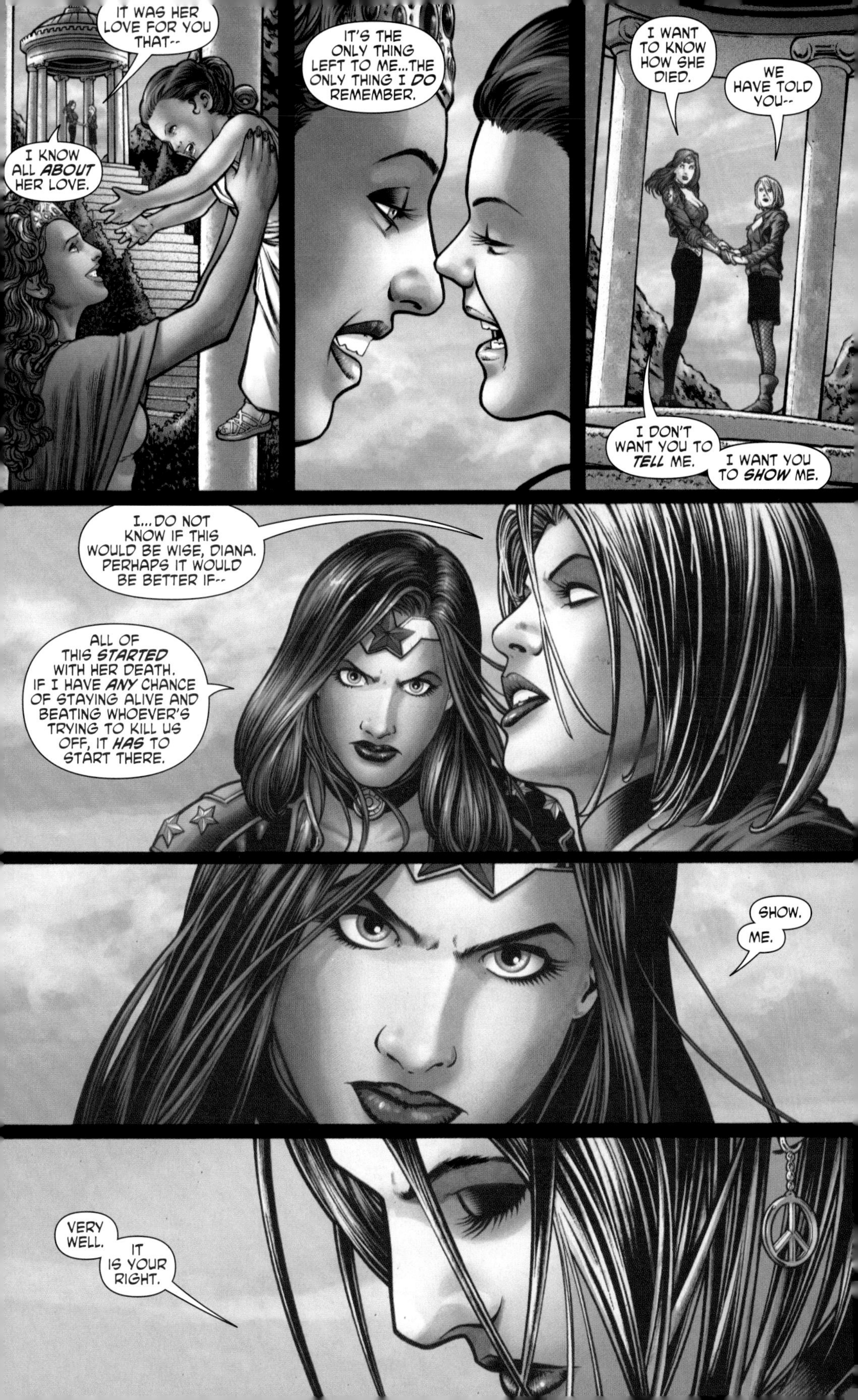
IT WAS HER LOVE FOR YOU THAT--
I KNOW ALL ABOUT HER LOVE.
IT'S THE ONLY THING LEFT TO ME...THE ONLY THING I DO REMEMBER.
I WANT TO KNOW HOW SHE DIED.
WE HAVE TOLD YOU--
I DON'T WANT YOU TO TELL ME.
I WANT YOU TO SHOW ME.
I...DO NOT KNOW IF THIS WOULD BE WISE, DIANA. PERHAPS IT WOULD BE BETTER IF--
ALL OF THIS STARTED WITH HER DEATH. IF I HAVE ANY CHANCE OF STAYING ALIVE AND BEATING WHOEVER'S TRYING TO KILL US OFF, IT HAS TO START THERE.
SHOW. ME.
VERY WELL.
IT IS YOUR RIGHT.

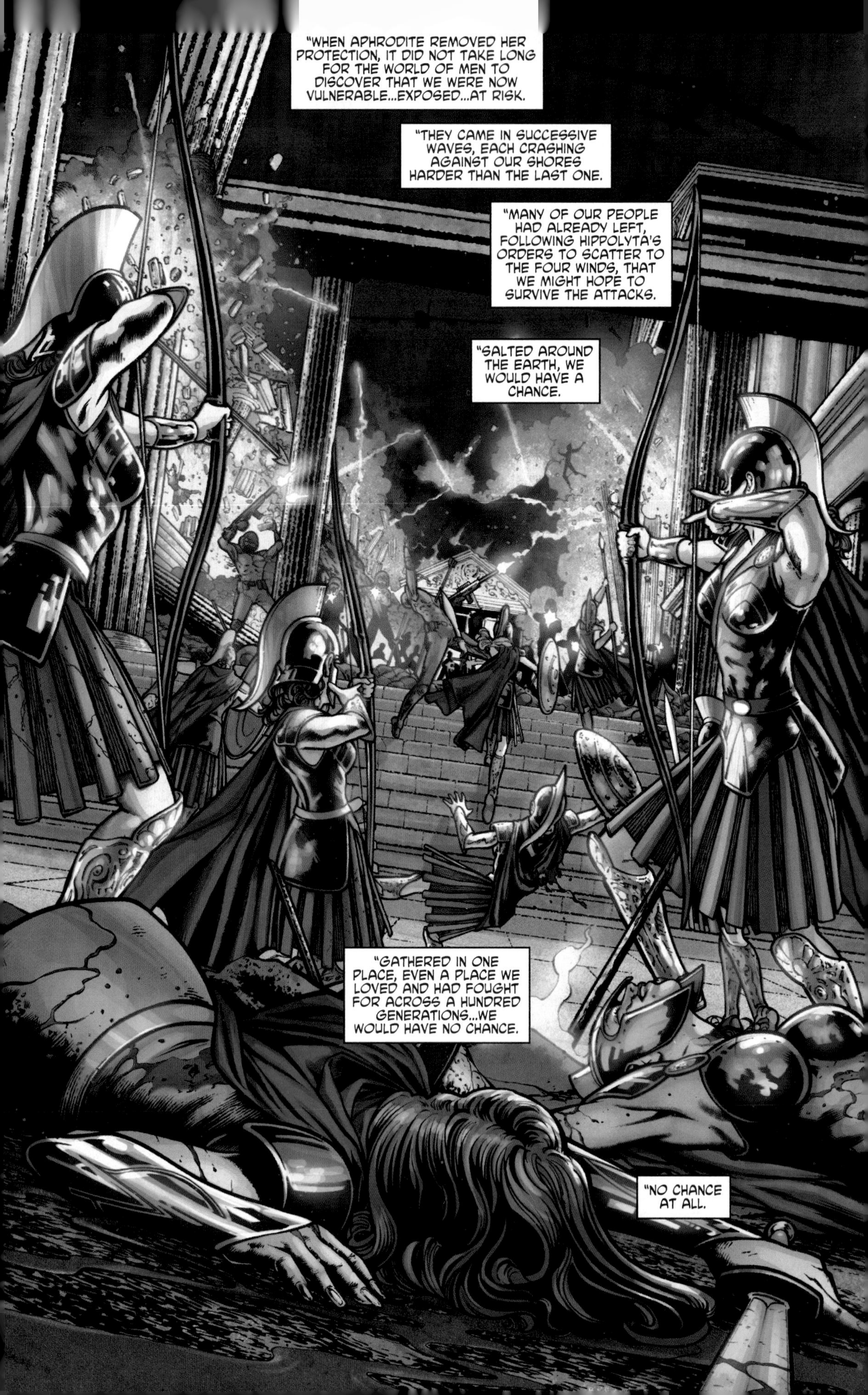
"WHEN APHRODITE REMOVED HER PROTECTION, IT DID NOT TAKE LONG FOR THE WORLD OF MEN TO DISCOVER THAT WE WERE NOW VULNERABLE...EXPOSED...AT RISK.
"THEY CAME IN SUCCESSIVE WAVES, EACH CRASHING AGAINST OUR SHORES HARDER THAN THE LAST ONE.
"MANY OF OUR PEOPLE HAD ALREADY LEFT, FOLLOWING HIPPOLYTA'S ORDERS TO SCATTER TO THE FOUR WINDS, THAT WE MIGHT HOPE TO SURVIVE THE ATTACKS.
"SALTED AROUND THE EARTH, WE WOULD HAVE A CHANCE.
"GATHERED IN ONE PLACE, EVEN A PLACE WE LOVED AND HAD FOUGHT FOR ACROSS A HUNDRED GENERATIONS...WE WOULD HAVE NO CHANCE.
"NO CHANCE AT ALL.

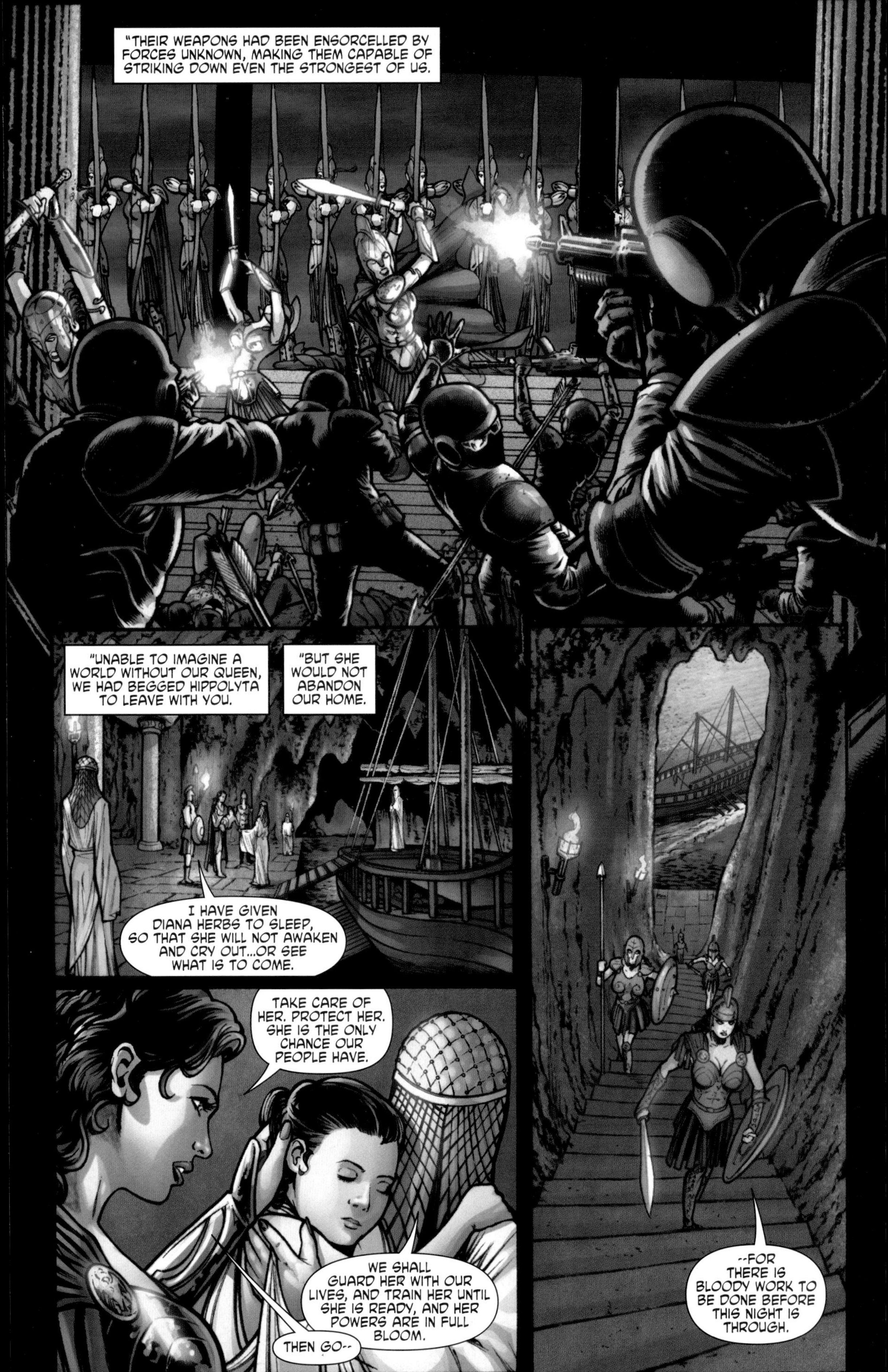
"THEIR WEAPONS HAD BEEN ENSORCELLED BY FORCES UNKNOWN, MAKING THEM CAPABLE OF STRIKING DOWN EVEN THE STRONGEST OF US.
"UNABLE TO IMAGINE A WORLD WITHOUT OUR QUEEN, WE HAD BEGGED HIPPOLYTA TO LEAVE WITH YOU.
"BUT SHE WOULD NOT ABANDON OUR HOME.
I HAVE GIVEN DIANA HERBS TO SLEEP, SO THAT SHE WILL NOT AWAKEN AND CRY OUT...OR SEE WHAT IS TO COME.
TAKE CARE OF HER. PROTECT HER. SHE IS THE ONLY CHANCE OUR PEOPLE HAVE.
WE SHALL GUARD HER WITH OUR LIVES, AND TRAIN HER UNTIL SHE IS READY, AND HER POWERS ARE IN FULL BLOOM.
THEN GO--
--FOR THERE IS BLOODY WORK TO BE DONE BEFORE THIS NIGHT IS THROUGH.

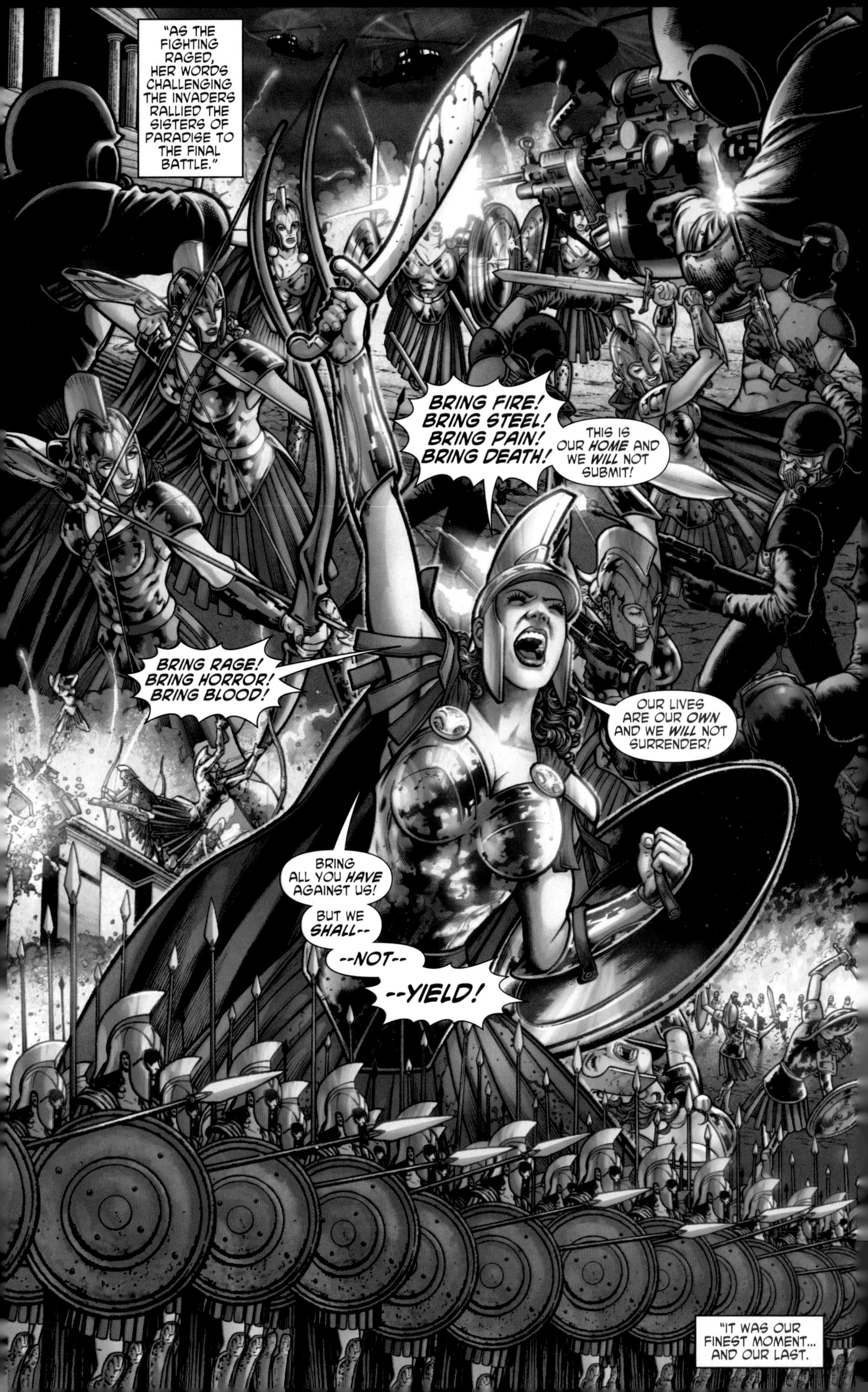
"AS THE FIGHTING RAGED, HER WORDS CHALLENGING THE INVADERS RALLIED THE SISTERS OF PARADISE TO THE FINAL BATTLE."
BRING FIRE! BRING STEEL! BRING PAIN! BRING DEATH!
THIS IS OUR HOME AND WE WILL NOT SUBMIT!
BRING RAGE! BRING HORROR! BRING BLOOD!
OUR LIVES ARE OUR OWN AND WE WILL NOT SURRENDER!
BRING ALL YOU HAVE AGAINST US!
BUT WE SHALL--
--NOT--
--YIELD!
"IT WAS OUR FINEST MOMENT... AND OUR LAST.

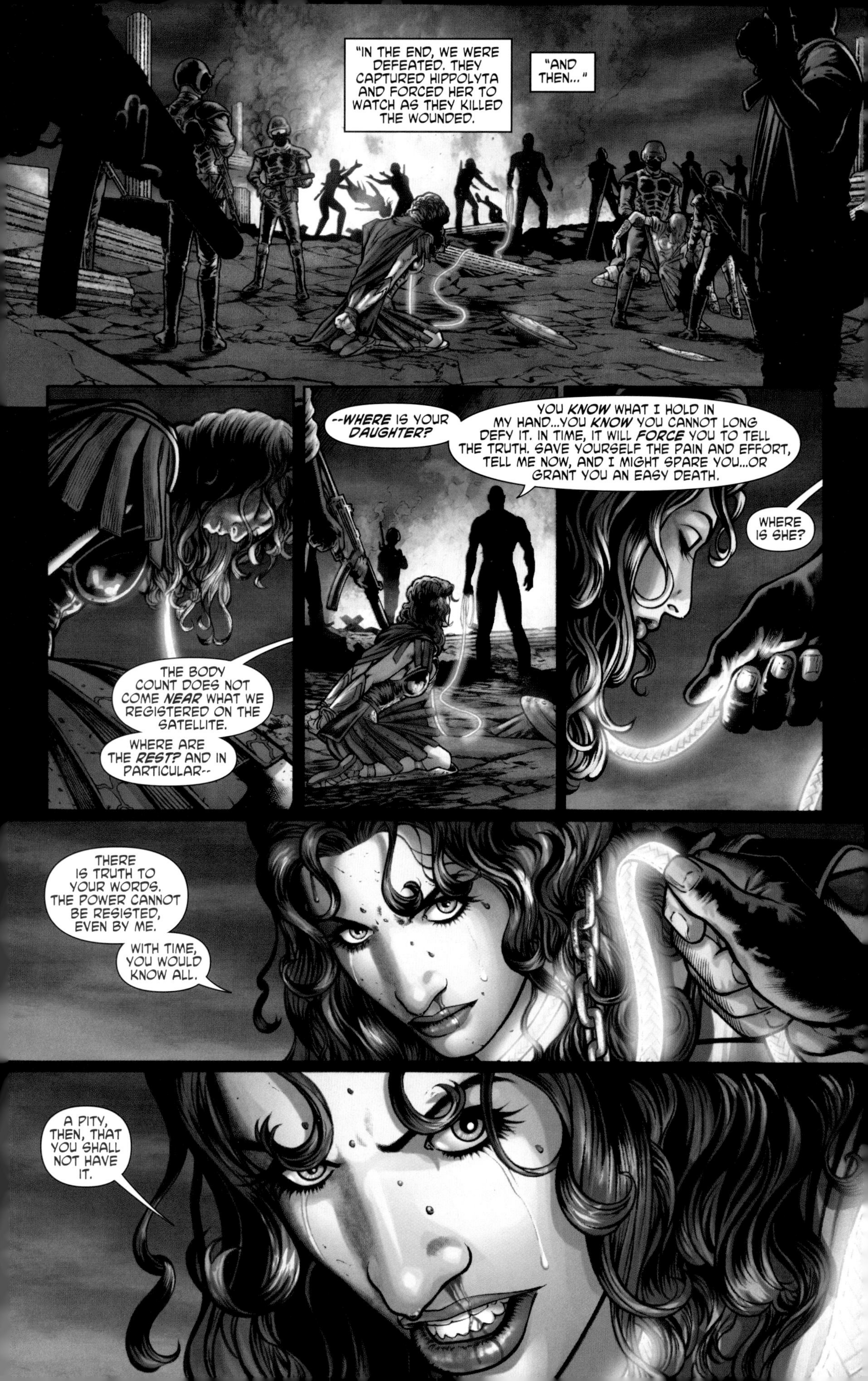
"IN THE END, WE WERE DEFEATED. THEY CAPTURED HIPPOLYTA AND FORCED HER TO WATCH AS THEY KILLED THE WOUNDED.
"AND THEN..."
THE BODY COUNT DOES NOT COME *NEAR* WHAT WE REGISTERED ON THE SATELLITE.
WHERE ARE THE *REST?* AND IN PARTICULAR--
--*WHERE* IS YOUR *DAUGHTER?*
YOU *KNOW* WHAT I HOLD IN MY HAND...YOU *KNOW* YOU CANNOT LONG DEFY IT. IN TIME, IT WILL *FORCE* YOU TO TELL THE TRUTH. SAVE YOURSELF THE PAIN AND EFFORT, TELL ME NOW, AND I MIGHT SPARE YOU...OR GRANT YOU AN EASY DEATH.
WHERE IS SHE?
THERE IS TRUTH TO YOUR WORDS. THE POWER CANNOT BE RESISTED, EVEN BY ME.
WITH TIME, YOU WOULD KNOW ALL.
A PITY, THEN, THAT YOU SHALL NOT HAVE IT.

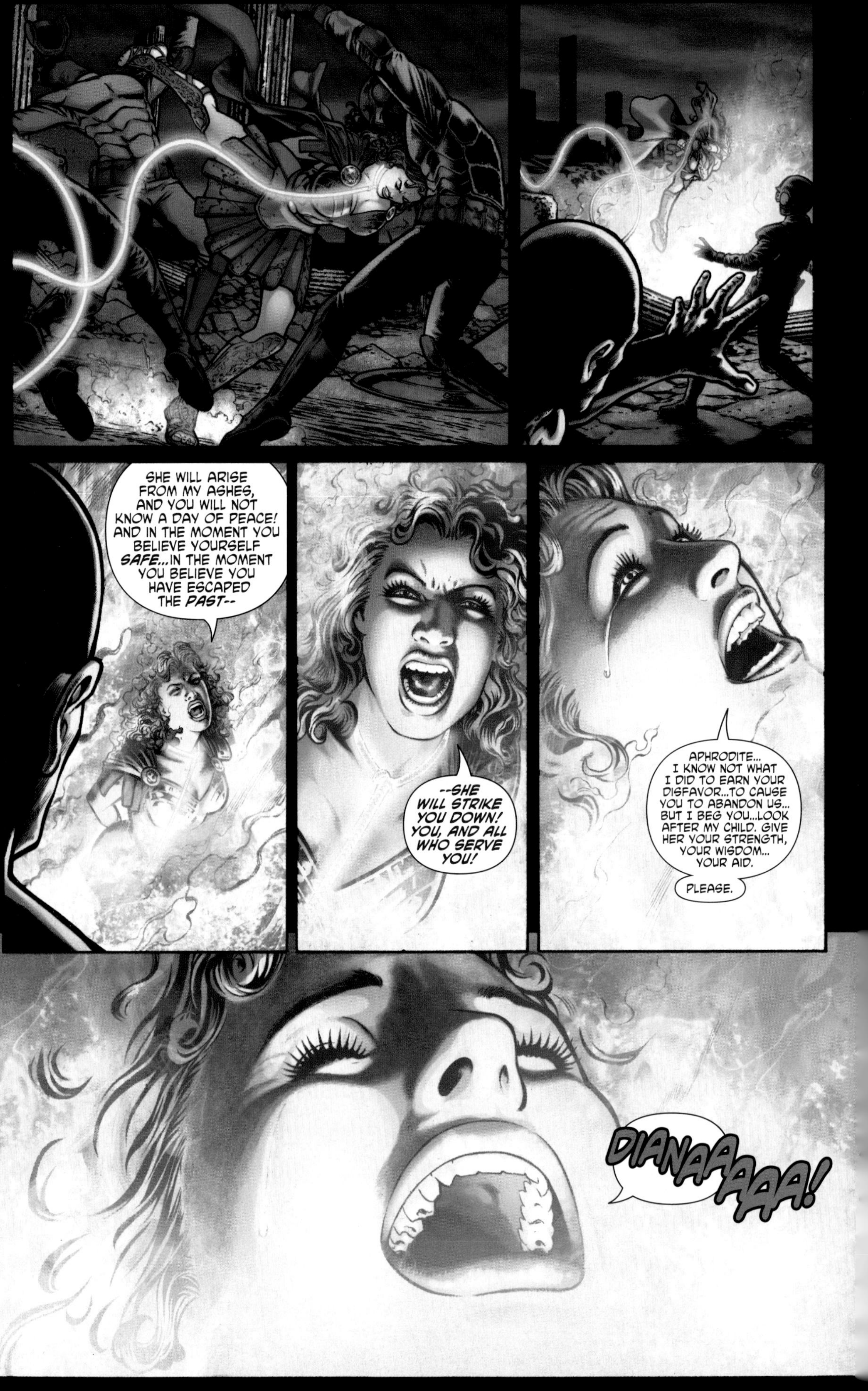
SHE WILL ARISE FROM MY ASHES, AND YOU WILL NOT KNOW A DAY OF PEACE! AND IN THE MOMENT YOU BELIEVE YOURSELF *SAFE*...IN THE MOMENT YOU BELIEVE YOU HAVE ESCAPED THE *PAST*--
--SHE WILL STRIKE YOU DOWN! YOU, AND ALL WHO SERVE YOU!
APHRODITE... I KNOW NOT WHAT I DID TO EARN YOUR DISFAVOR...TO CAUSE YOU TO ABANDON US... BUT I BEG YOU...LOOK AFTER MY CHILD. GIVE HER YOUR STRENGTH, YOUR WISDOM... YOUR AID.
PLEASE.
DIANAAAAAA!

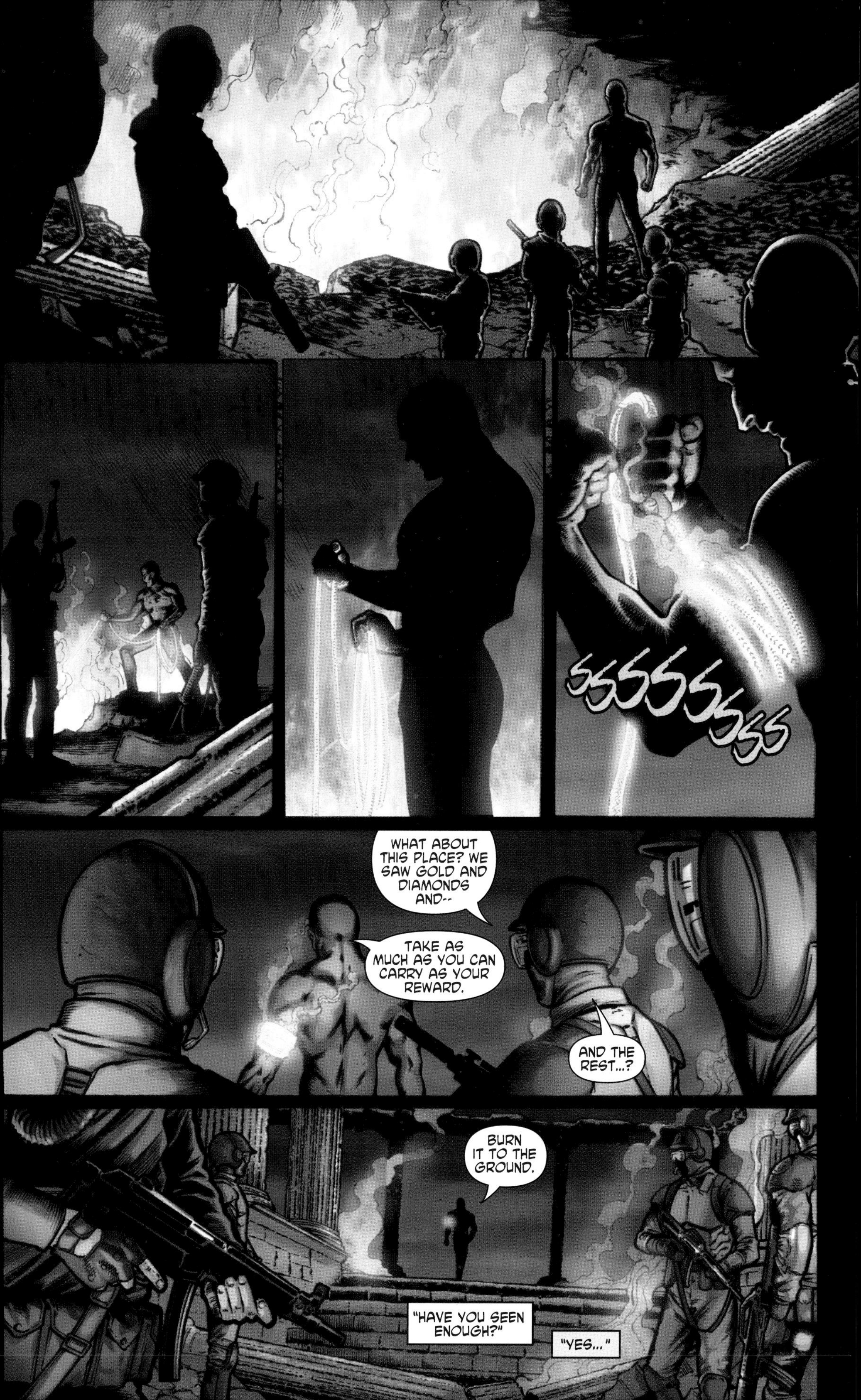

SSSSSSSSS
WHAT ABOUT THIS PLACE? WE SAW GOLD AND DIAMONDS AND--
TAKE AS MUCH AS YOU CAN CARRY AS YOUR REWARD.
AND THE REST...?
BURN IT TO THE GROUND.
"HAVE YOU SEEN ENOUGH?"
"YES..."

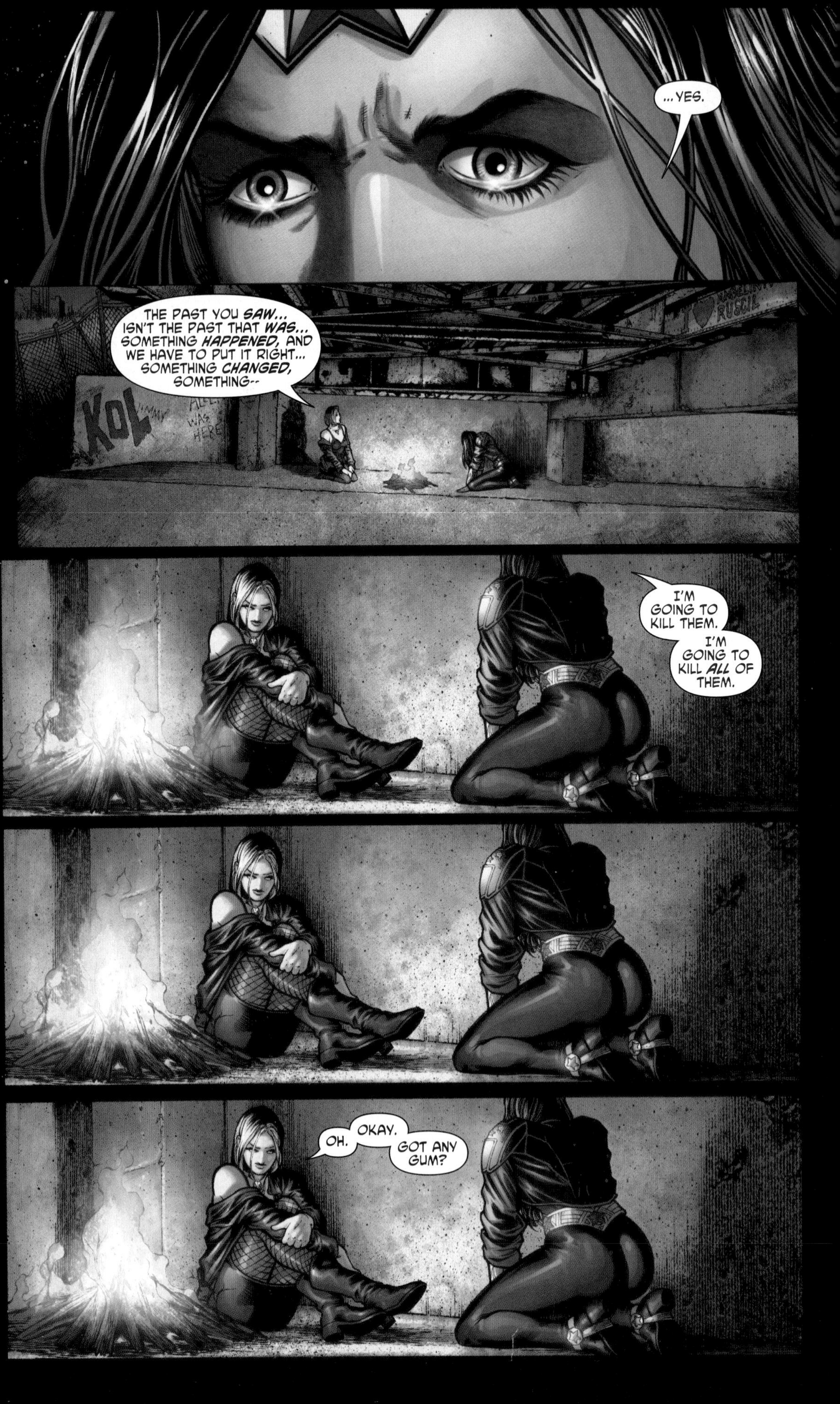

...YES.
THE PAST YOU SAW... ISN'T THE PAST THAT WAS... SOMETHING HAPPENED, AND WE HAVE TO PUT IT RIGHT... SOMETHING CHANGED, SOMETHING--
KOL
I'M GOING TO KILL THEM.
I'M GOING TO KILL ALL OF THEM.
OH.
OKAY.
GOT ANY GUM?

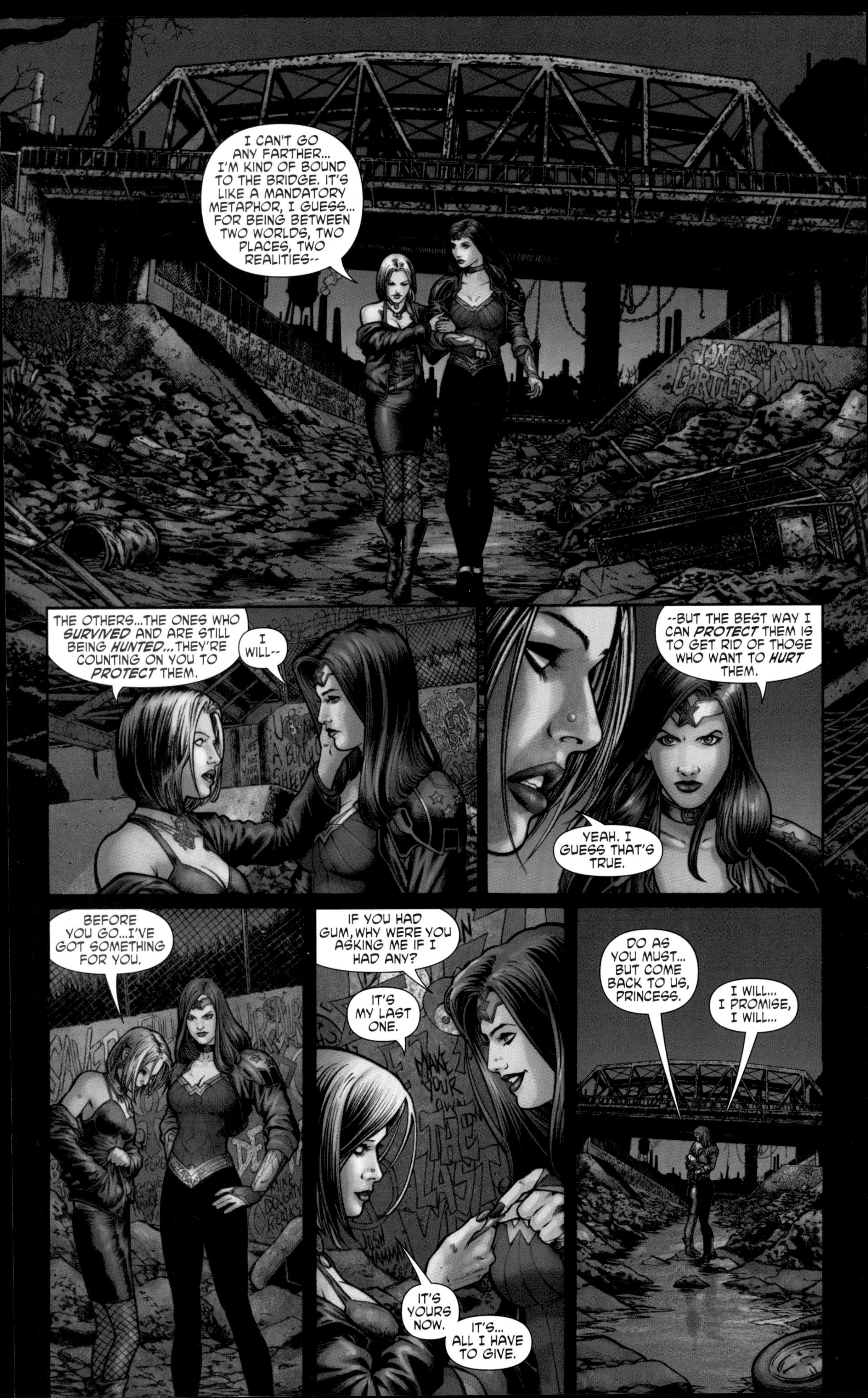
I CAN'T GO ANY FARTHER... I'M KIND OF BOUND TO THE BRIDGE. IT'S LIKE A MANDATORY METAPHOR, I GUESS... FOR BEING BETWEEN TWO WORLDS, TWO PLACES, TWO REALITIES--
THE OTHERS...THE ONES WHO SURVIVED AND ARE STILL BEING HUNTED...THEY'RE COUNTING ON YOU TO PROTECT THEM.
I WILL--
--BUT THE BEST WAY I CAN PROTECT THEM IS TO GET RID OF THOSE WHO WANT TO HURT THEM.
YEAH. I GUESS THAT'S TRUE.
BEFORE YOU GO...I'VE GOT SOMETHING FOR YOU.
IF YOU HAD GUM, WHY WERE YOU ASKING ME IF I HAD ANY?
IT'S MY LAST ONE.
IT'S YOURS NOW.
IT'S... ALL I HAVE TO GIVE.
DO AS YOU MUST... BUT COME BACK TO US, PRINCESS.
I WILL... I PROMISE, I WILL...

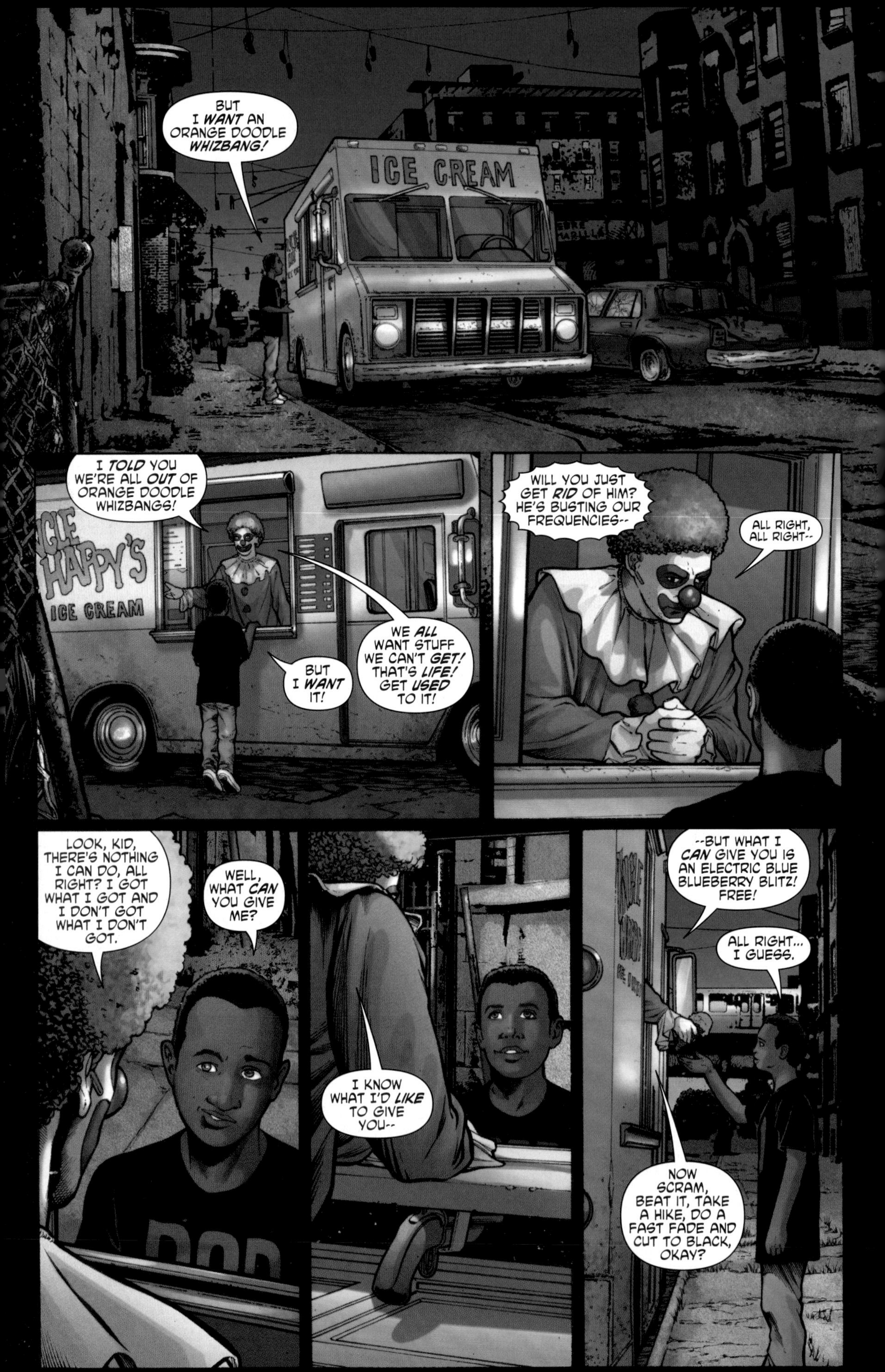

BUT I *WANT* AN ORANGE DOODLE *WHIZBANG!*
ICE CREAM
I *TOLD* YOU WE'RE ALL *OUT* OF ORANGE DOODLE WHIZBANGS!
HAPPY'S ICE CREAM
BUT I *WANT* IT!
WE *ALL* WANT STUFF WE CAN'T *GET!* THAT'S *LIFE!* GET *USED* TO IT!
WILL YOU JUST GET *RID* OF HIM? HE'S BUSTING OUR FREQUENCIES--
ALL RIGHT, ALL RIGHT--
LOOK, KID, THERE'S NOTHING I CAN DO, ALL RIGHT? I GOT WHAT I GOT AND I DON'T GOT WHAT I DON'T GOT.
WELL, WHAT *CAN* YOU GIVE ME?
I KNOW WHAT I'D *LIKE* TO GIVE YOU--
--BUT WHAT I *CAN* GIVE YOU IS AN ELECTRIC BLUE BLUEBERRY BLITZ! FREE!
ALL RIGHT... I GUESS.
NOW SCRAM, BEAT IT, TAKE A HIKE, DO A FAST FADE AND CUT TO BLACK, OKAY?

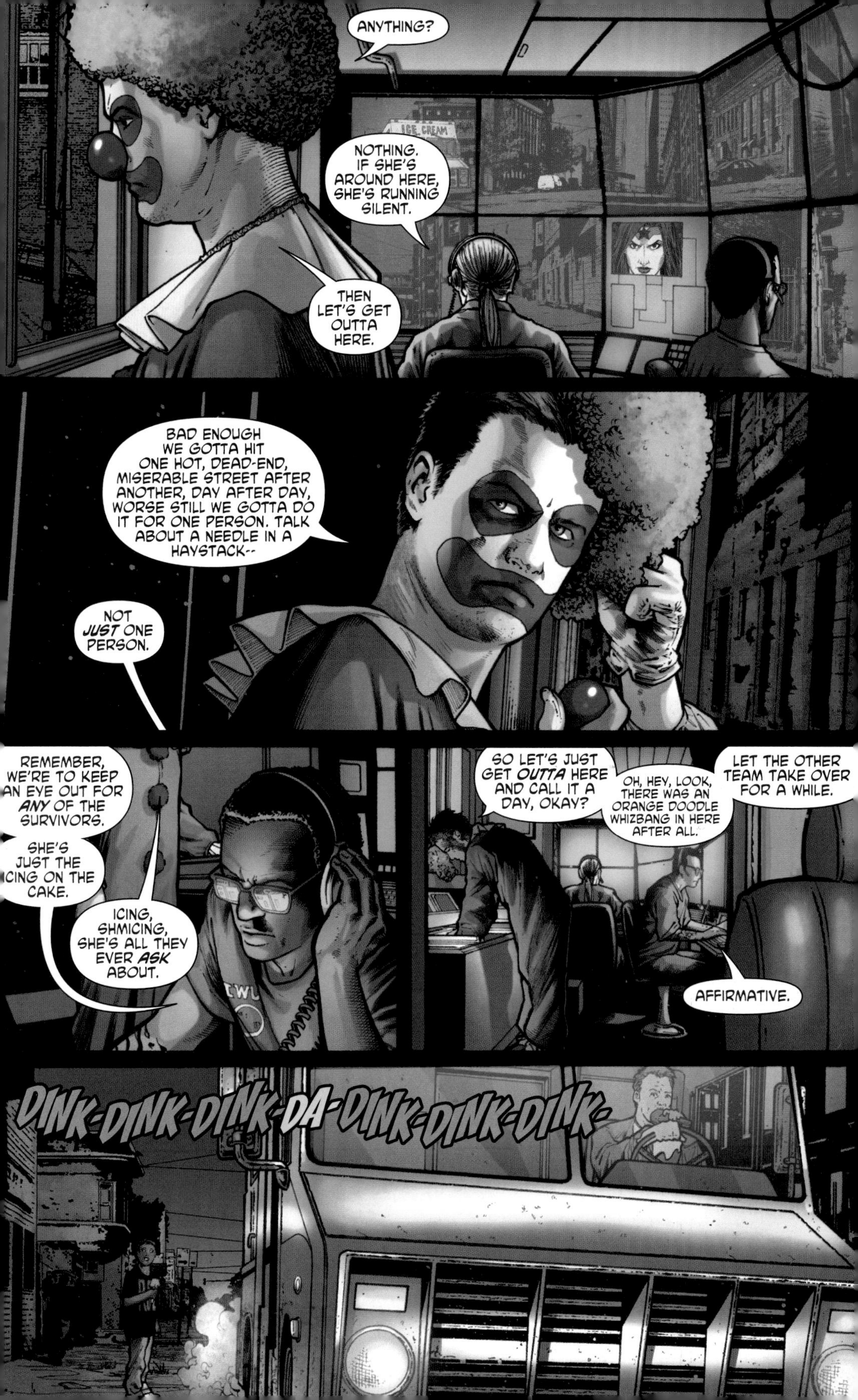
ANYTHING?
ICE CREAM
NOTHING. IF SHE'S AROUND HERE, SHE'S RUNNING SILENT.
THEN LET'S GET OUTTA HERE.
BAD ENOUGH WE GOTTA HIT ONE HOT, DEAD-END, MISERABLE STREET AFTER ANOTHER, DAY AFTER DAY, WORSE STILL WE GOTTA DO IT FOR ONE PERSON. TALK ABOUT A NEEDLE IN A HAYSTACK--
NOT *JUST* ONE PERSON.
REMEMBER, WE'RE TO KEEP AN EYE OUT FOR *ANY* OF THE SURVIVORS.
SHE'S JUST THE ICING ON THE CAKE.
ICING, SHMICING, SHE'S ALL THEY EVER *ASK* ABOUT.
SO LET'S JUST GET *OUTTA* HERE AND CALL IT A DAY, OKAY?
OH, HEY, LOOK, THERE WAS AN ORANGE DOODLE WHIZBANG IN HERE AFTER ALL.
LET THE OTHER TEAM TAKE OVER FOR A WHILE.
AFFIRMATIVE.
DINK-DINK-DINK-DA-DINK-DINK-DINK-

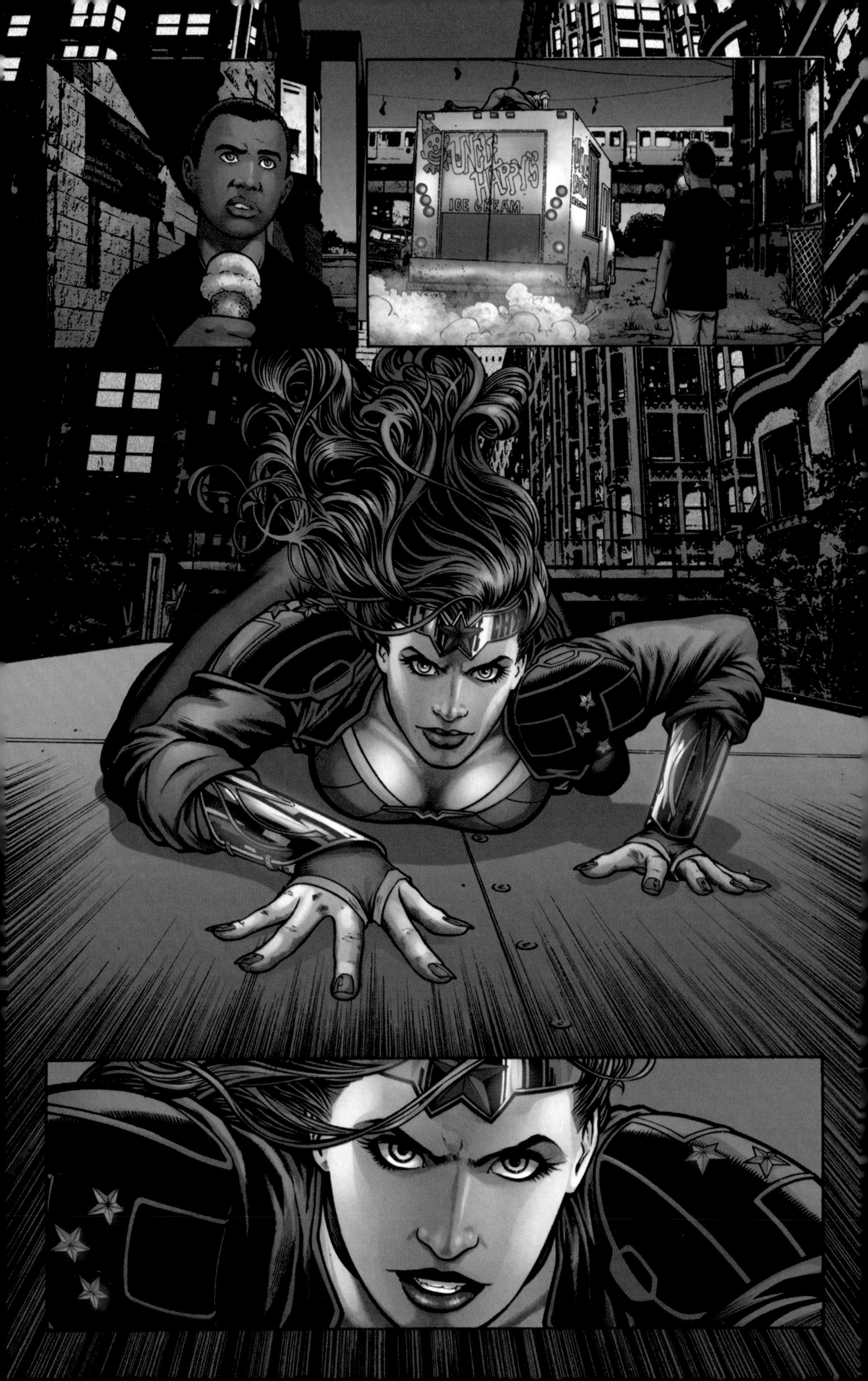
UNCLE HAPPY'S
ICE CREAM

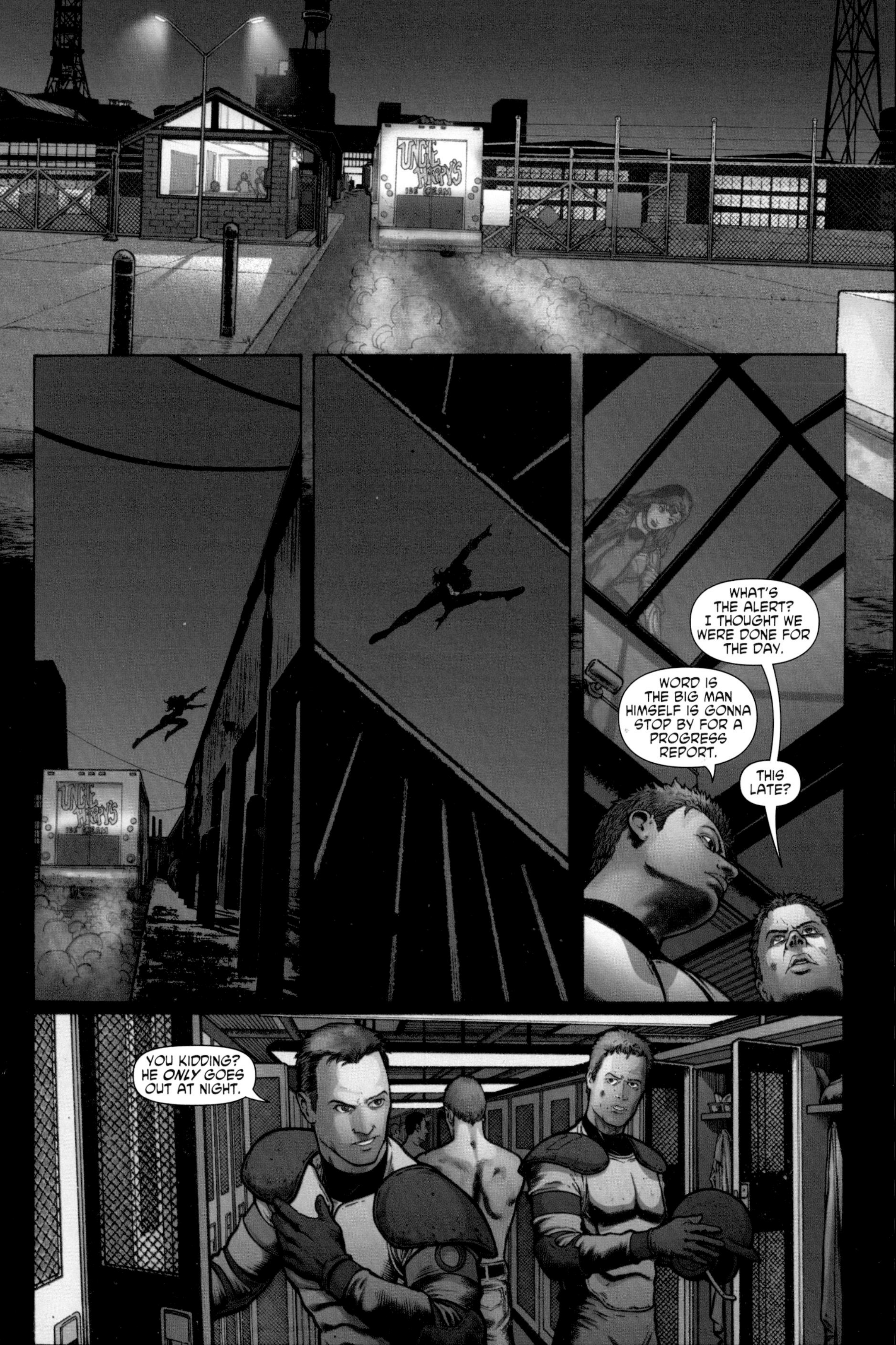
UNCLE HARRY'S ICE CREAM
WHAT'S THE ALERT? I THOUGHT WE WERE DONE FOR THE DAY.
WORD IS THE BIG MAN HIMSELF IS GONNA STOP BY FOR A PROGRESS REPORT.
THIS LATE?
YOU KIDDING? HE *ONLY* GOES OUT AT NIGHT.

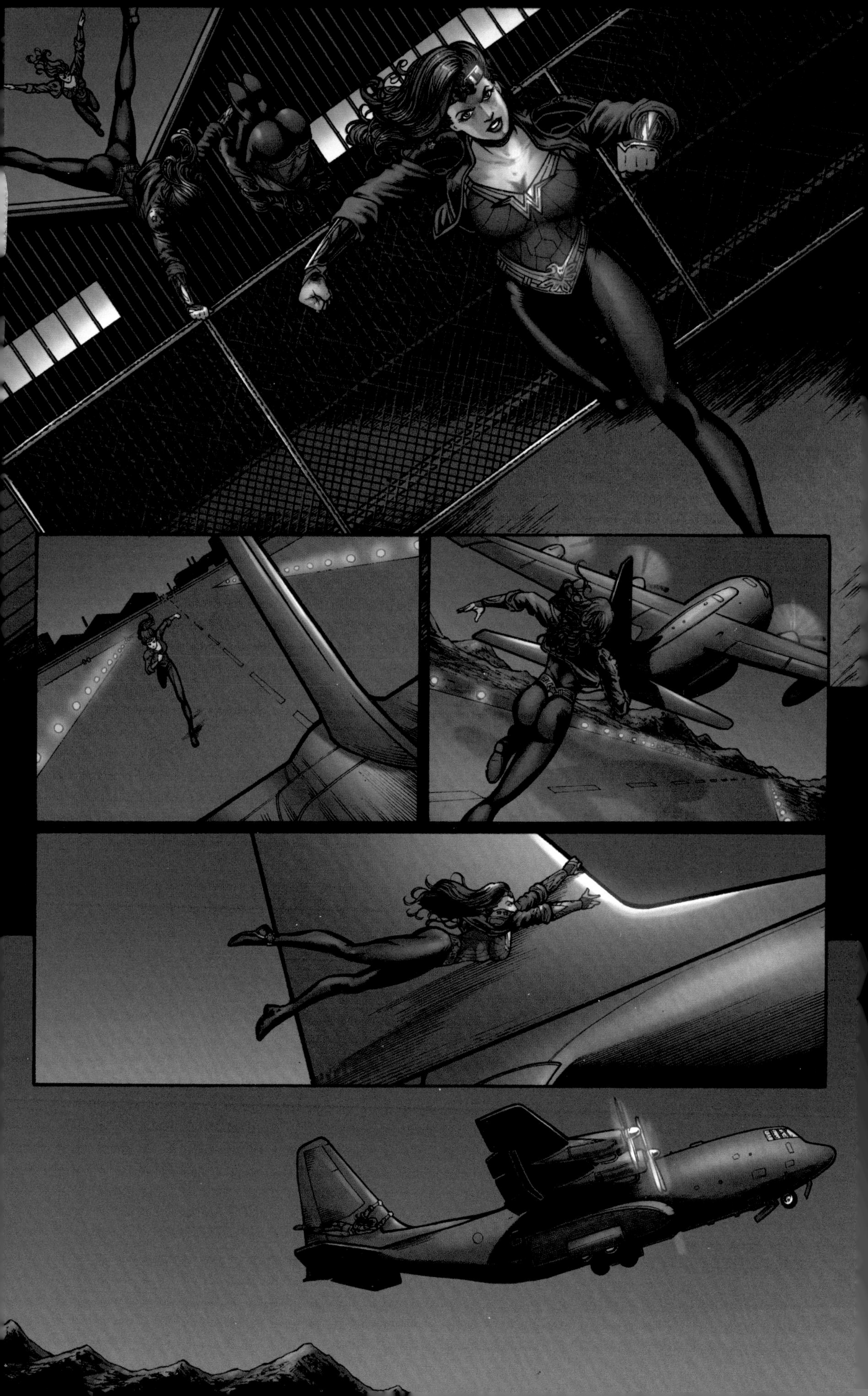

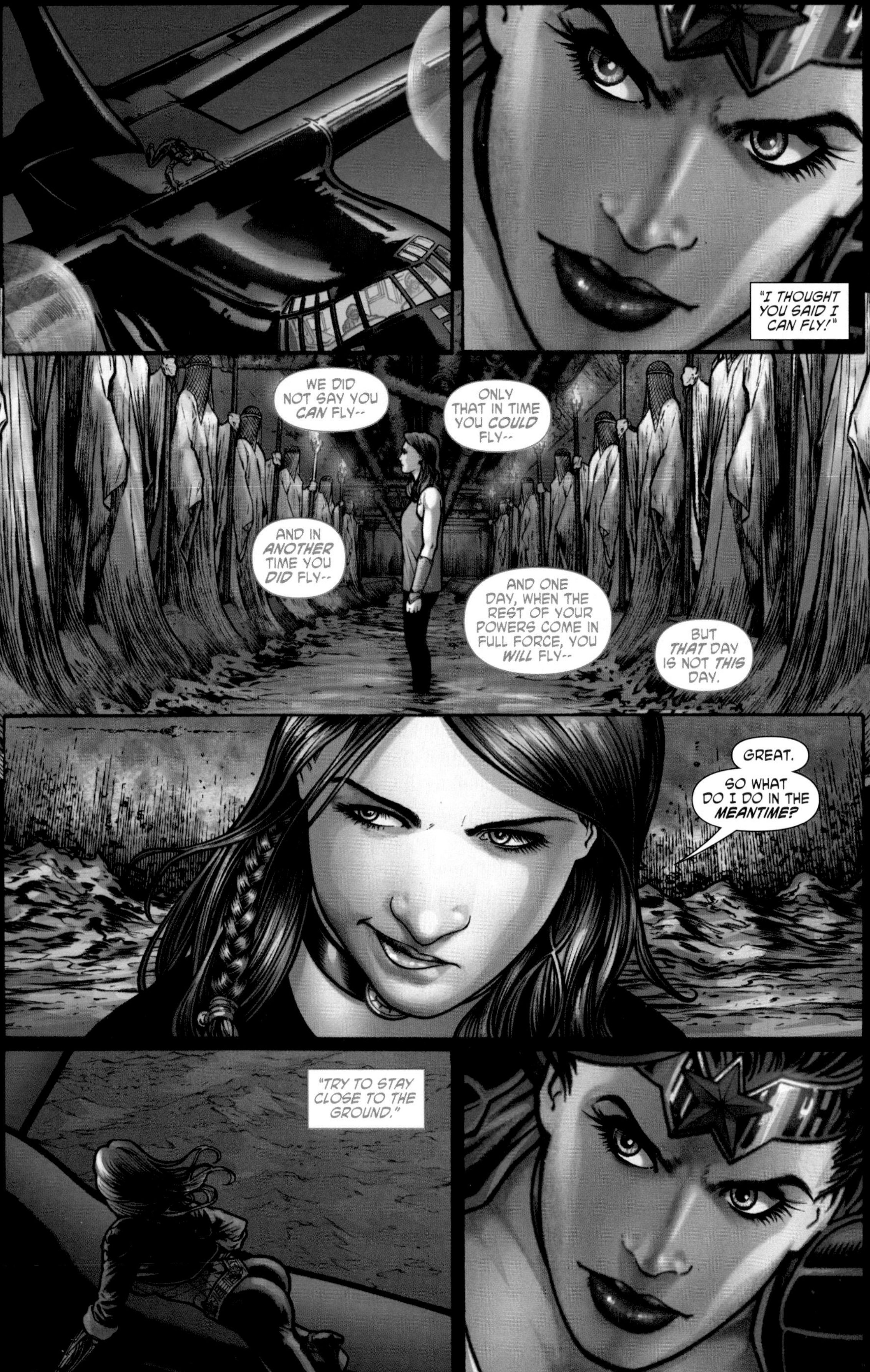
"I THOUGHT YOU SAID I CAN FLY!"
WE DID NOT SAY YOU CAN FLY--
ONLY THAT IN TIME YOU COULD FLY--
AND IN ANOTHER TIME YOU DID FLY--
AND ONE DAY, WHEN THE REST OF YOUR POWERS COME IN FULL FORCE, YOU WILL FLY--
BUT THAT DAY IS NOT THIS DAY.
GREAT.
SO WHAT DO I DO IN THE MEANTIME?
"TRY TO STAY CLOSE TO THE GROUND."

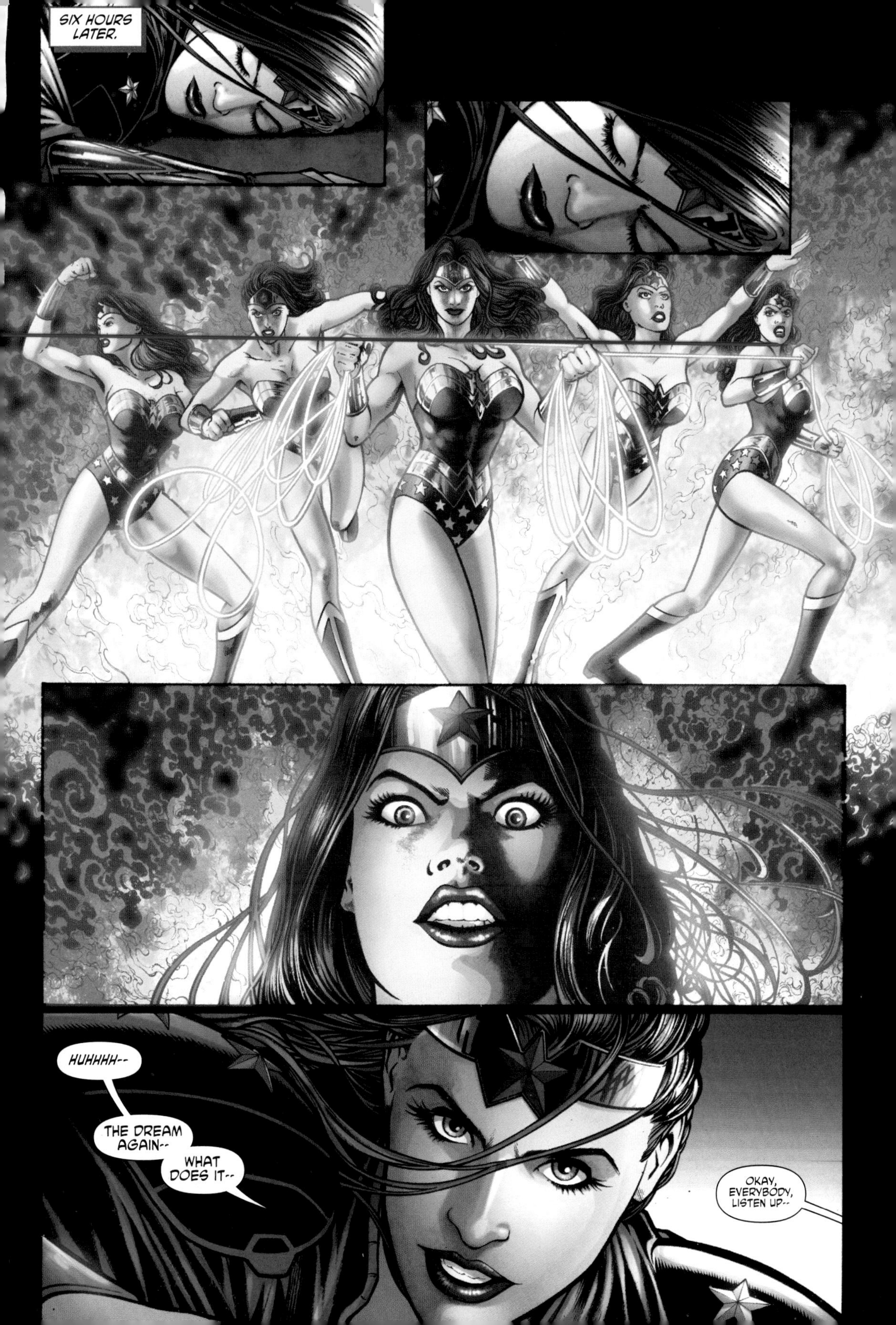
SIX HOURS LATER.
HUHHHH--
THE DREAM AGAIN--
WHAT DOES IT--
OKAY, EVERYBODY, LISTEN UP--

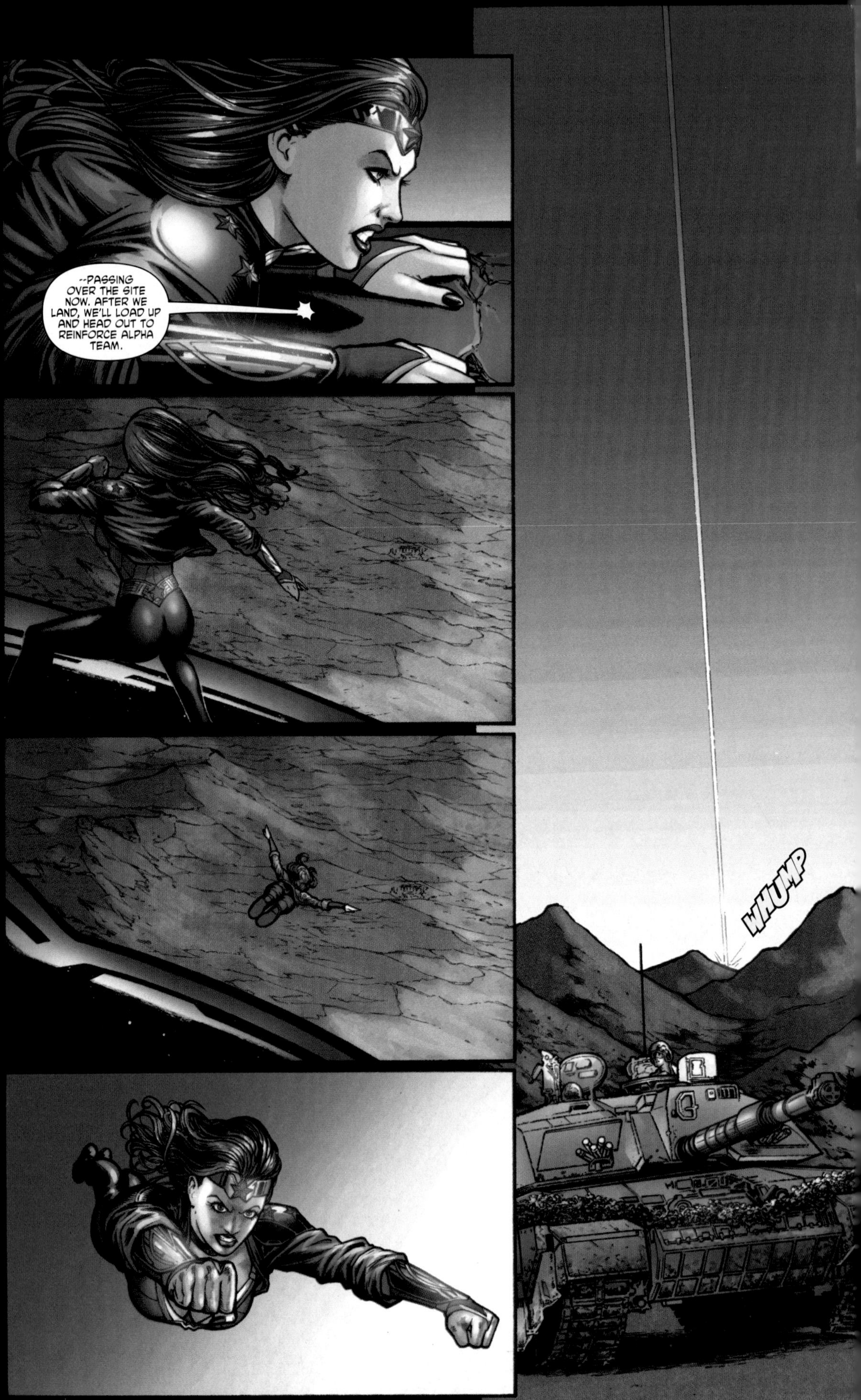
--PASSING OVER THE SITE NOW. AFTER WE LAND, WE'LL LOAD UP AND HEAD OUT TO REINFORCE ALPHA TEAM.
WHUMP

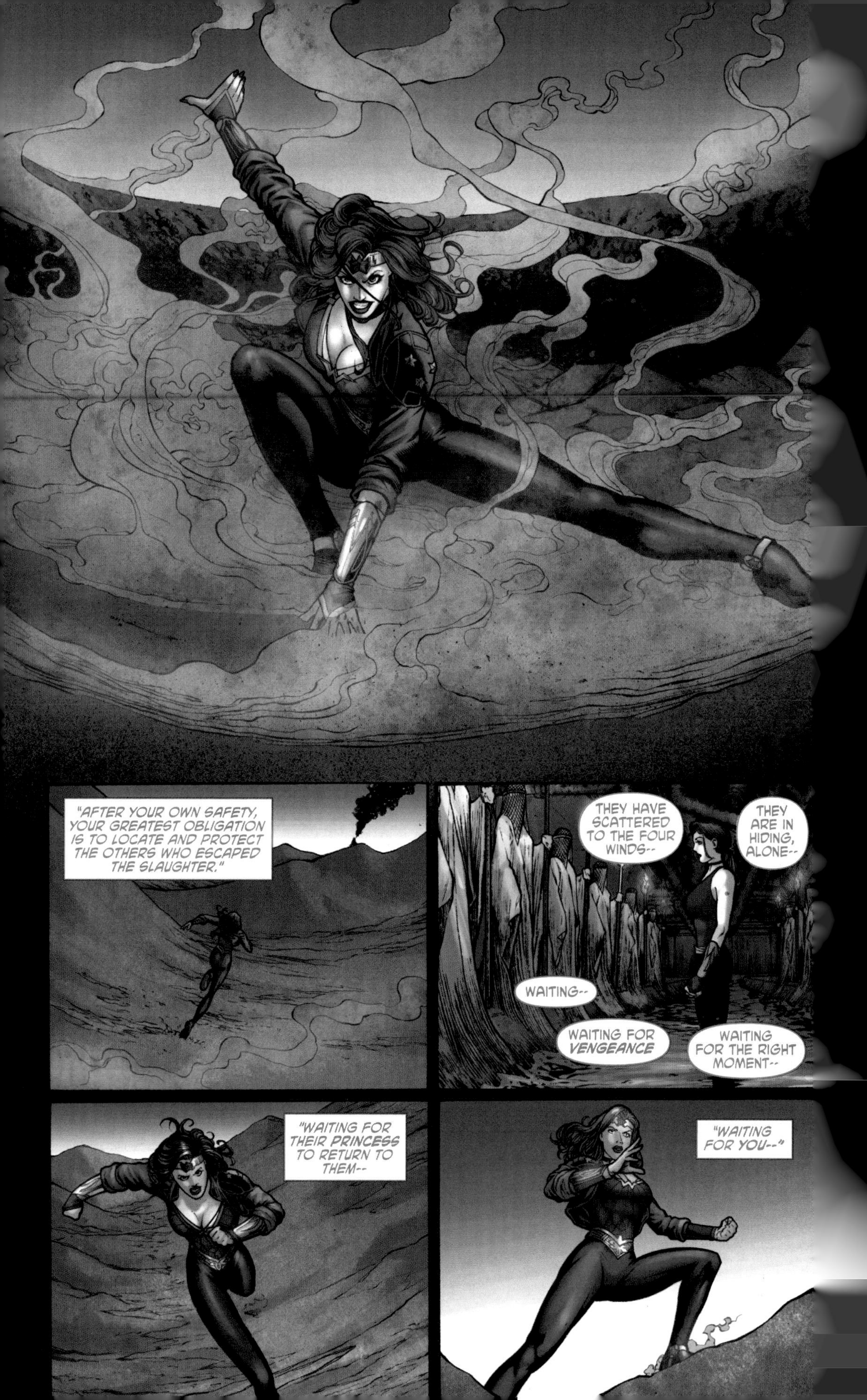
"AFTER YOUR OWN SAFETY, YOUR GREATEST OBLIGATION IS TO LOCATE AND PROTECT THE OTHERS WHO ESCAPED THE SLAUGHTER."
THEY HAVE SCATTERED TO THE FOUR WINDS--
THEY ARE IN HIDING, ALONE--
WAITING--
WAITING FOR VENGEANCE
WAITING FOR THE RIGHT MOMENT--
"WAITING FOR THEIR PRINCESS TO RETURN TO THEM--
"WAITING FOR YOU--"

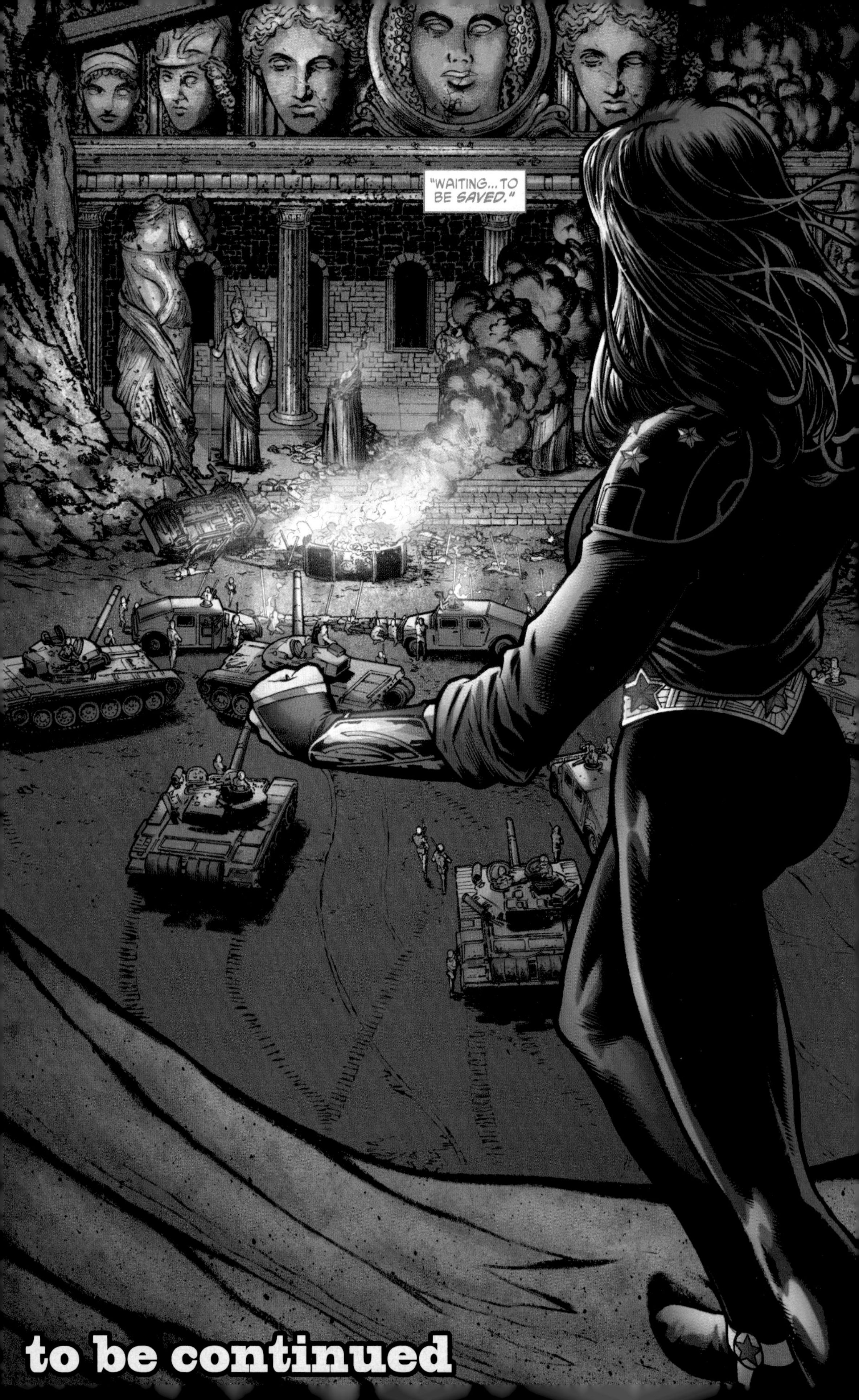
"WAITING... TO BE SAVED."
to be continued

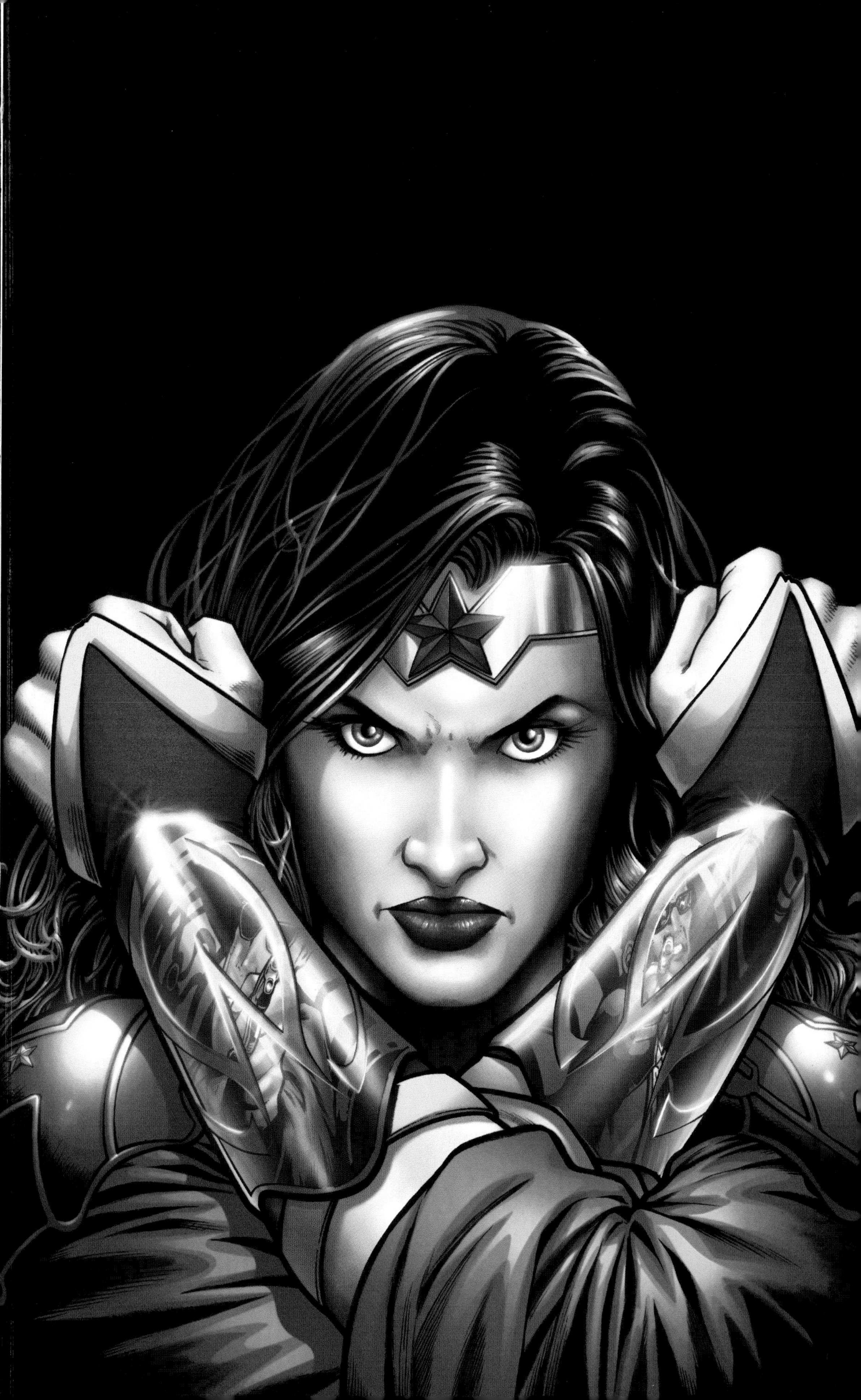

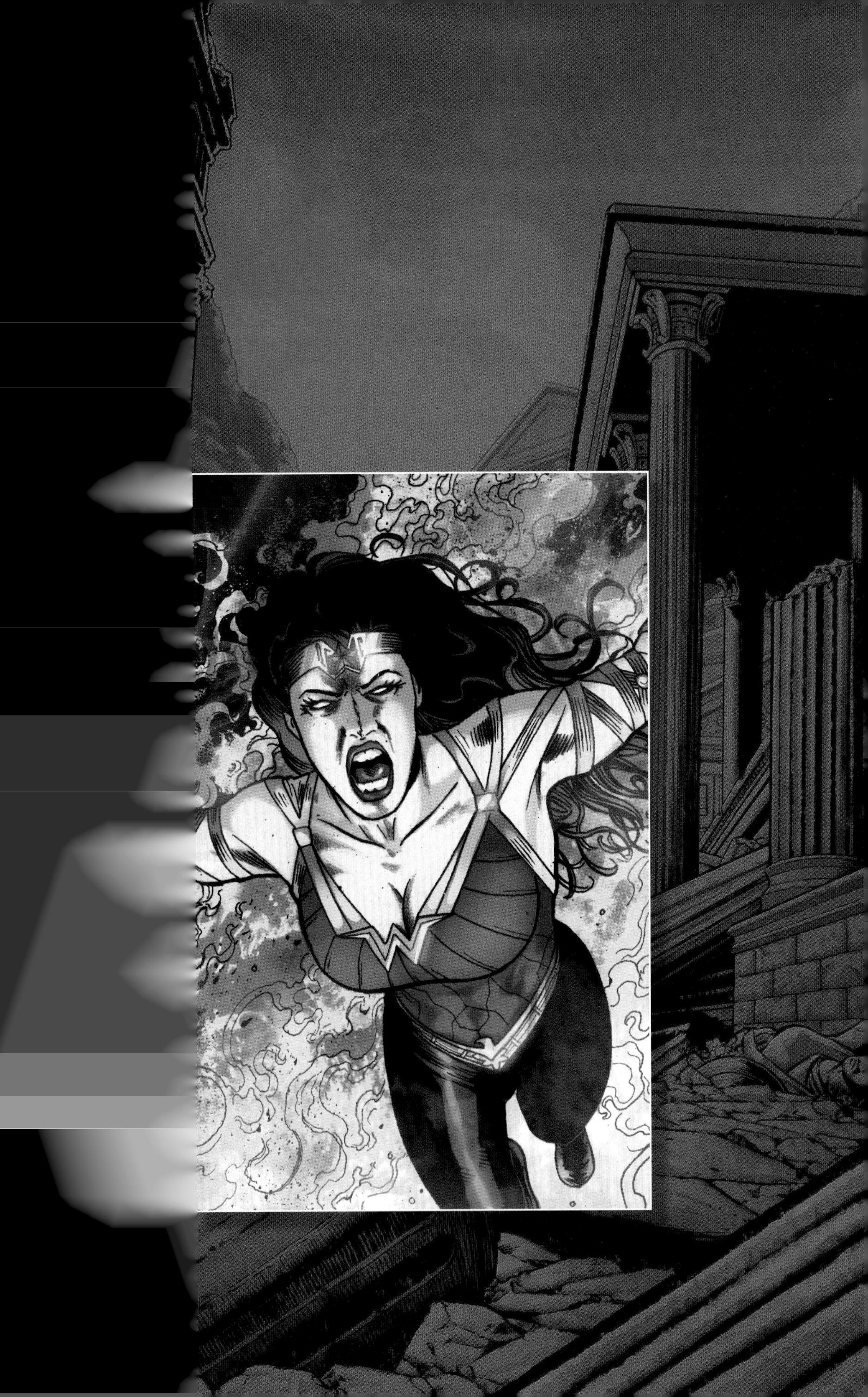

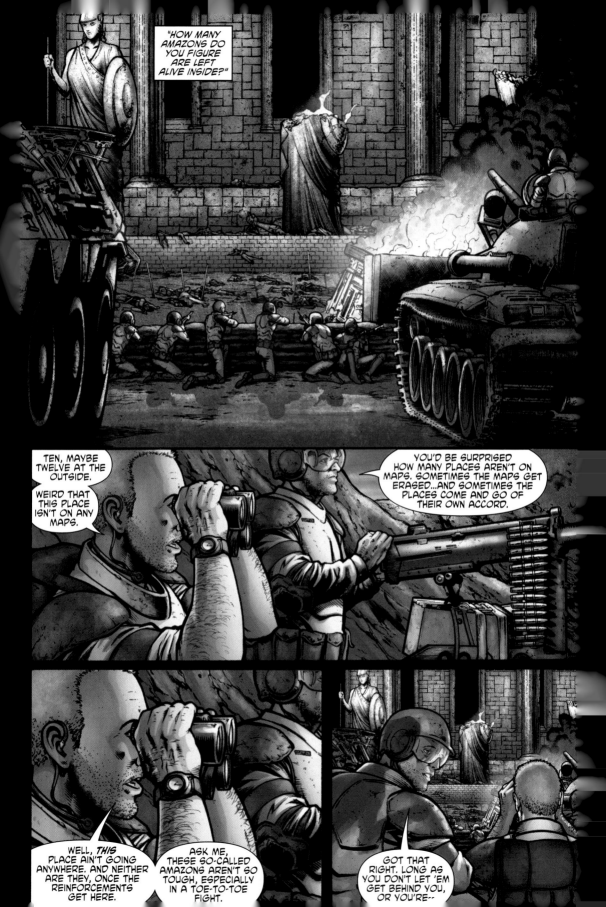

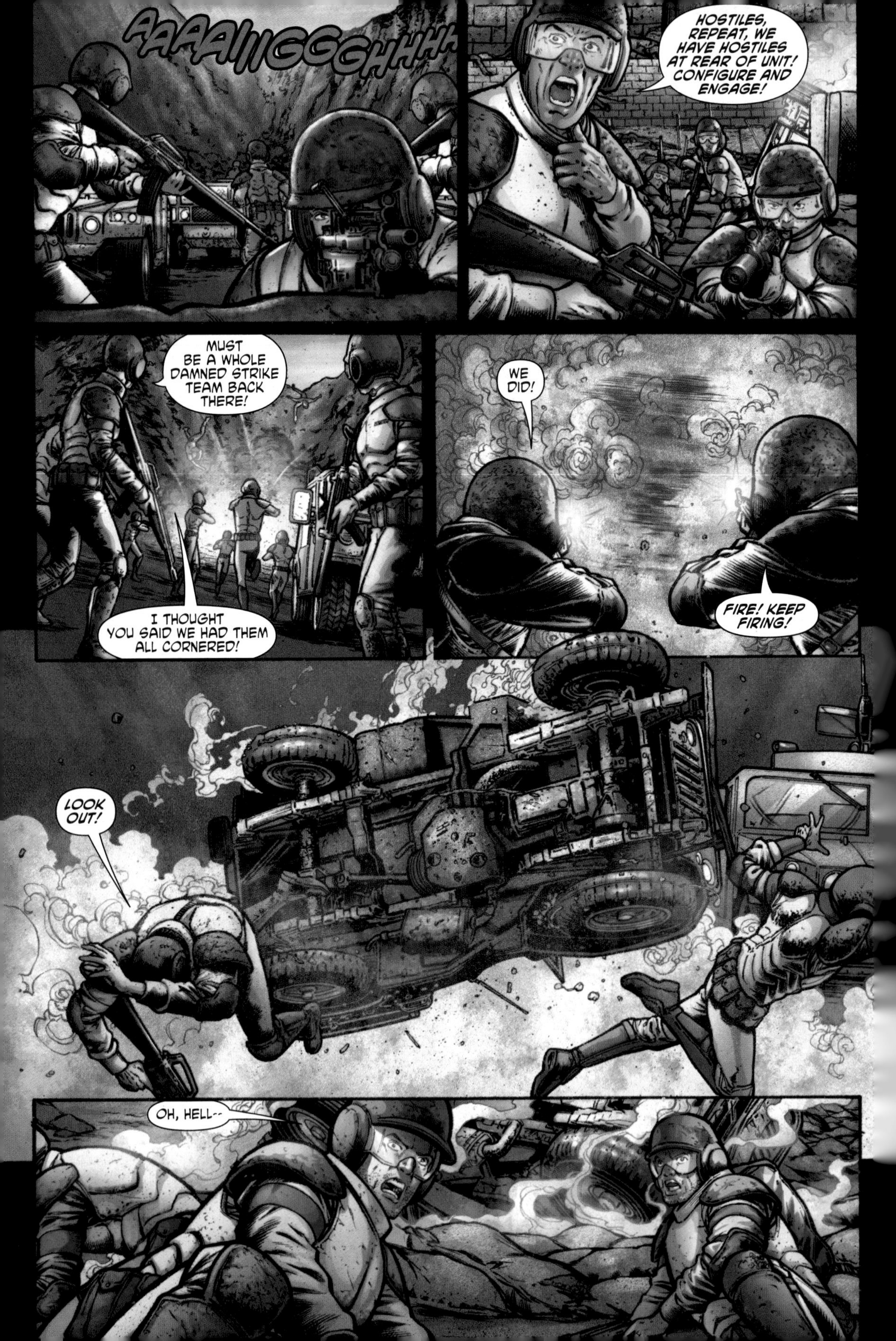
AAAAIIIGGGHHH
HOSTILES, REPEAT, WE HAVE HOSTILES AT REAR OF UNIT! CONFIGURE AND ENGAGE!
MUST BE A WHOLE DAMNED STRIKE TEAM BACK THERE!
I THOUGHT YOU SAID WE HAD THEM ALL CORNERED!
WE DID!
FIRE! KEEP FIRING!
LOOK OUT!
OH, HELL--

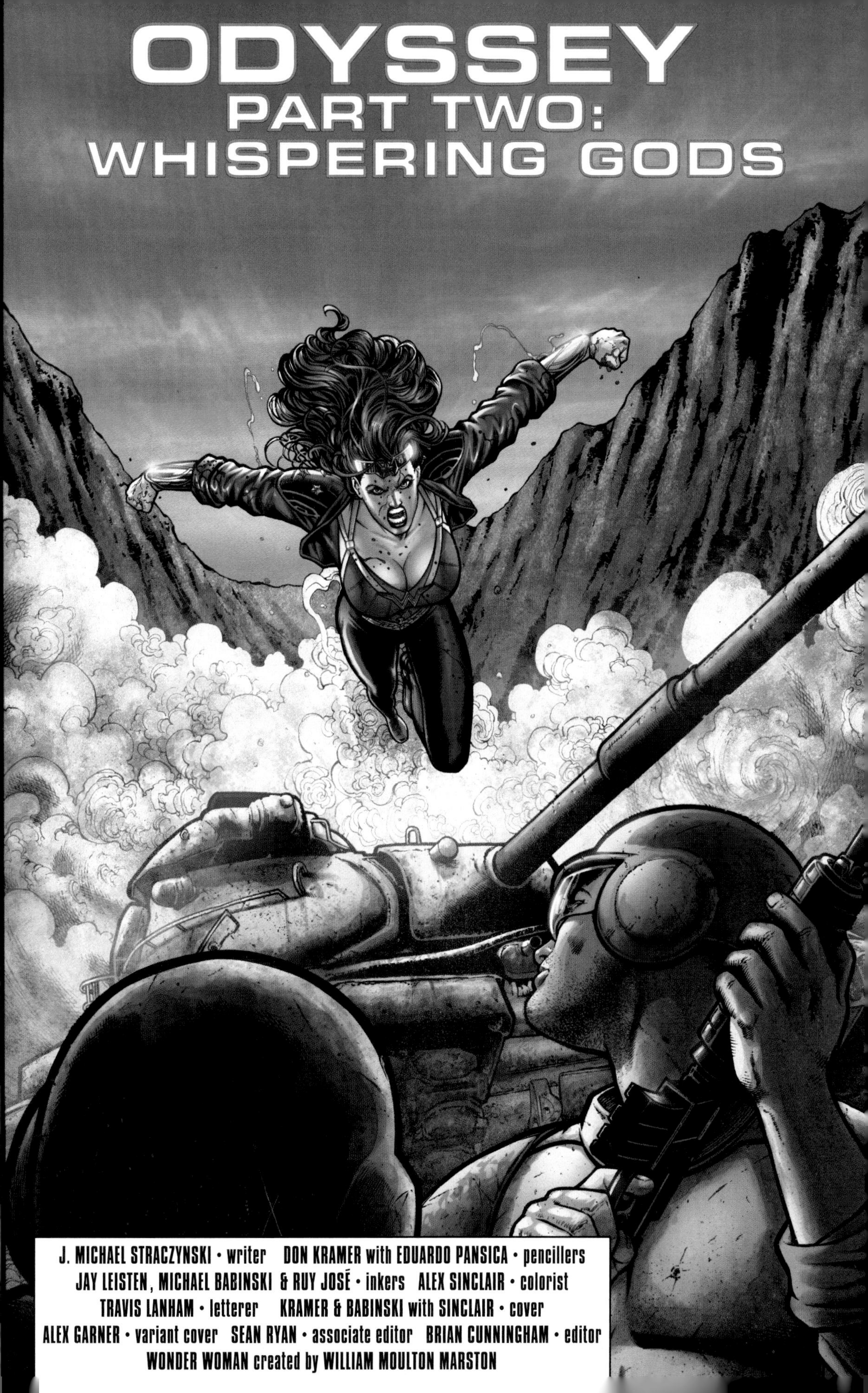
ODYSSEY
PART TWO:
WHISPERING GODS
J. MICHAEL STRACZYNSKI • writer DON KRAMER with EDUARDO PANSICA • pencillers
JAY LEISTEN, MICHAEL BABINSKI & RUY JOSÉ • inkers ALEX SINCLAIR • colorist
TRAVIS LANHAM • letterer KRAMER & BABINSKI with SINCLAIR • cover
ALEX GARNER • variant cover SEAN RYAN • associate editor BRIAN CUNNINGHAM • editor
WONDER WOMAN created by WILLIAM MOULTON MARSTON

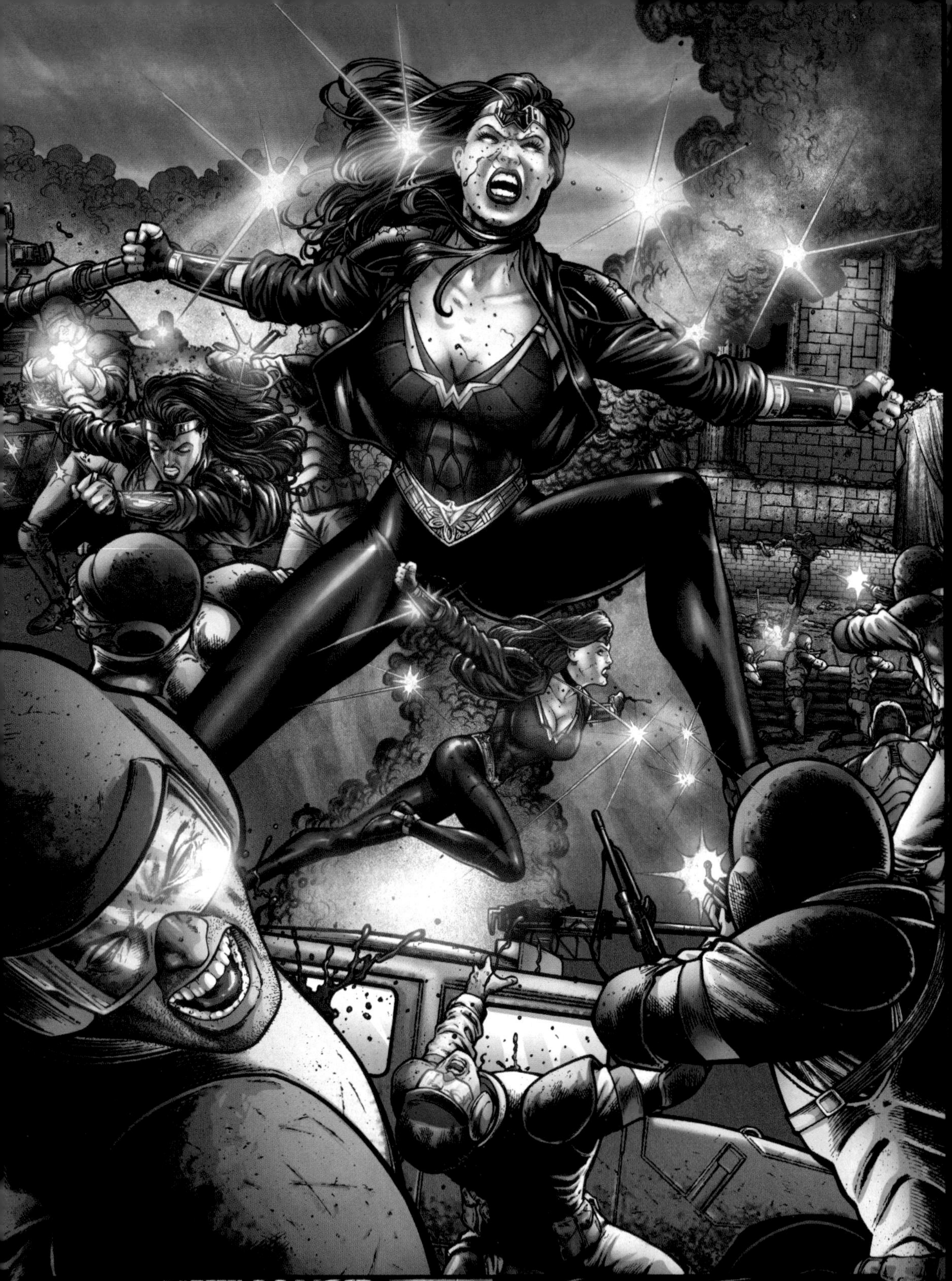

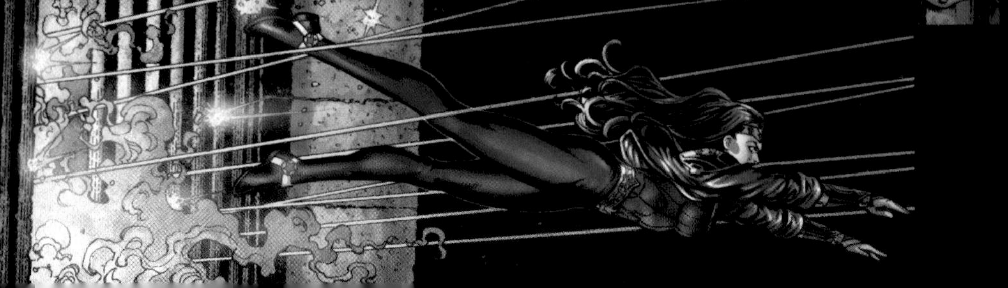

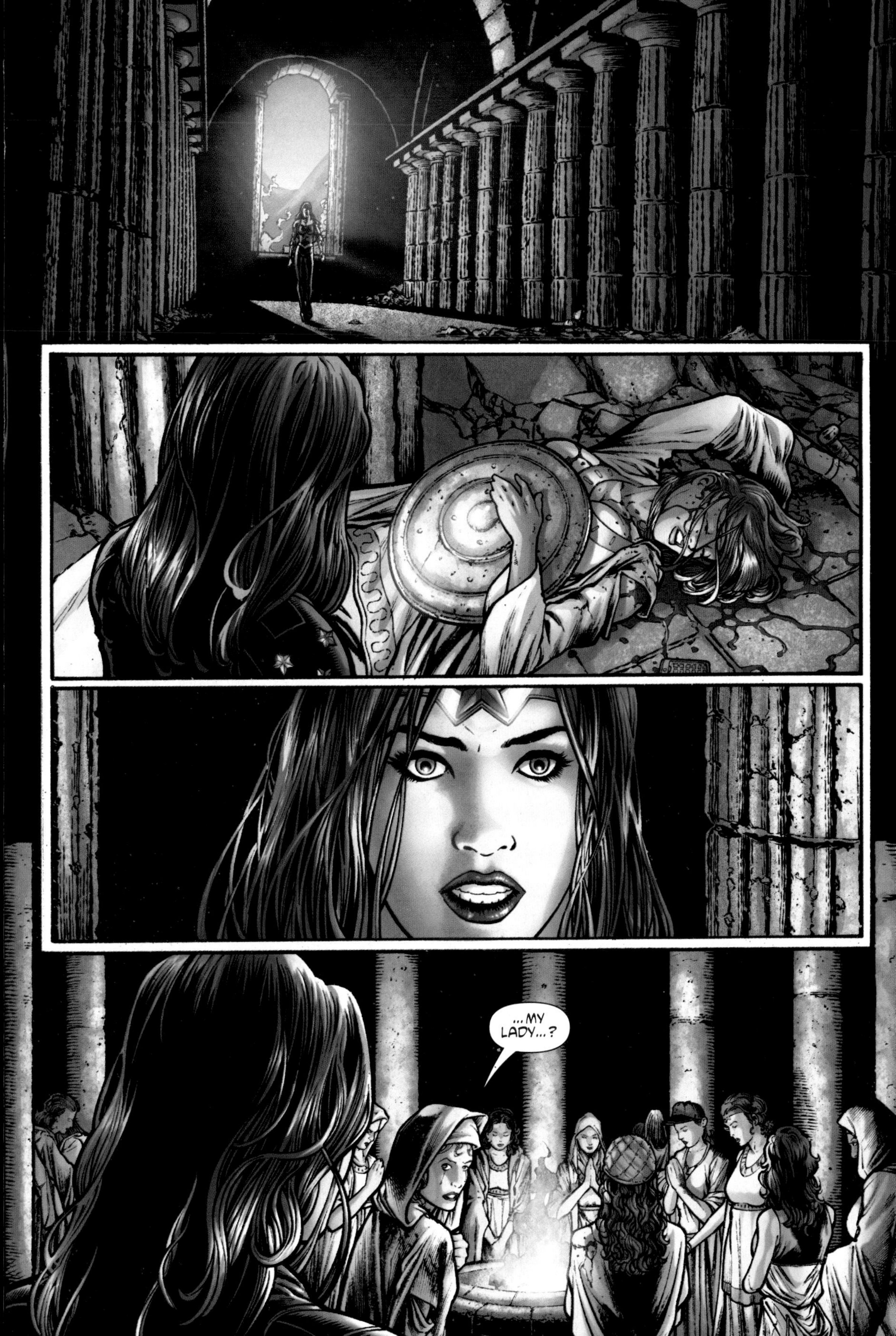
...MY LADY...?

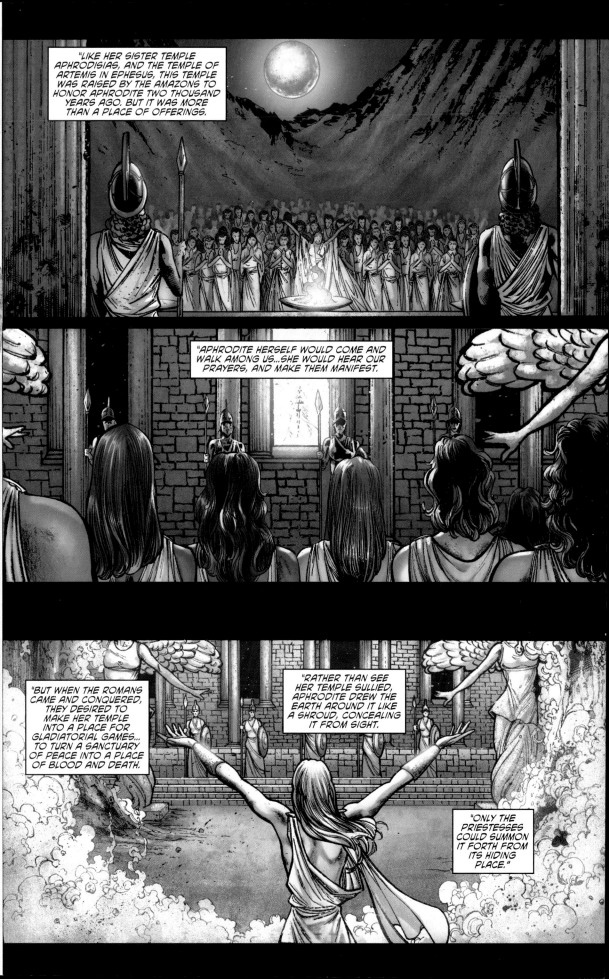

"LIKE HER SISTER TEMPLE APHRODISIAS, AND THE TEMPLE OF ARTEMIS IN EPHESUS, THIS TEMPLE WAS RAISED BY THE AMAZONS TO HONOR APHRODITE TWO THOUSAND YEARS AGO. BUT IT WAS MORE THAN A PLACE OF OFFERINGS.

"APHRODITE HERSELF WOULD COME AND WALK AMONG US...SHE WOULD HEAR OUR PRAYERS, AND MAKE THEM MANIFEST.

"BUT WHEN THE ROMANS CAME AND CONQUERED, THEY DESIRED TO MAKE HER TEMPLE INTO A PLACE FOR GLADIATORIAL GAMES... TO TURN A SANCTUARY OF PEACE INTO A PLACE OF BLOOD AND DEATH.

"RATHER THAN SEE HER TEMPLE SULLIED, APHRODITE DREW THE EARTH AROUND IT LIKE A SHROUD, CONCEALING IT FROM SIGHT.

"ONLY THE PRIESTESSES COULD SUMMON IT FORTH FROM ITS HIDING PLACE."

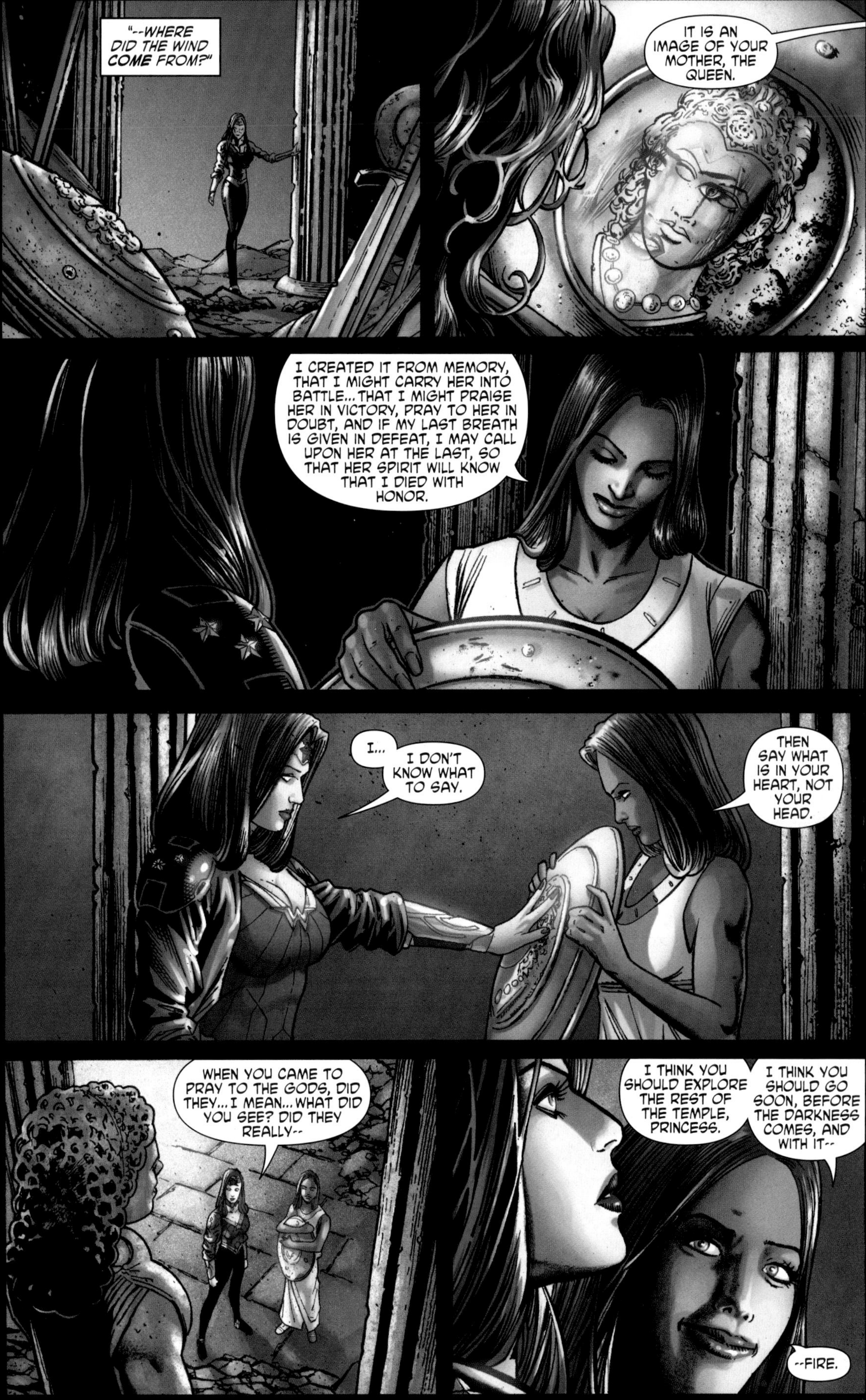
"--WHERE DID THE WIND COME FROM?"
IT IS AN IMAGE OF YOUR MOTHER, THE QUEEN.
I CREATED IT FROM MEMORY, THAT I MIGHT CARRY HER INTO BATTLE... THAT I MIGHT PRAISE HER IN VICTORY, PRAY TO HER IN DOUBT, AND IF MY LAST BREATH IS GIVEN IN DEFEAT, I MAY CALL UPON HER AT THE LAST, SO THAT HER SPIRIT WILL KNOW THAT I DIED WITH HONOR.
I... I DON'T KNOW WHAT TO SAY.
THEN SAY WHAT IS IN YOUR HEART, NOT YOUR HEAD.
WHEN YOU CAME TO PRAY TO THE GODS, DID THEY... I MEAN... WHAT DID YOU SEE? DID THEY REALLY--
I THINK YOU SHOULD EXPLORE THE REST OF THE TEMPLE, PRINCESS.
I THINK YOU SHOULD GO SOON, BEFORE THE DARKNESS COMES, AND WITH IT--
--FIRE.

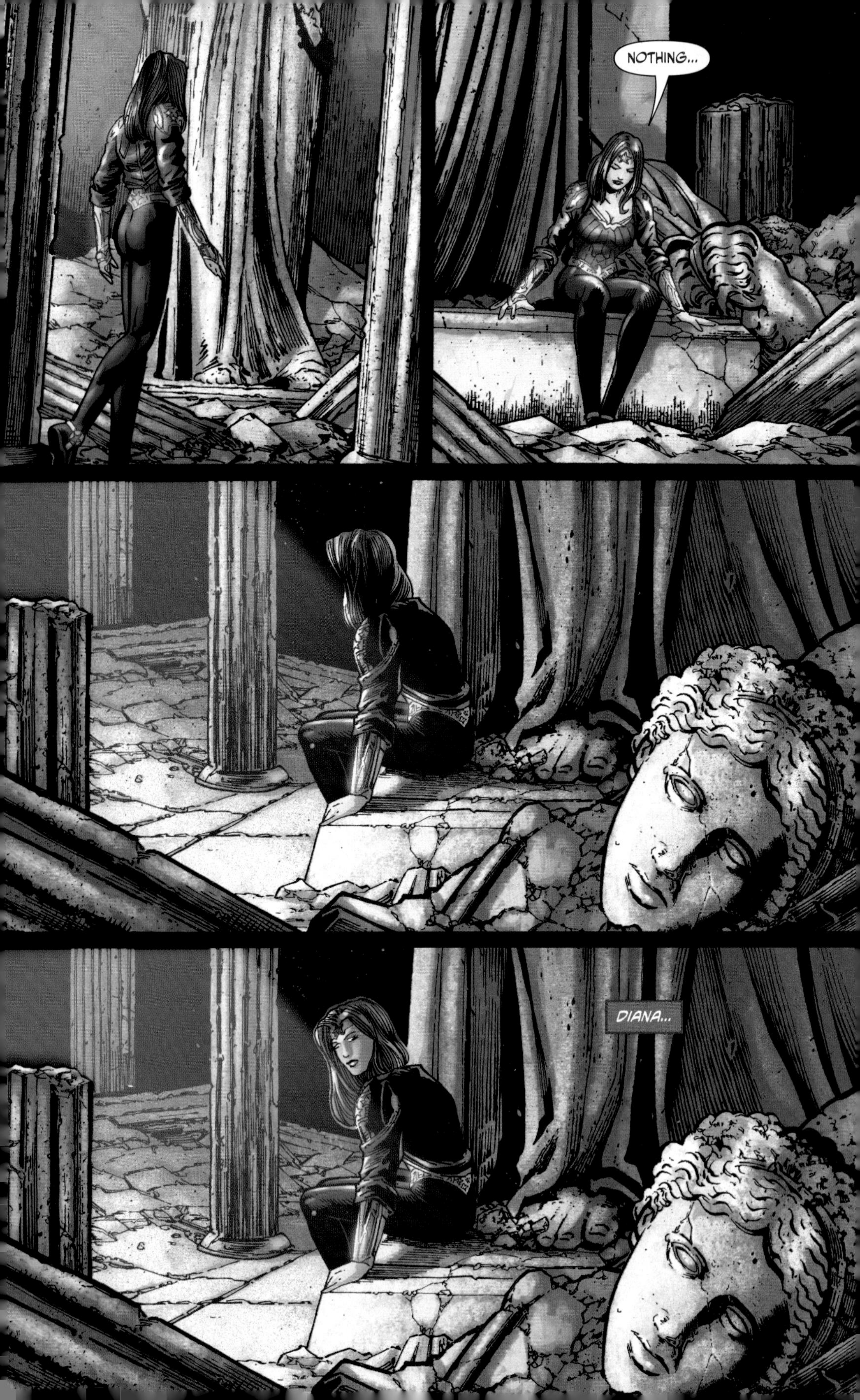
NOTHING...
DIANA...

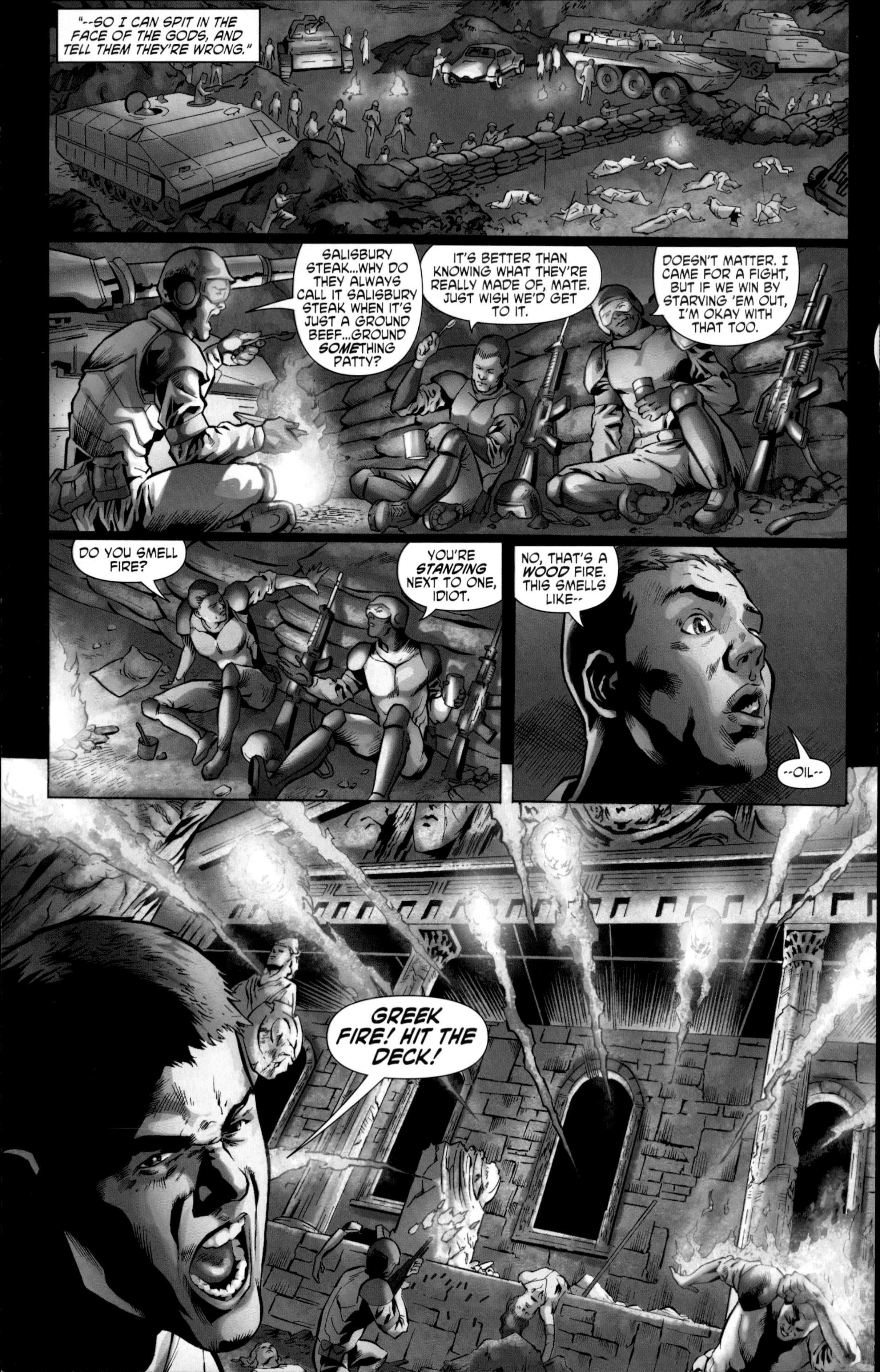
"--SO I CAN SPIT IN THE FACE OF THE GODS, AND TELL THEM THEY'RE WRONG."
SALISBURY STEAK...WHY DO THEY ALWAYS CALL IT SALISBURY STEAK WHEN IT'S JUST A GROUND BEEF...GROUND SOMETHING PATTY?
IT'S BETTER THAN KNOWING WHAT THEY'RE REALLY MADE OF, MATE. JUST WISH WE'D GET TO IT.
DOESN'T MATTER. I CAME FOR A FIGHT, BUT IF WE WIN BY STARVING 'EM OUT, I'M OKAY WITH THAT TOO.
DO YOU SMELL FIRE?
YOU'RE STANDING NEXT TO ONE, IDIOT.
NO, THAT'S A WOOD FIRE. THIS SMELLS LIKE--
--OIL--
GREEK FIRE! HIT THE DECK!

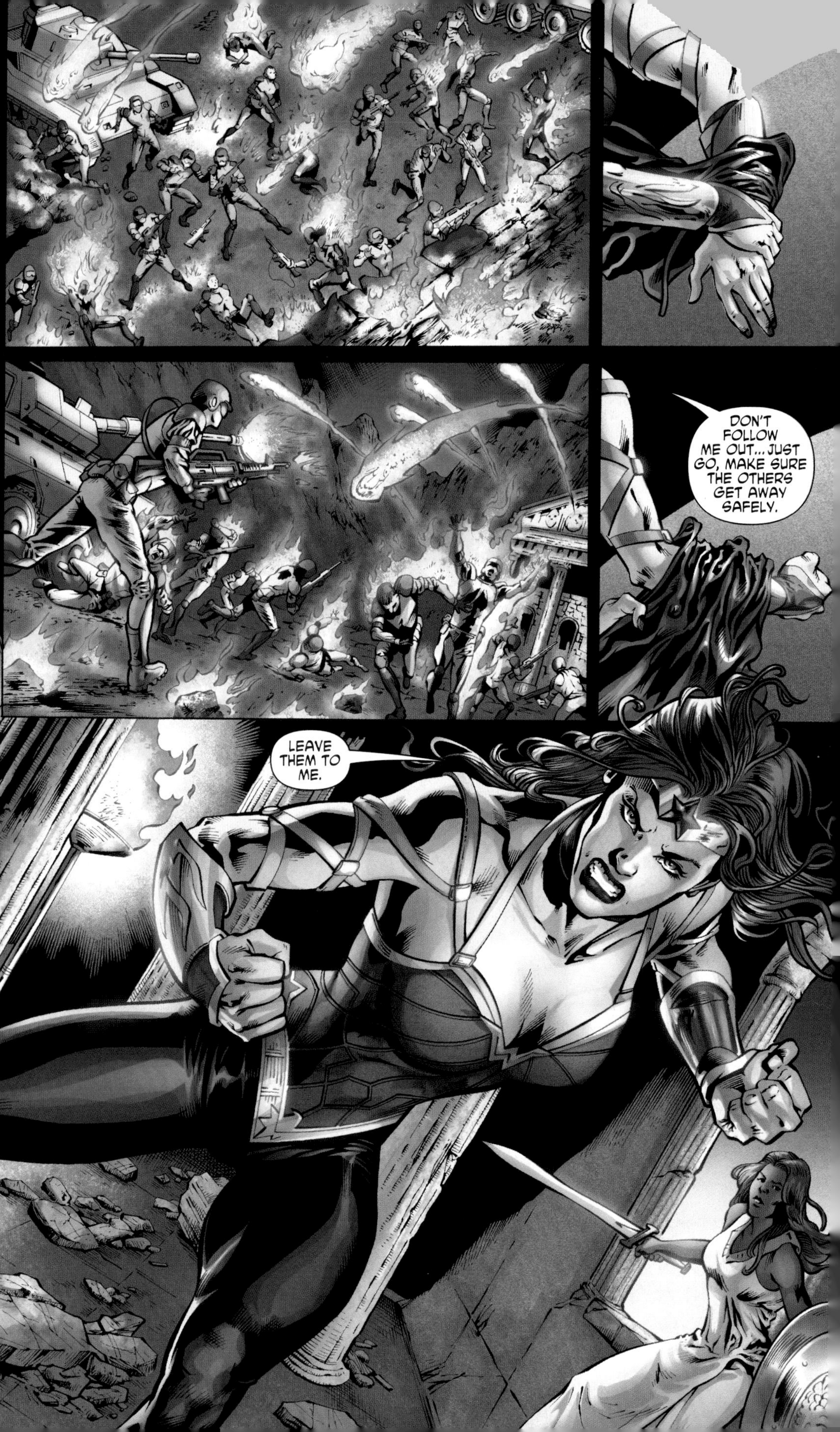
DON'T FOLLOW ME OUT... JUST GO, MAKE SURE THE OTHERS GET AWAY SAFELY.
LEAVE THEM TO ME.

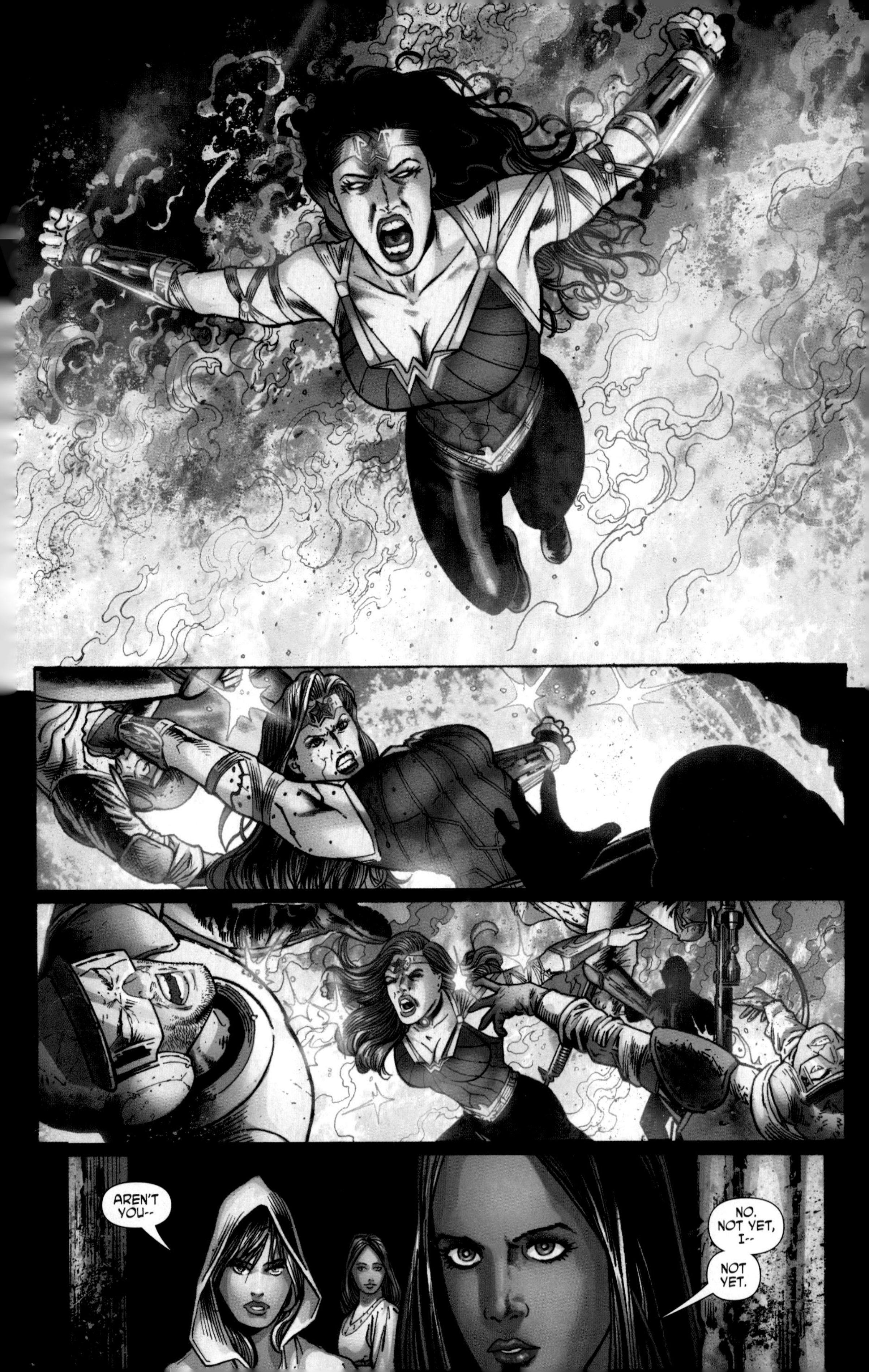
ARE'NT YOU--
NO. NOT YET, I--
NOT YET.

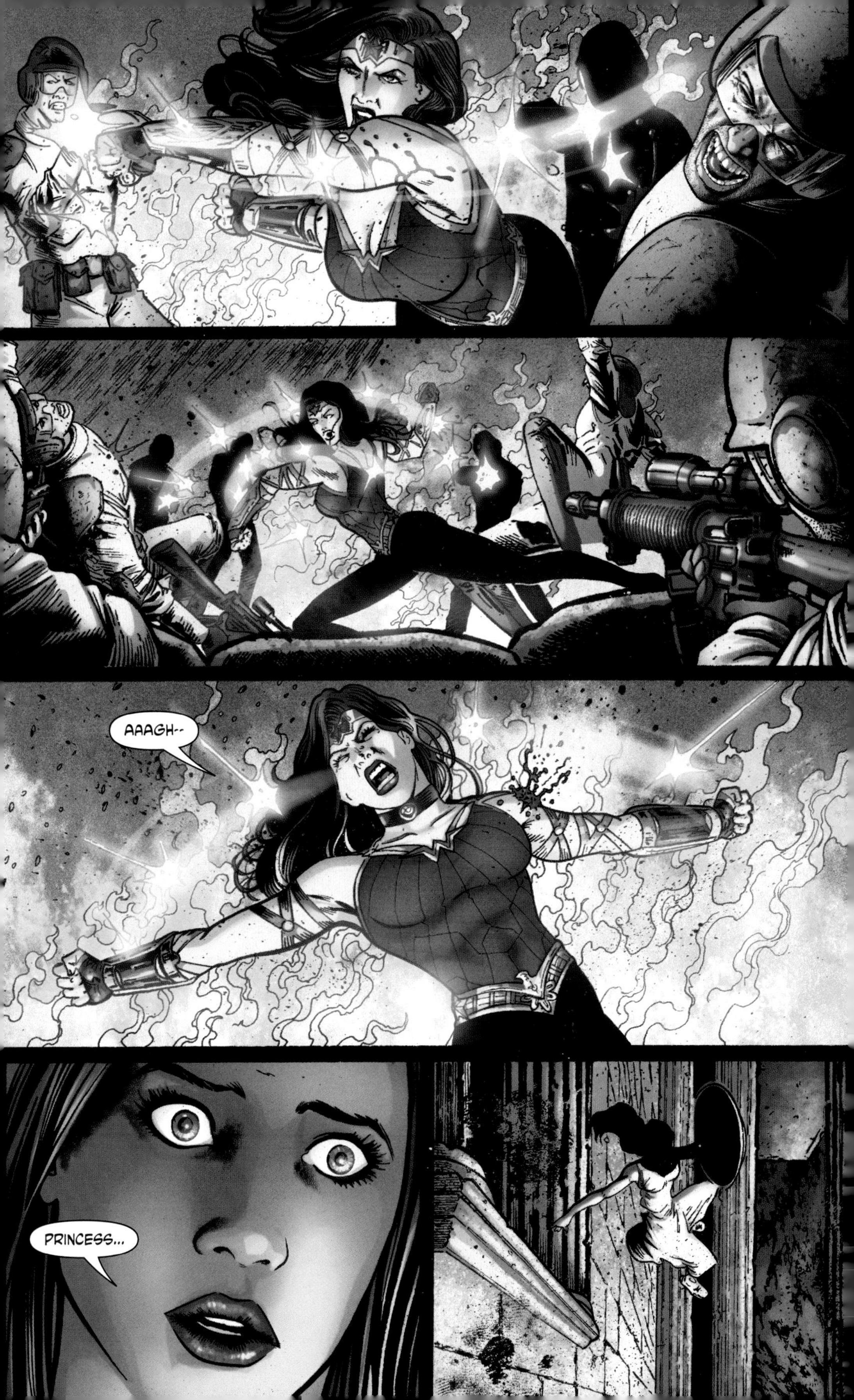
AAAGH--
PRINCESS...

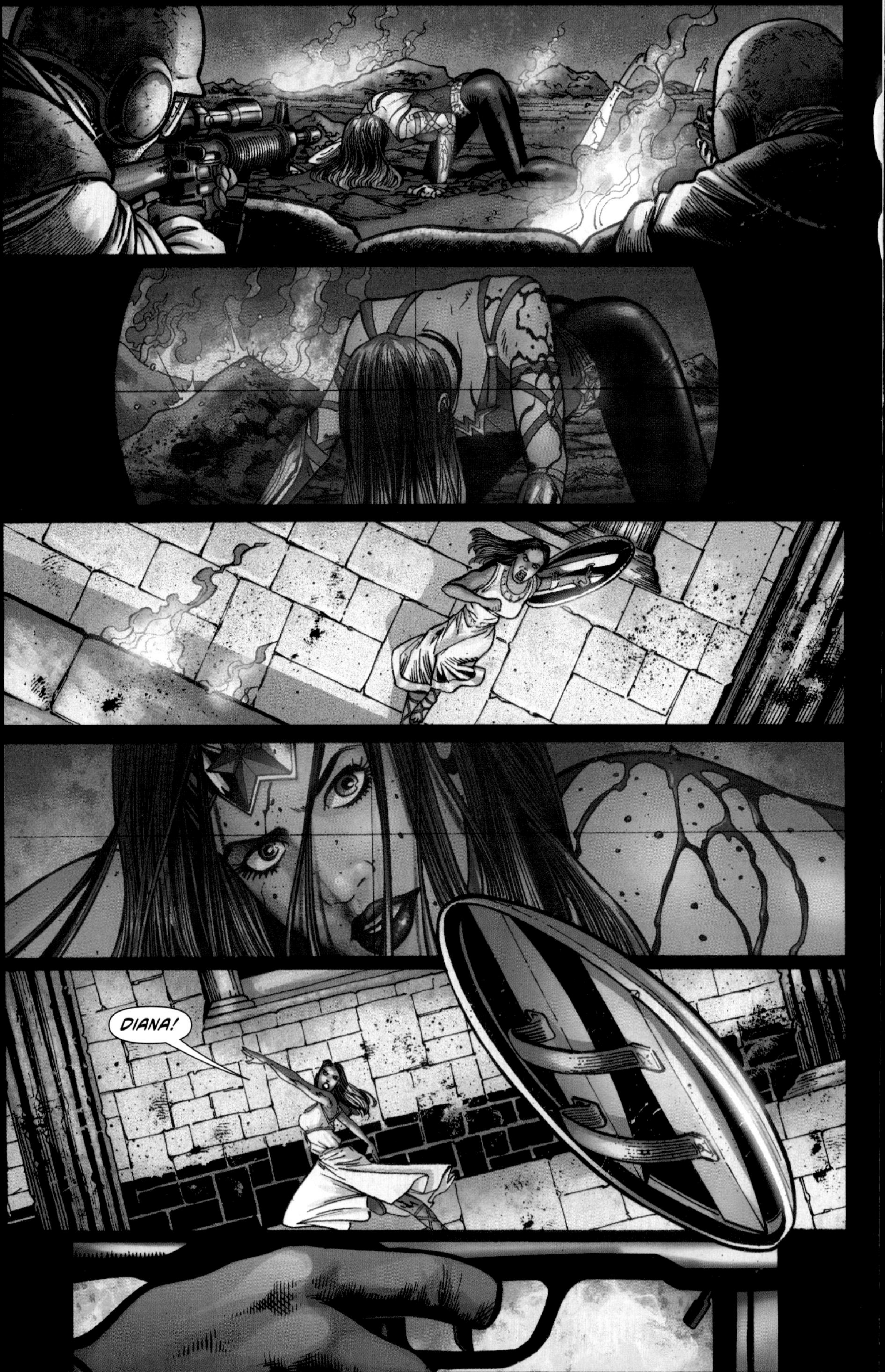
DIANA!

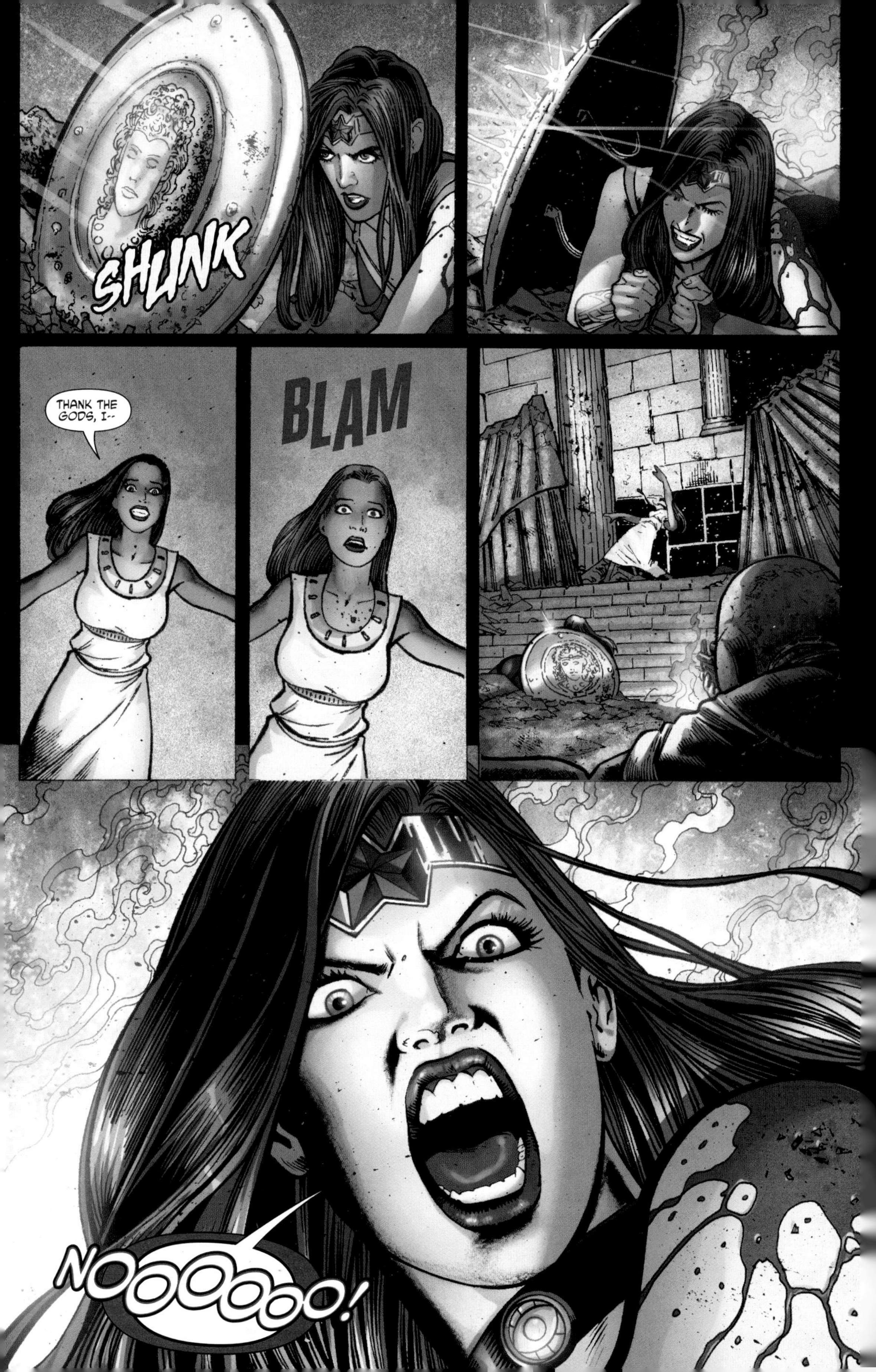
SHUNK
THANK THE GODS, I--
BLAM
NOOOOOOO!

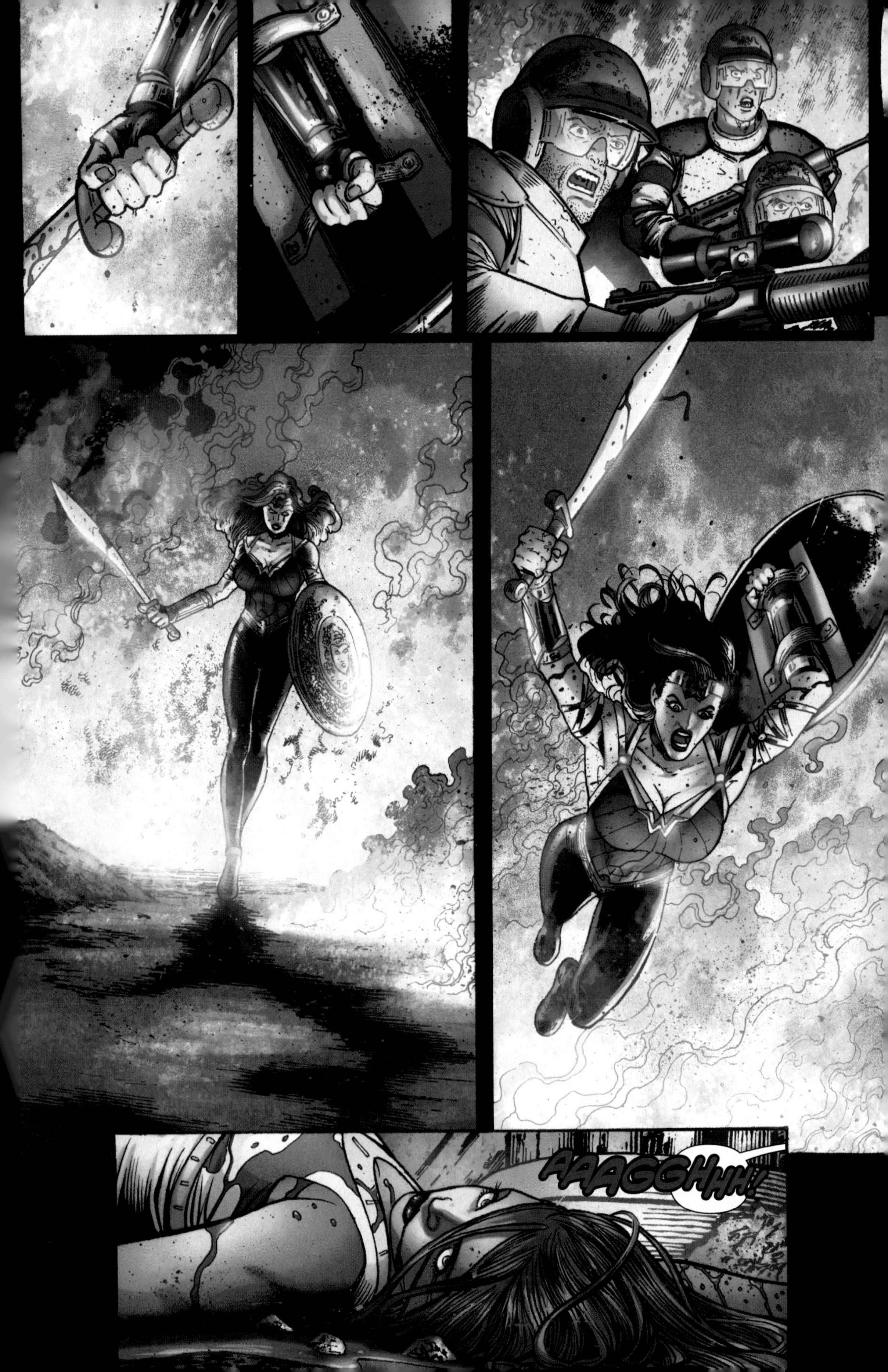

AAAAGGHHHH!

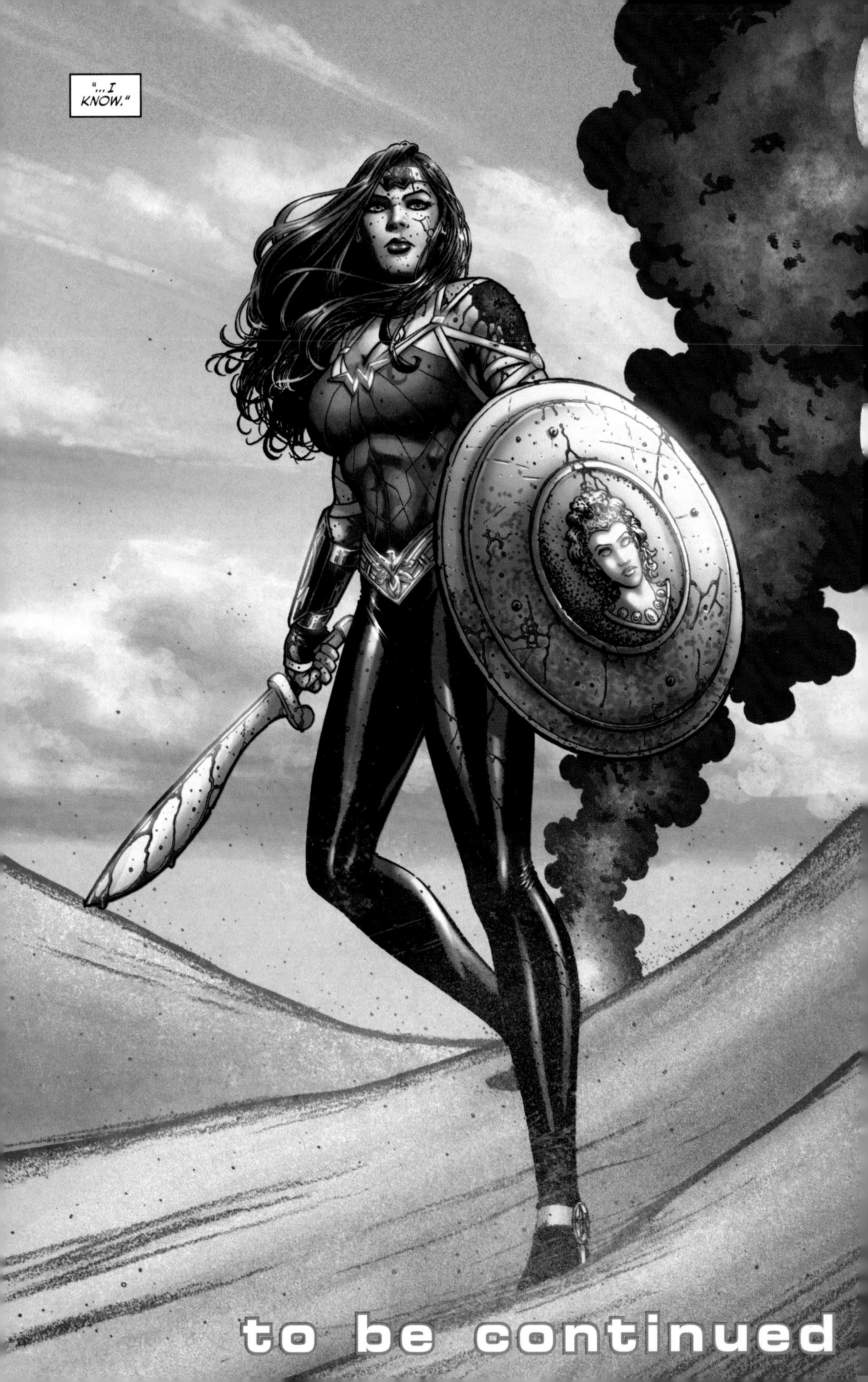
"...I KNOW."
to be continued

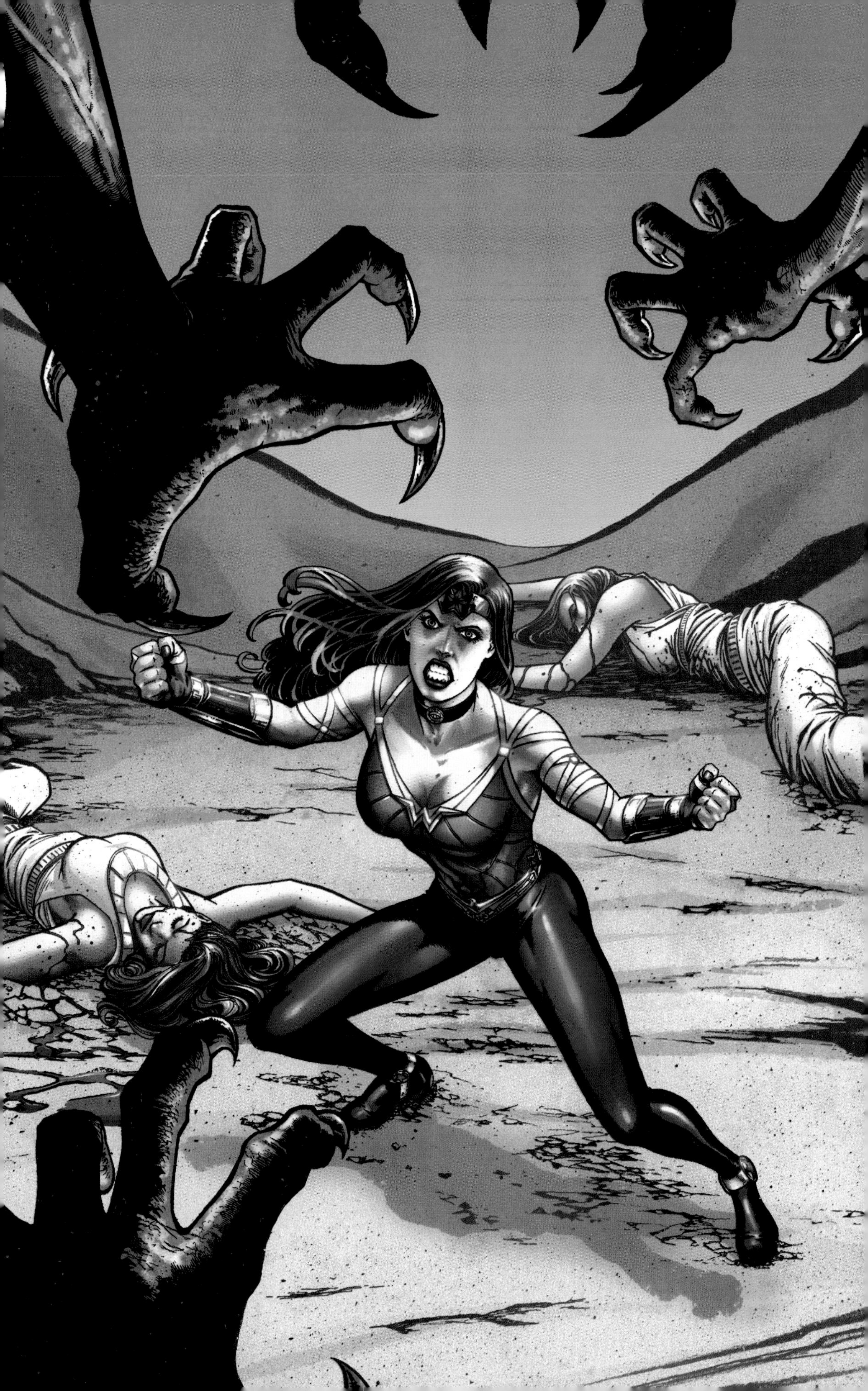

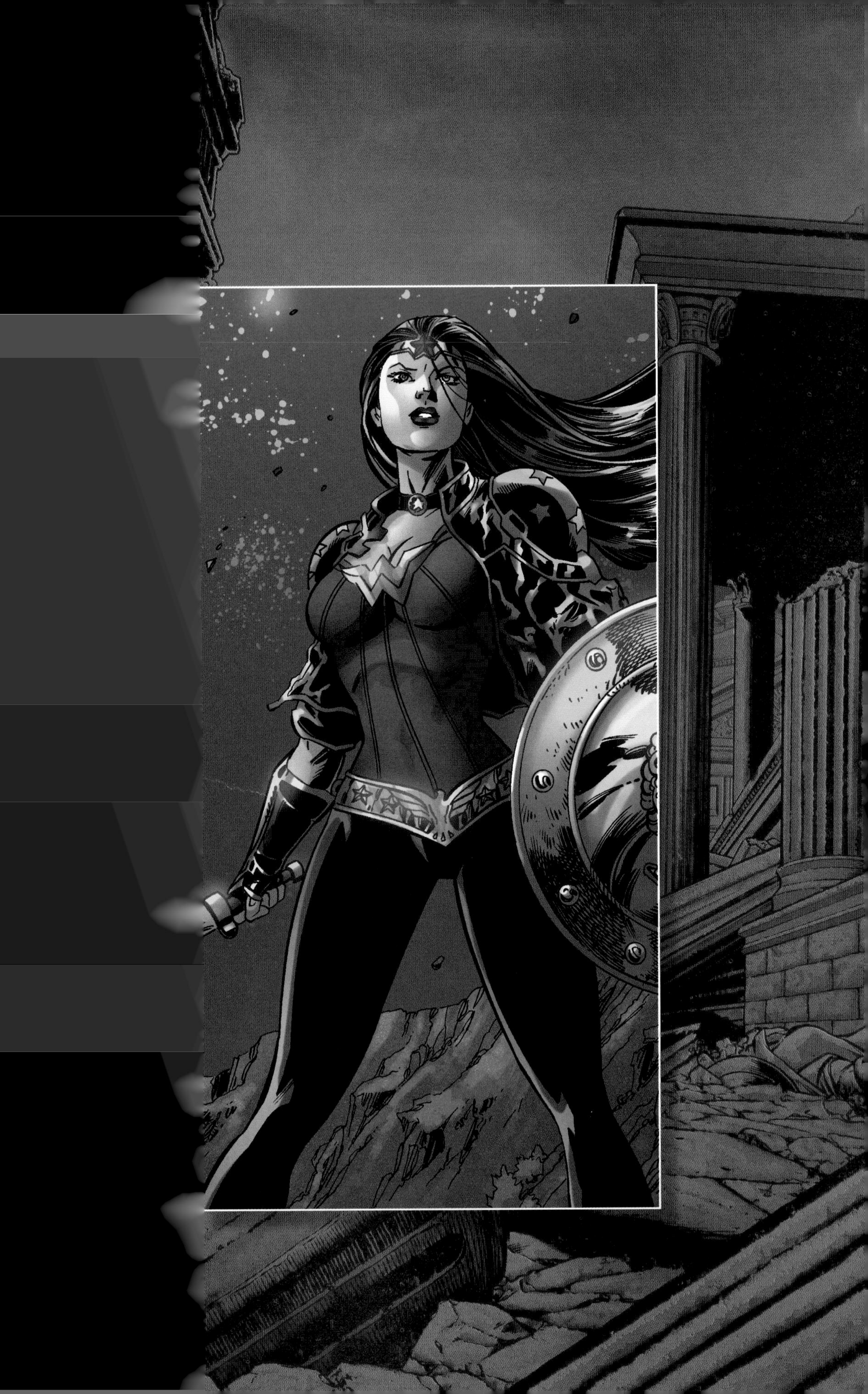

ODYSSEY: PART THREE
KERES

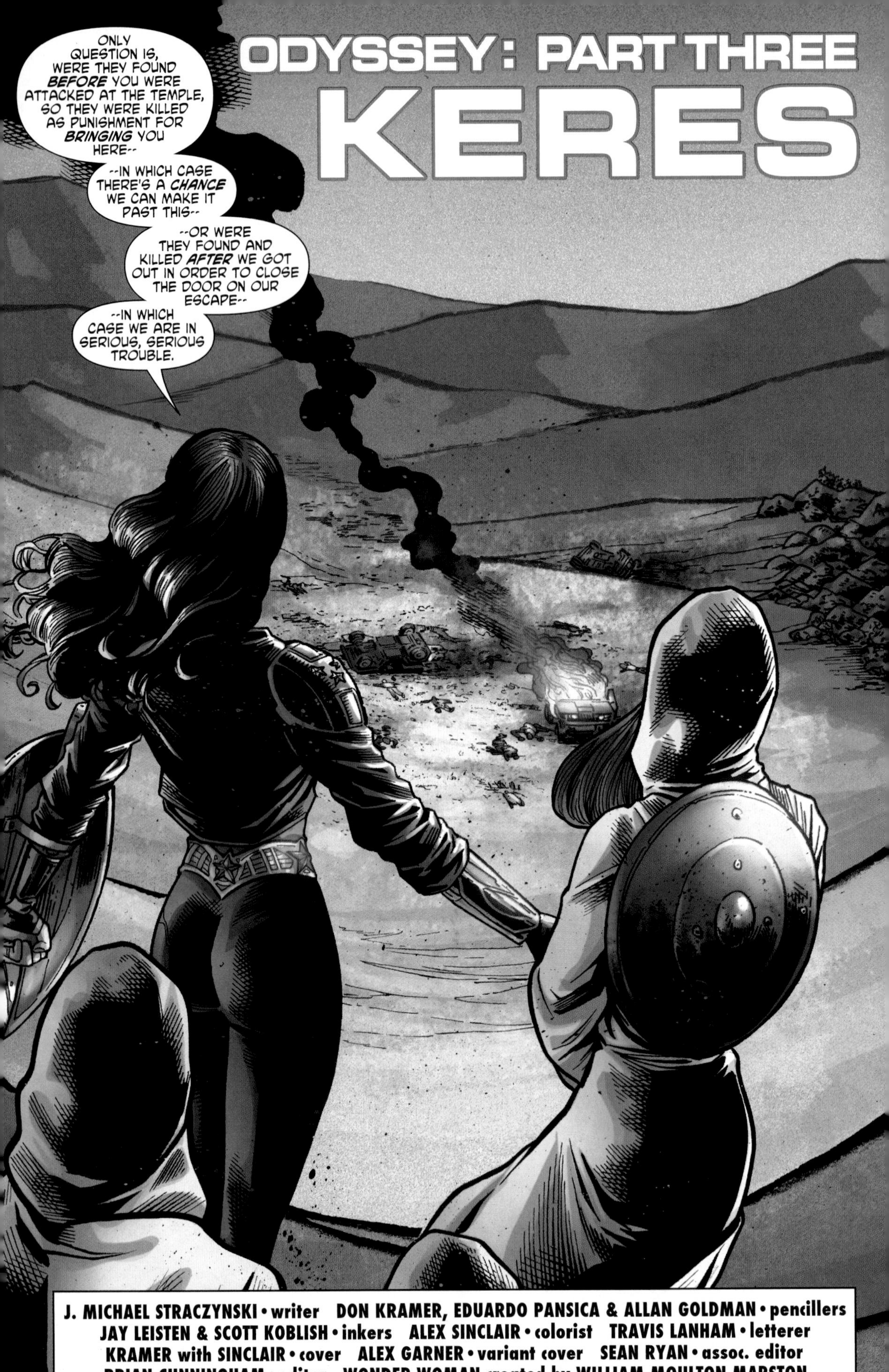
ONLY QUESTION IS, WERE THEY FOUND *BEFORE* YOU WERE ATTACKED AT THE TEMPLE, SO THEY WERE KILLED AS PUNISHMENT FOR *BRINGING* YOU HERE--
--IN WHICH CASE THERE'S A *CHANCE* WE CAN MAKE IT PAST THIS--
--OR WERE THEY FOUND AND KILLED *AFTER* WE GOT OUT IN ORDER TO CLOSE THE DOOR ON OUR ESCAPE--
--IN WHICH CASE WE ARE IN SERIOUS, SERIOUS TROUBLE.

J. MICHAEL STRACZYNSKI • writer **DON KRAMER, EDUARDO PANSICA & ALLAN GOLDMAN** • pencillers
JAY LEISTEN & SCOTT KOBLISH • inkers **ALEX SINCLAIR** • colorist **TRAVIS LANHAM** • letterer
KRAMER with SINCLAIR • cover **ALEX GARNER** • variant cover **SEAN RYAN** • assoc. editor
BRIAN CUNNINGHAM • editor **WONDER WOMAN** created by **WILLIAM MOULTON MARSTON**

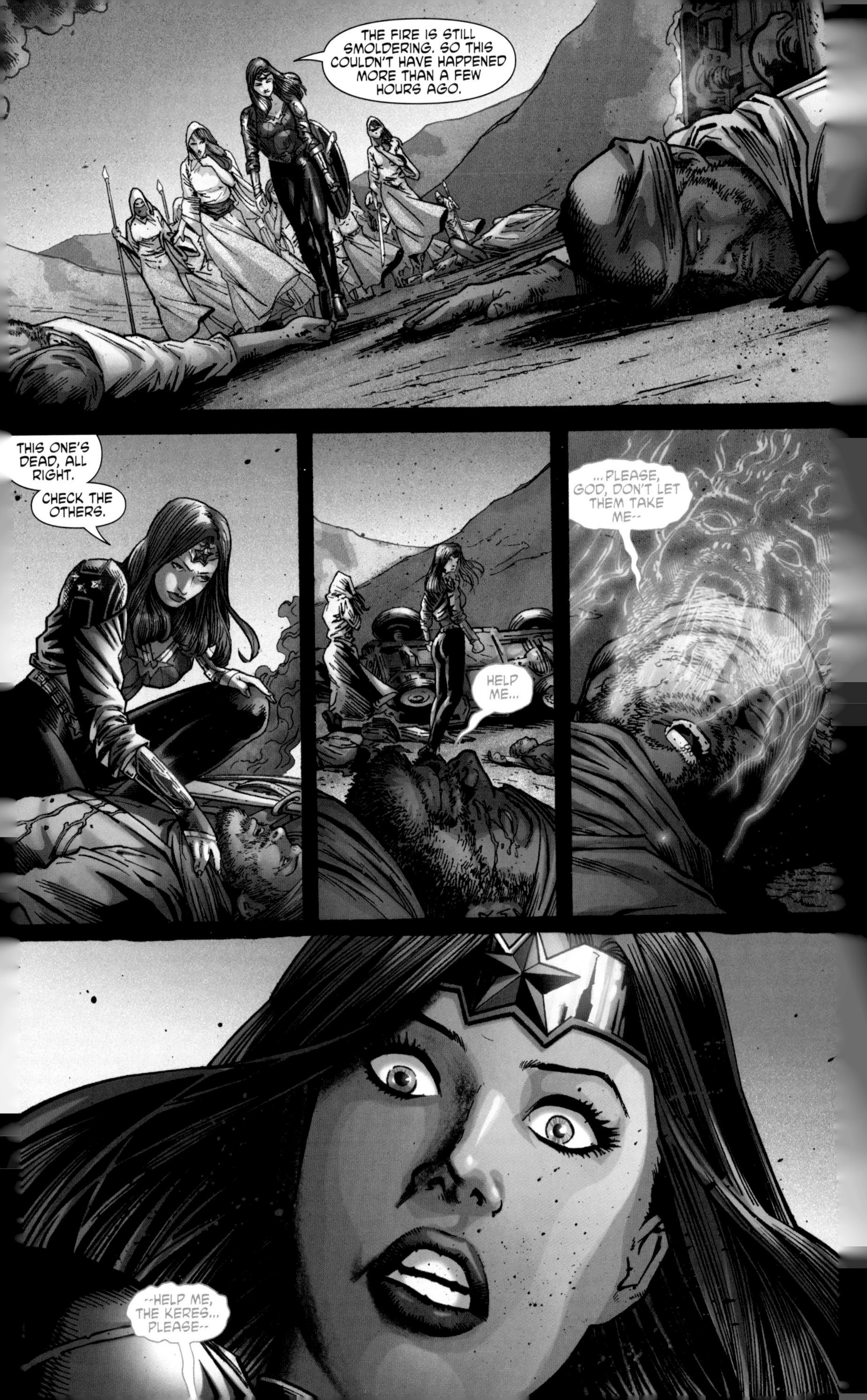
THE FIRE IS STILL SMOLDERING. SO THIS COULDN'T HAVE HAPPENED MORE THAN A FEW HOURS AGO.
THIS ONE'S DEAD, ALL RIGHT.
CHECK THE OTHERS.
HELP ME...
...PLEASE, GOD, DON'T LET THEM TAKE ME--
--HELP ME, THE KERES... PLEASE--

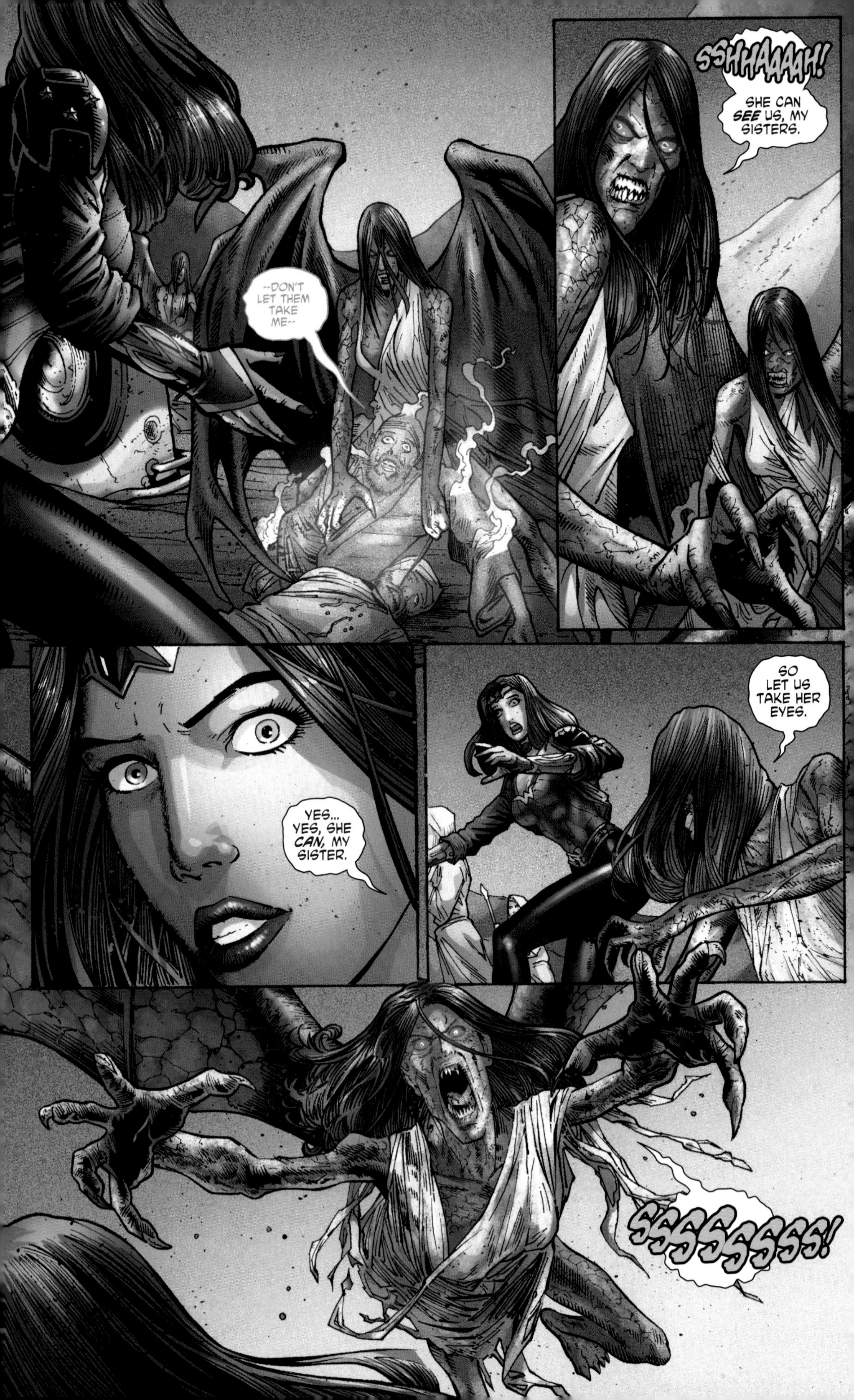
--DON'T LET THEM TAKE ME--
SSHHAAAAH!
SHE CAN SEE US, MY SISTERS.
YES... YES, SHE CAN, MY SISTER.
SO LET US TAKE HER EYES.
SSSSSSSSS!

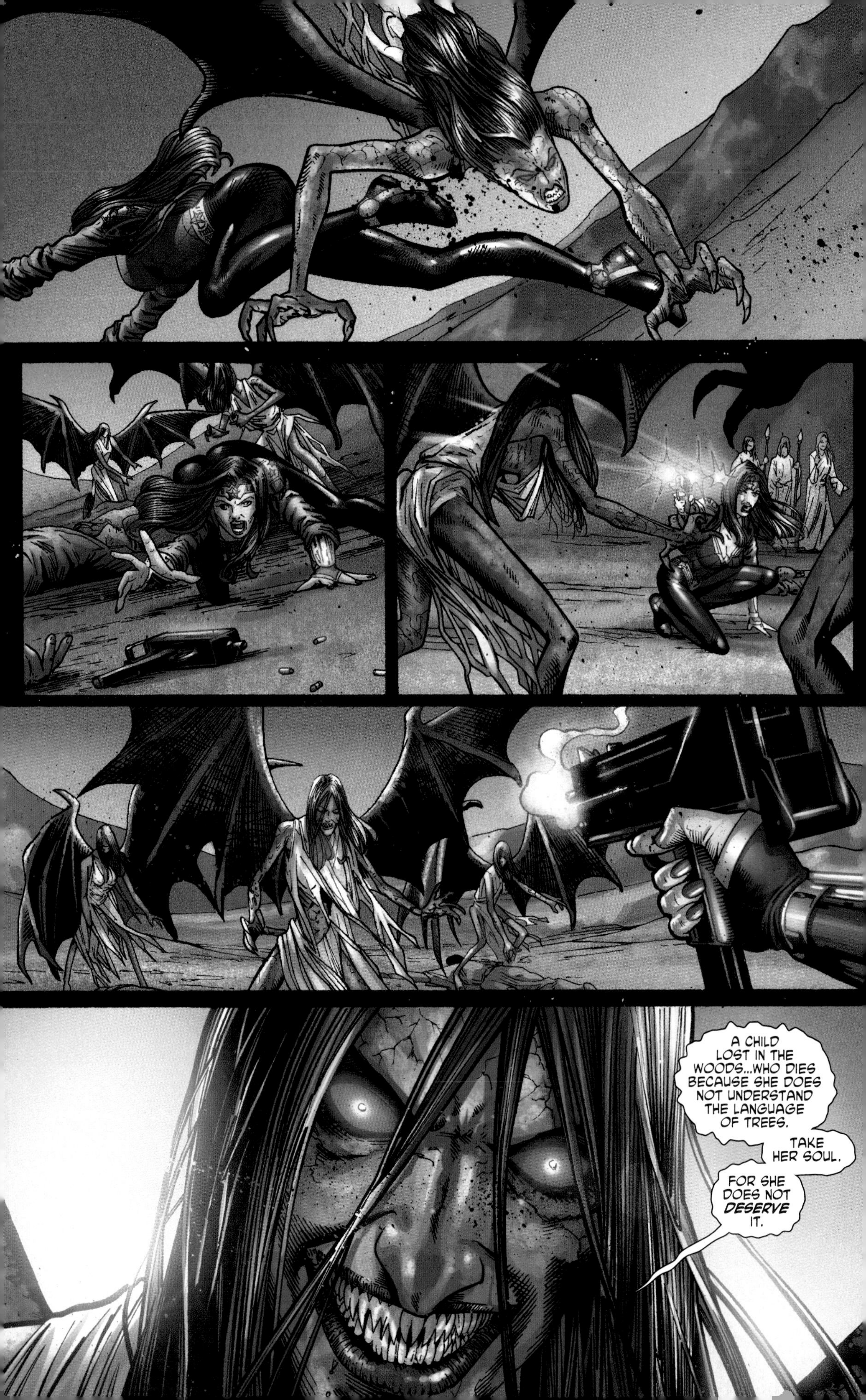

A CHILD LOST IN THE WOODS...WHO DIES BECAUSE SHE DOES NOT UNDERSTAND THE LANGUAGE OF TREES.
TAKE HER SOUL.
FOR SHE DOES NOT *DESERVE* IT.

SSAAAAHH!

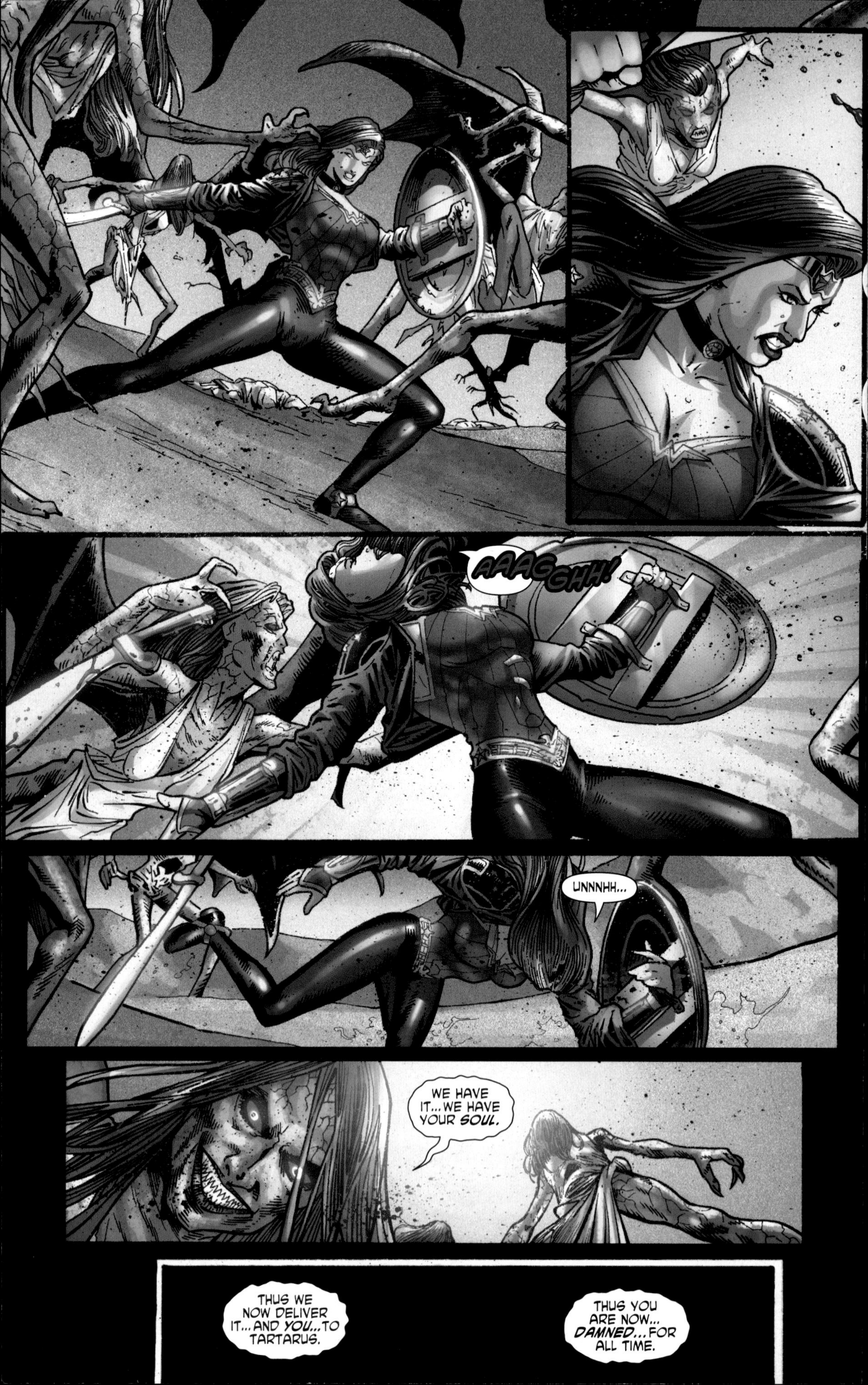
AAAGGHH!
UNNNHH...
WE HAVE IT...WE HAVE YOUR SOUL.
THUS WE NOW DELIVER IT...AND YOU...TO TARTARUS.
THUS YOU ARE NOW... DAMNED...FOR ALL TIME.

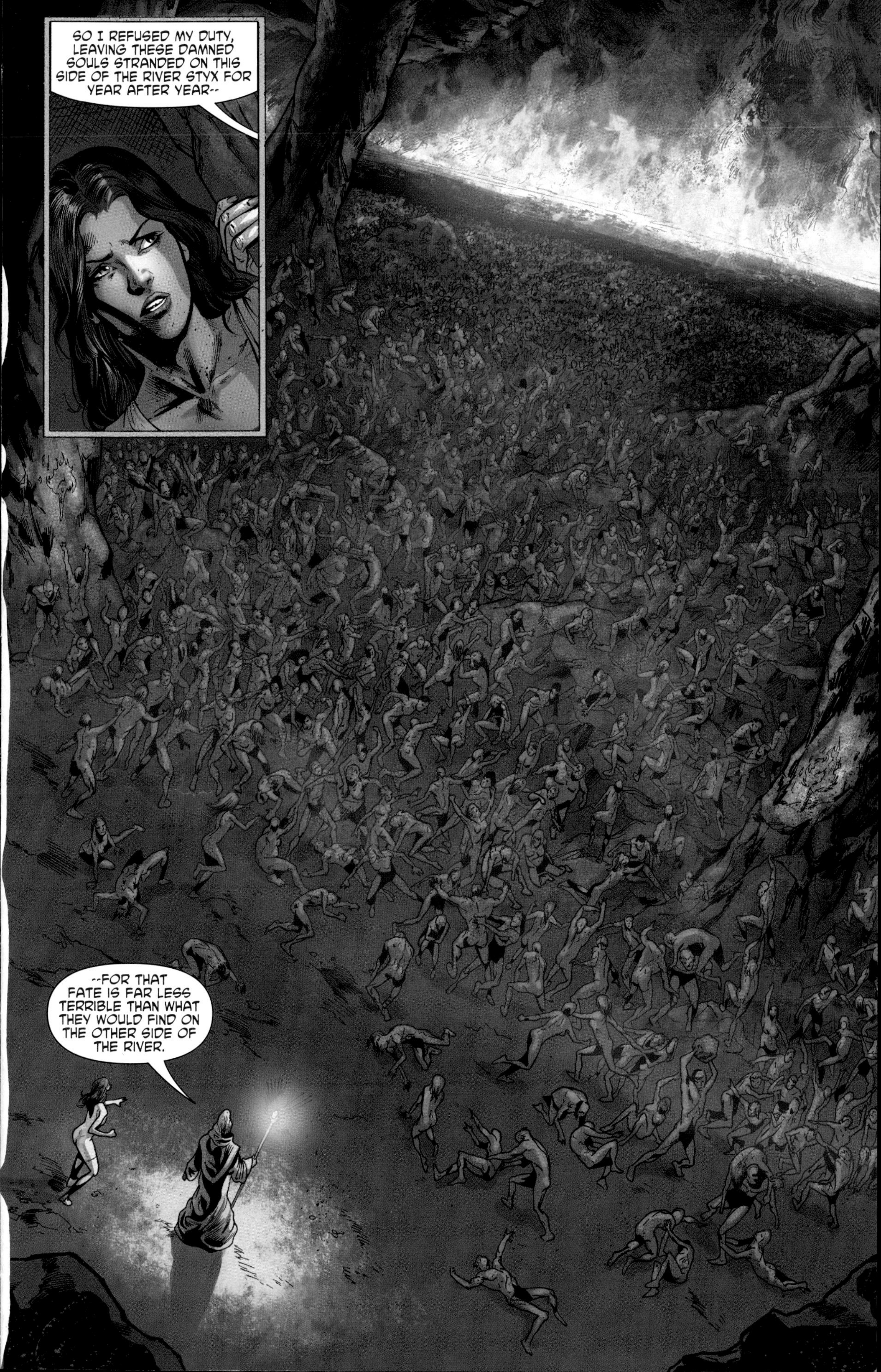
SO I REFUSED MY DUTY, LEAVING THESE DAMNED SOULS STRANDED ON THIS SIDE OF THE RIVER STYX FOR YEAR AFTER YEAR--
--FOR THAT FATE IS FAR LESS TERRIBLE THAN WHAT THEY WOULD FIND ON THE OTHER SIDE OF THE RIVER.

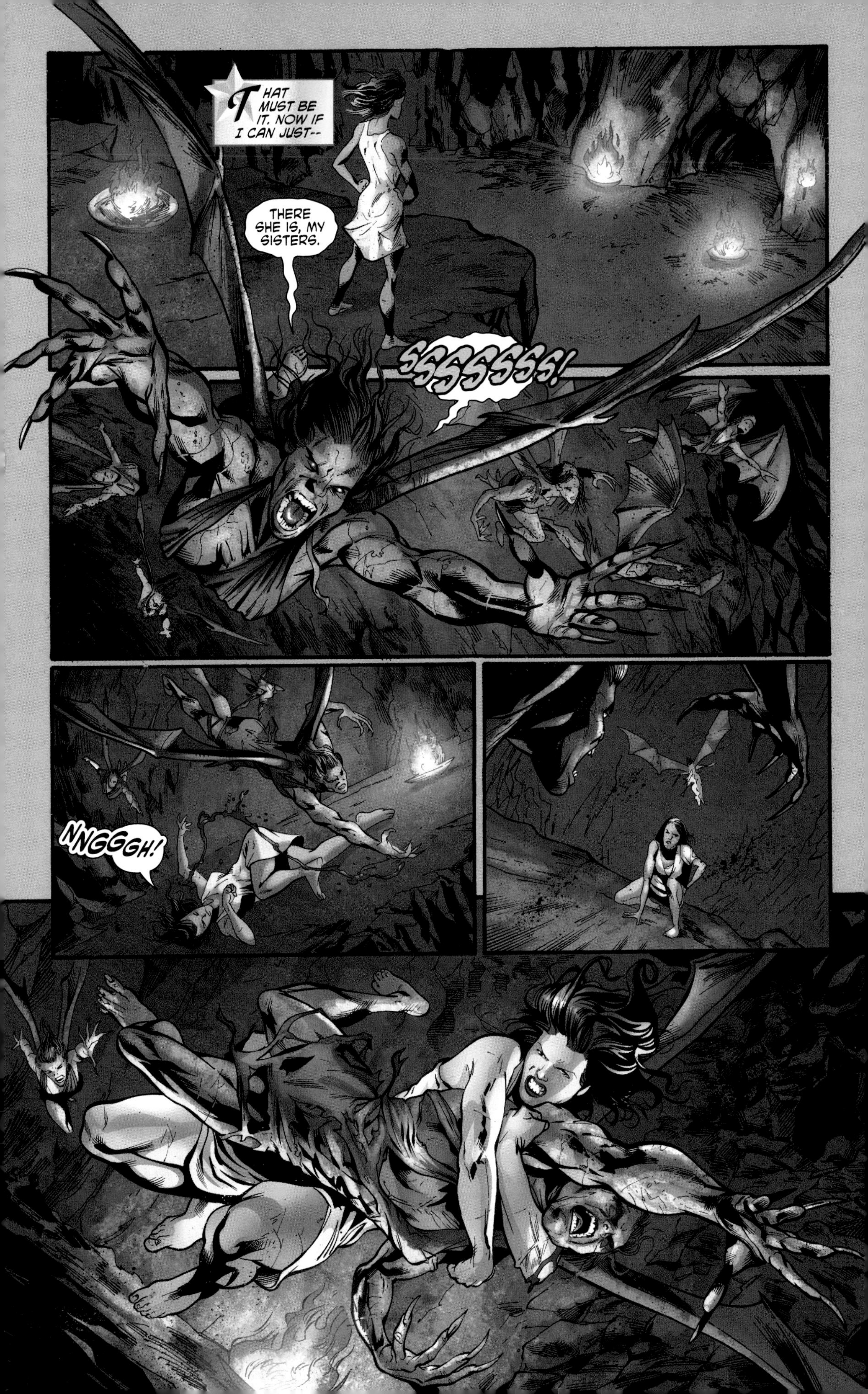

THAT MUST BE IT. NOW IF I CAN JUST--
THERE SHE IS, MY SISTERS.
SSSSSSS!
NNGGGH!

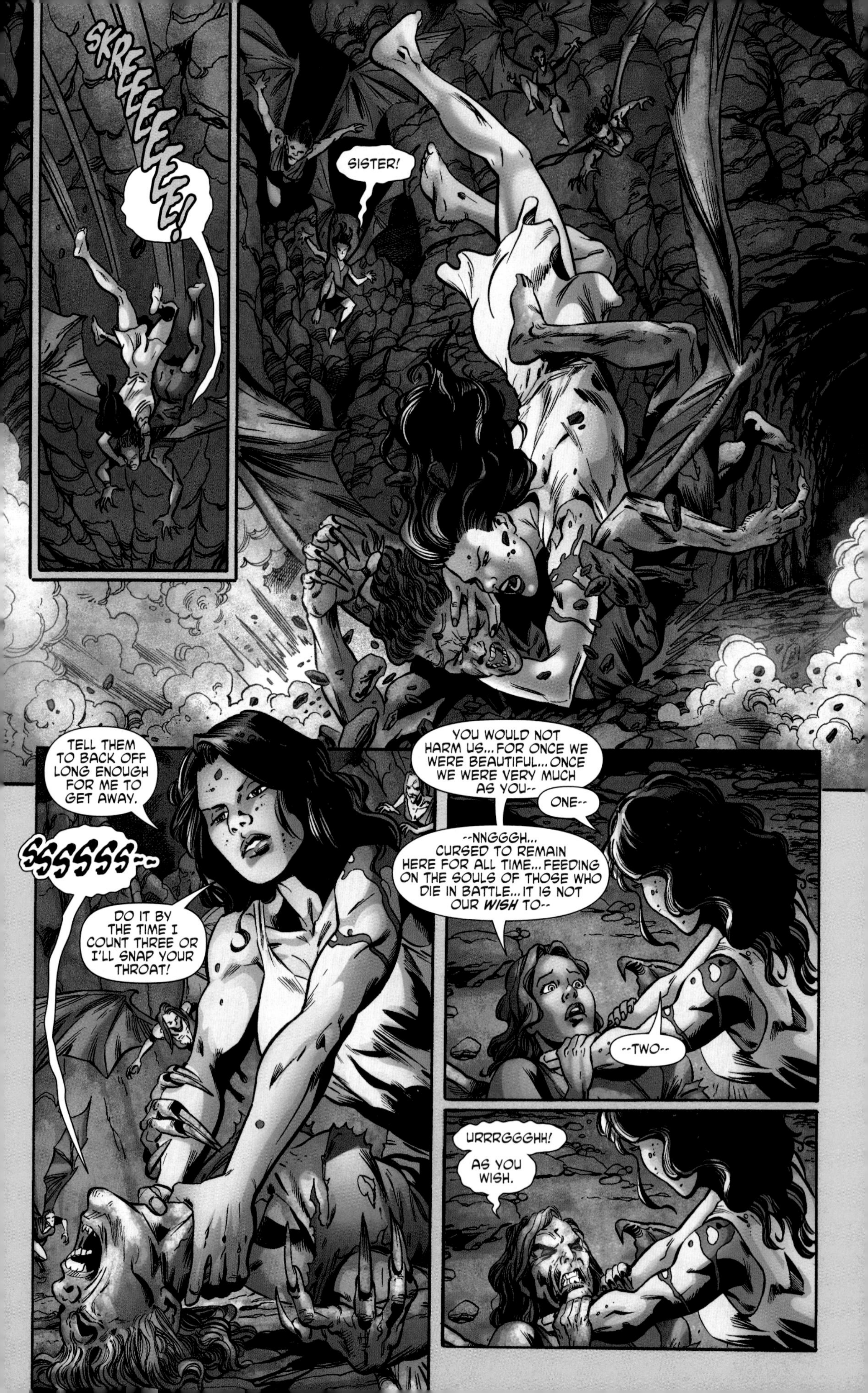
SKREEEEEEEE!
SISTER!
TELL THEM TO BACK OFF LONG ENOUGH FOR ME TO GET AWAY.
SSSSSS--
DO IT BY THE TIME I COUNT THREE OR I'LL SNAP YOUR THROAT!
YOU WOULD NOT HARM US...FOR ONCE WE WERE BEAUTIFUL...ONCE WE WERE VERY MUCH AS YOU--
ONE--
--NNGGGH... CURSED TO REMAIN HERE FOR ALL TIME... FEEDING ON THE SOULS OF THOSE WHO DIE IN BATTLE... IT IS NOT OUR WISH TO--
--TWO--
URRRGGGHH!
AS YOU WISH.

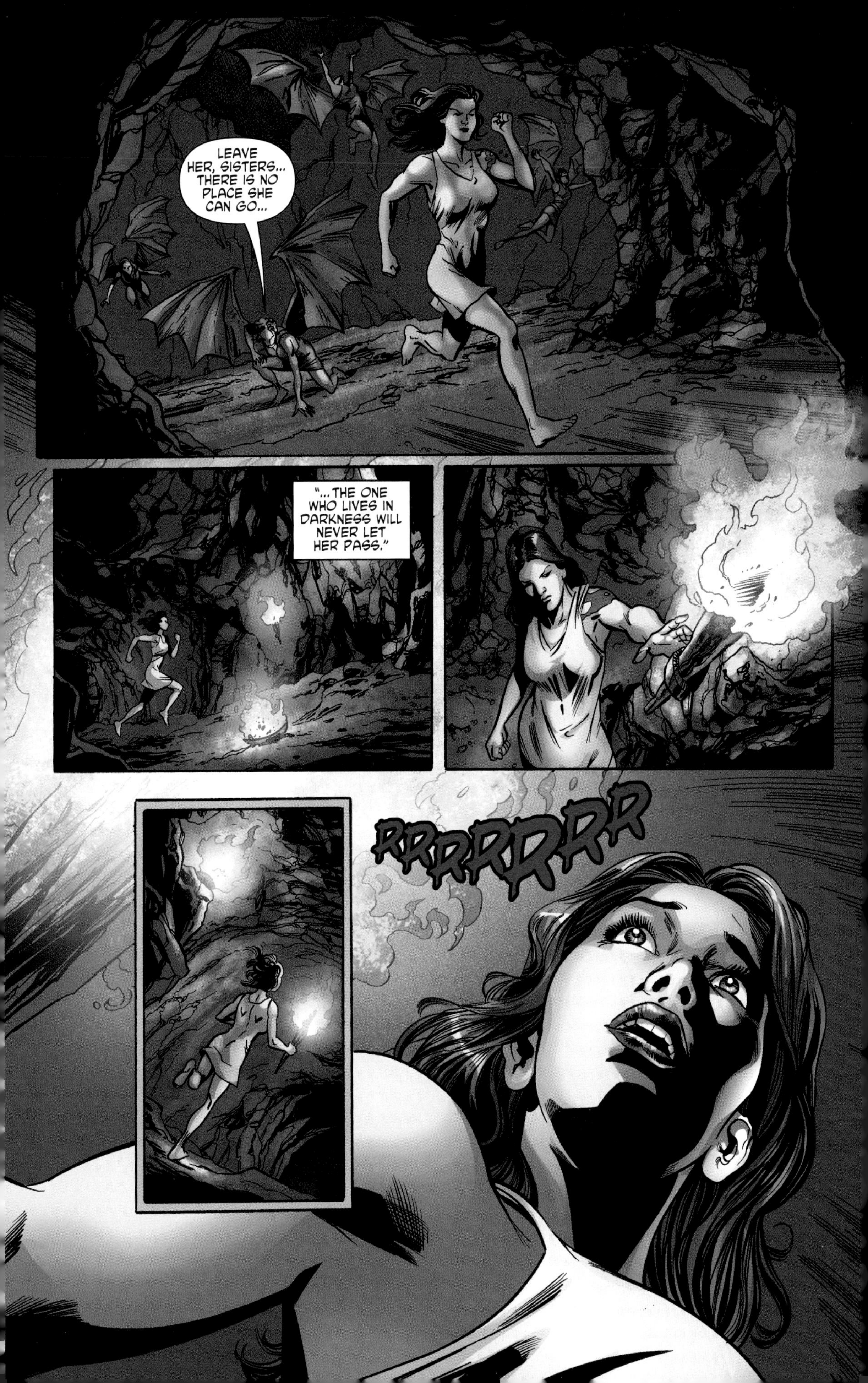
LEAVE HER, SISTERS... THERE IS NO PLACE SHE CAN GO...
"...THE ONE WHO LIVES IN DARKNESS WILL NEVER LET HER PASS."
RRRRRRR

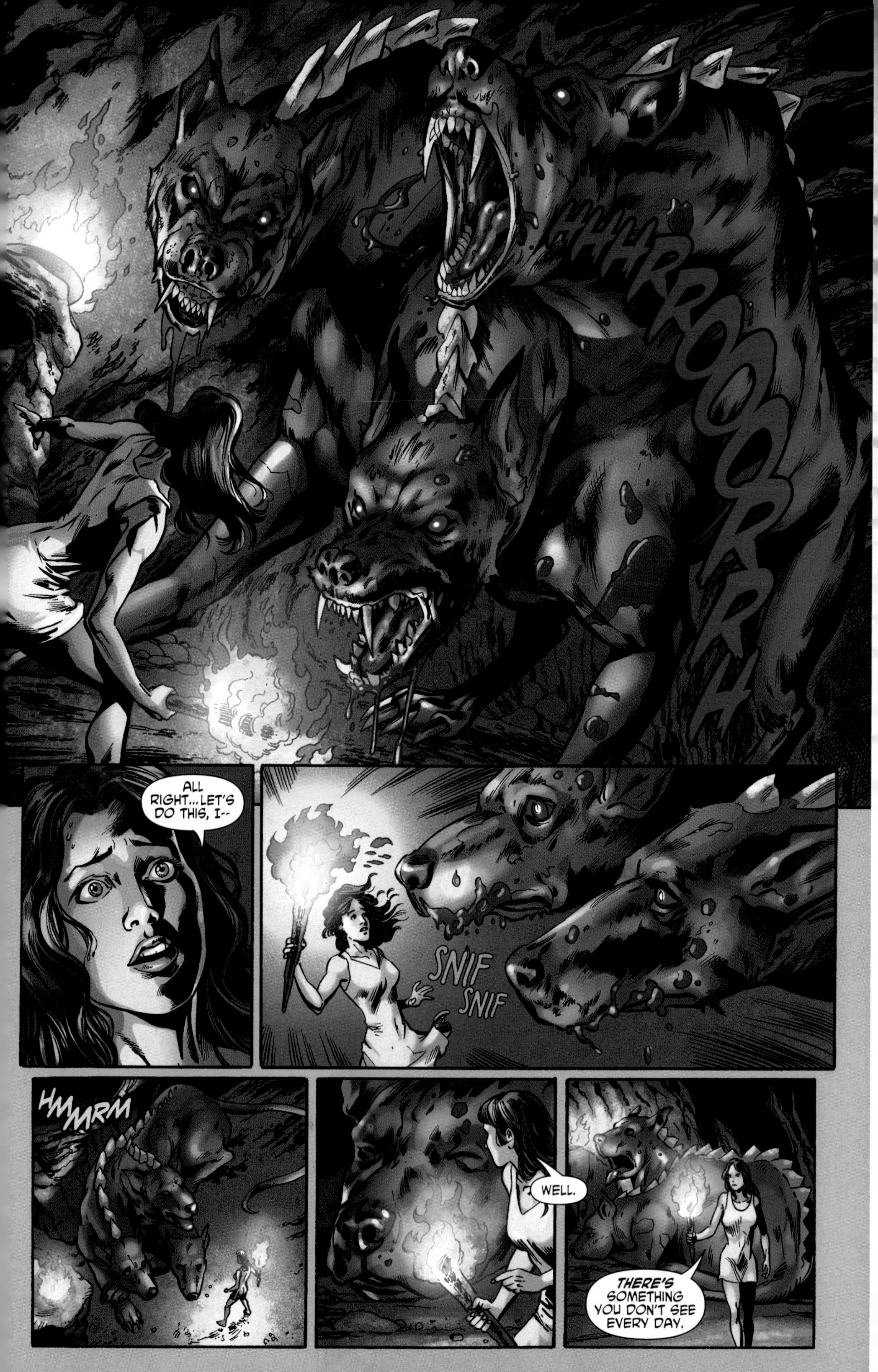
HHHRROOOORRH
ALL RIGHT... LET'S DO THIS, I--
SNIF
SNIF
HMMRM
WELL.
THERE'S SOMETHING YOU DON'T SEE EVERY DAY.

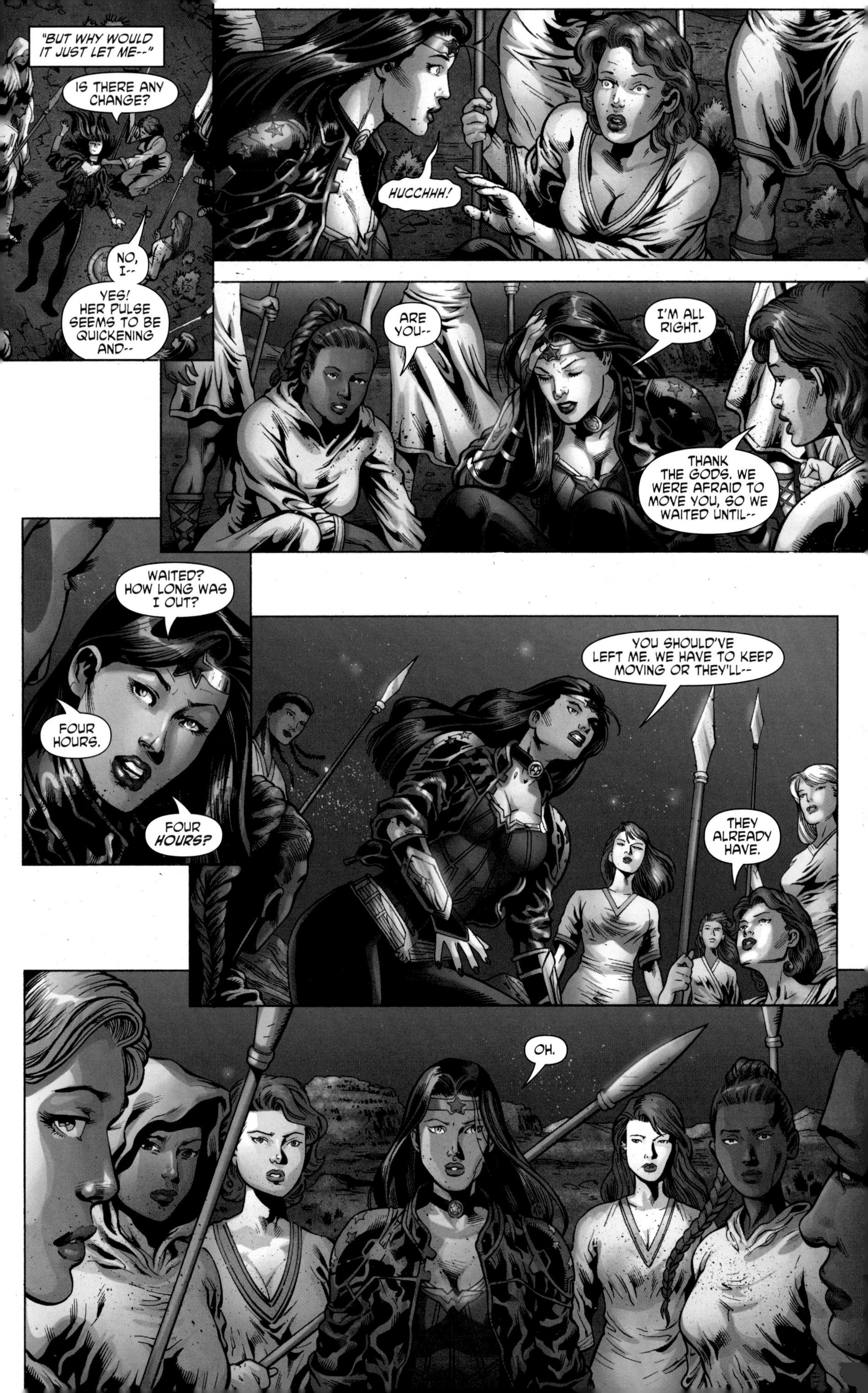
"BUT WHY WOULD IT JUST LET ME--"
IS THERE ANY CHANGE?
NO, I--
YES! HER PULSE SEEMS TO BE QUICKENING AND--
HUCCHHH!
ARE YOU--
I'M ALL RIGHT.
THANK THE GODS. WE WERE AFRAID TO MOVE YOU, SO WE WAITED UNTIL--
WAITED? HOW LONG WAS I OUT?
FOUR HOURS.
FOUR *HOURS?*
YOU SHOULD'VE LEFT ME. WE HAVE TO KEEP MOVING OR THEY'LL--
THEY ALREADY HAVE.
OH.

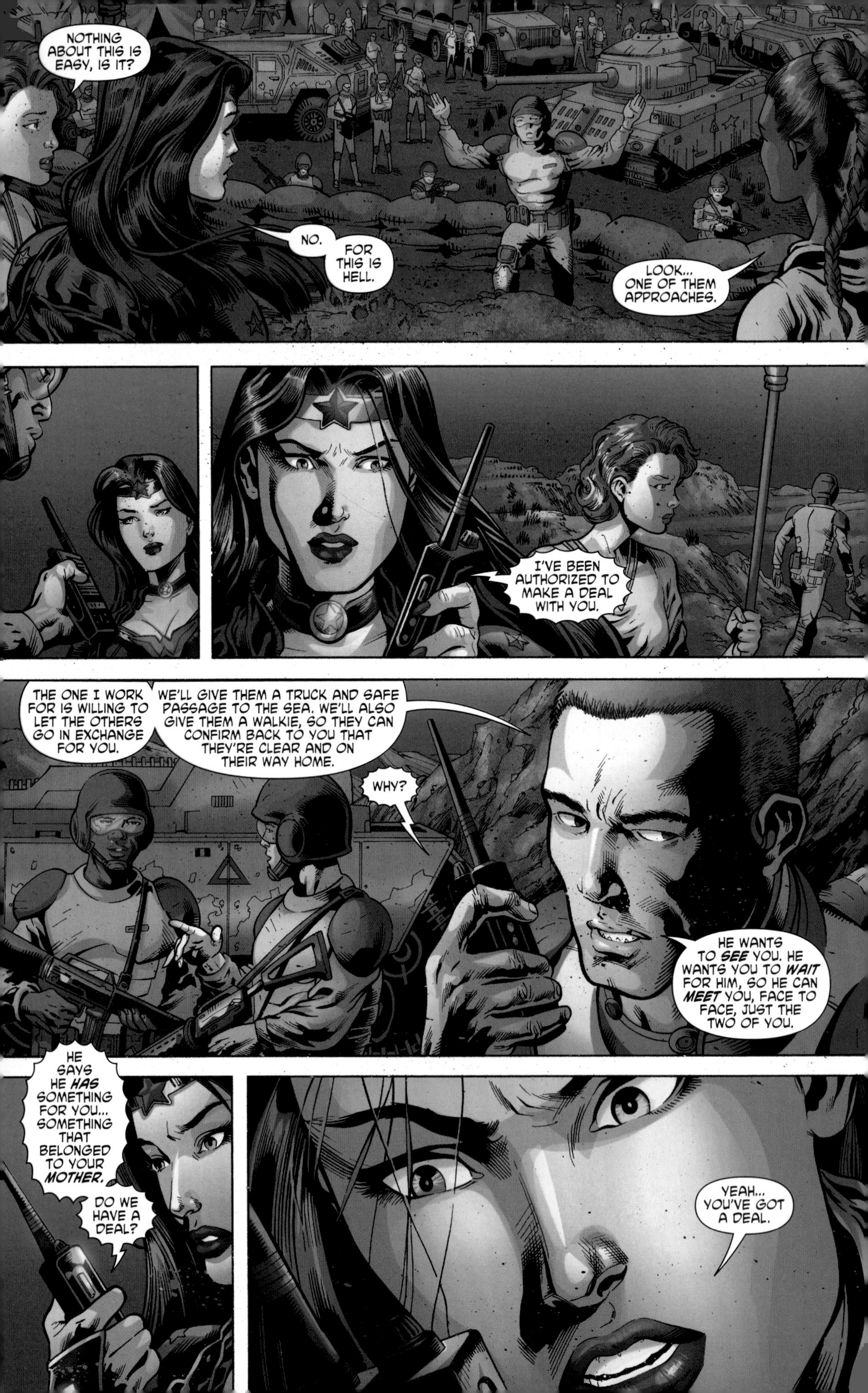
NOTHING ABOUT THIS IS EASY, IS IT?
NO.
FOR THIS IS HELL.
LOOK... ONE OF THEM APPROACHES.
I'VE BEEN AUTHORIZED TO MAKE A DEAL WITH YOU.
THE ONE I WORK FOR IS WILLING TO LET THE OTHERS GO IN EXCHANGE FOR YOU.
WE'LL GIVE THEM A TRUCK AND SAFE PASSAGE TO THE SEA. WE'LL ALSO GIVE THEM A WALKIE, SO THEY CAN CONFIRM BACK TO YOU THAT THEY'RE CLEAR AND ON THEIR WAY HOME.
WHY?
HE WANTS TO *SEE* YOU. HE WANTS YOU TO *WAIT* FOR HIM, SO HE CAN *MEET* YOU, FACE TO FACE, JUST THE TWO OF YOU.
HE SAYS HE *HAS* SOMETHING FOR YOU... SOMETHING THAT BELONGED TO YOUR *MOTHER.*
DO WE HAVE A DEAL?
YEAH... YOU'VE GOT A DEAL.

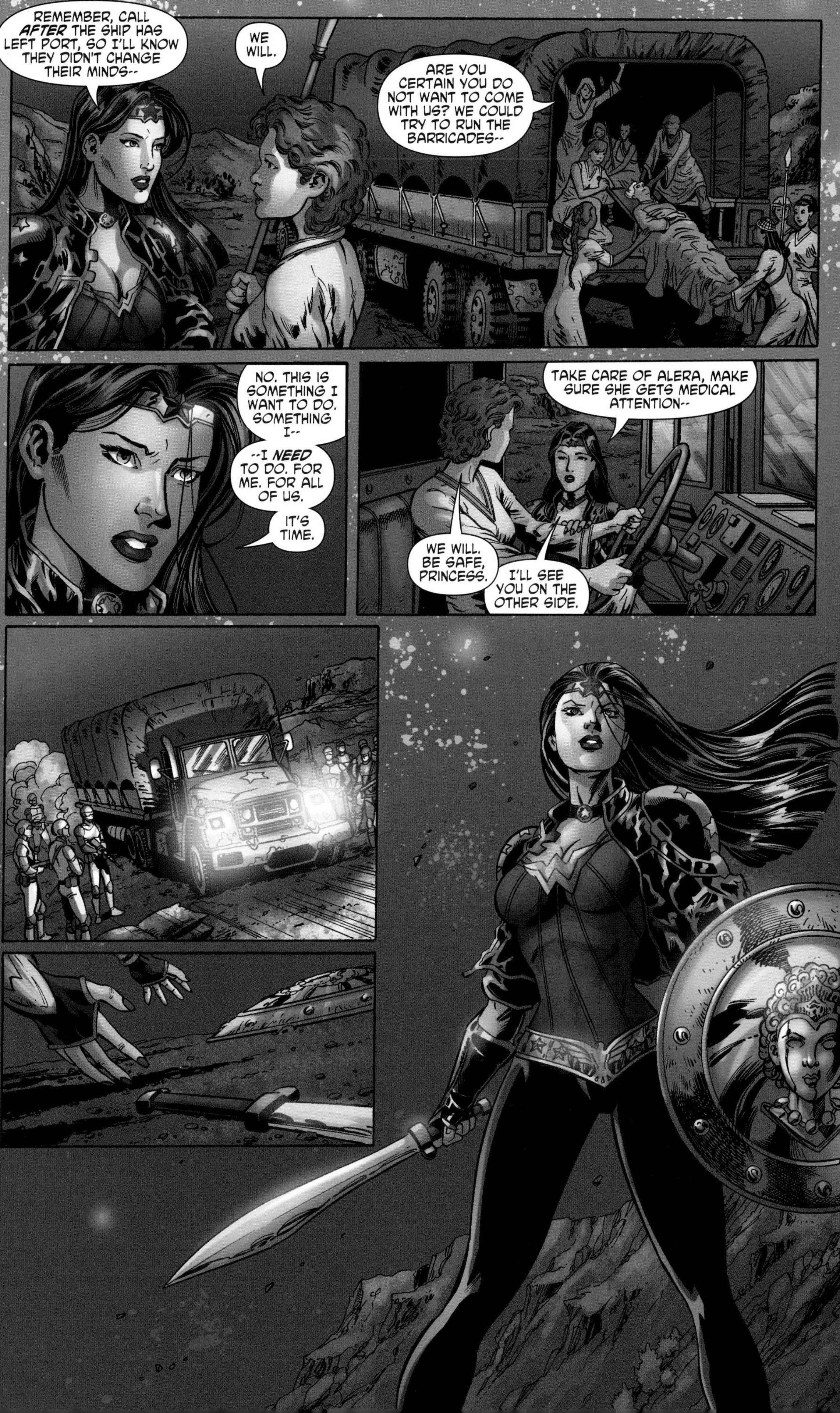
REMEMBER, CALL AFTER THE SHIP HAS LEFT PORT, SO I'LL KNOW THEY DIDN'T CHANGE THEIR MINDS--
WE WILL.
ARE YOU CERTAIN YOU DO NOT WANT TO COME WITH US? WE COULD TRY TO RUN THE BARRICADES--
NO. THIS IS SOMETHING I WANT TO DO. SOMETHING I--
--I NEED TO DO. FOR ME. FOR ALL OF US.
IT'S TIME.
TAKE CARE OF ALERA, MAKE SURE SHE GETS MEDICAL ATTENTION--
WE WILL. BE SAFE, PRINCESS.
I'LL SEE YOU ON THE OTHER SIDE.

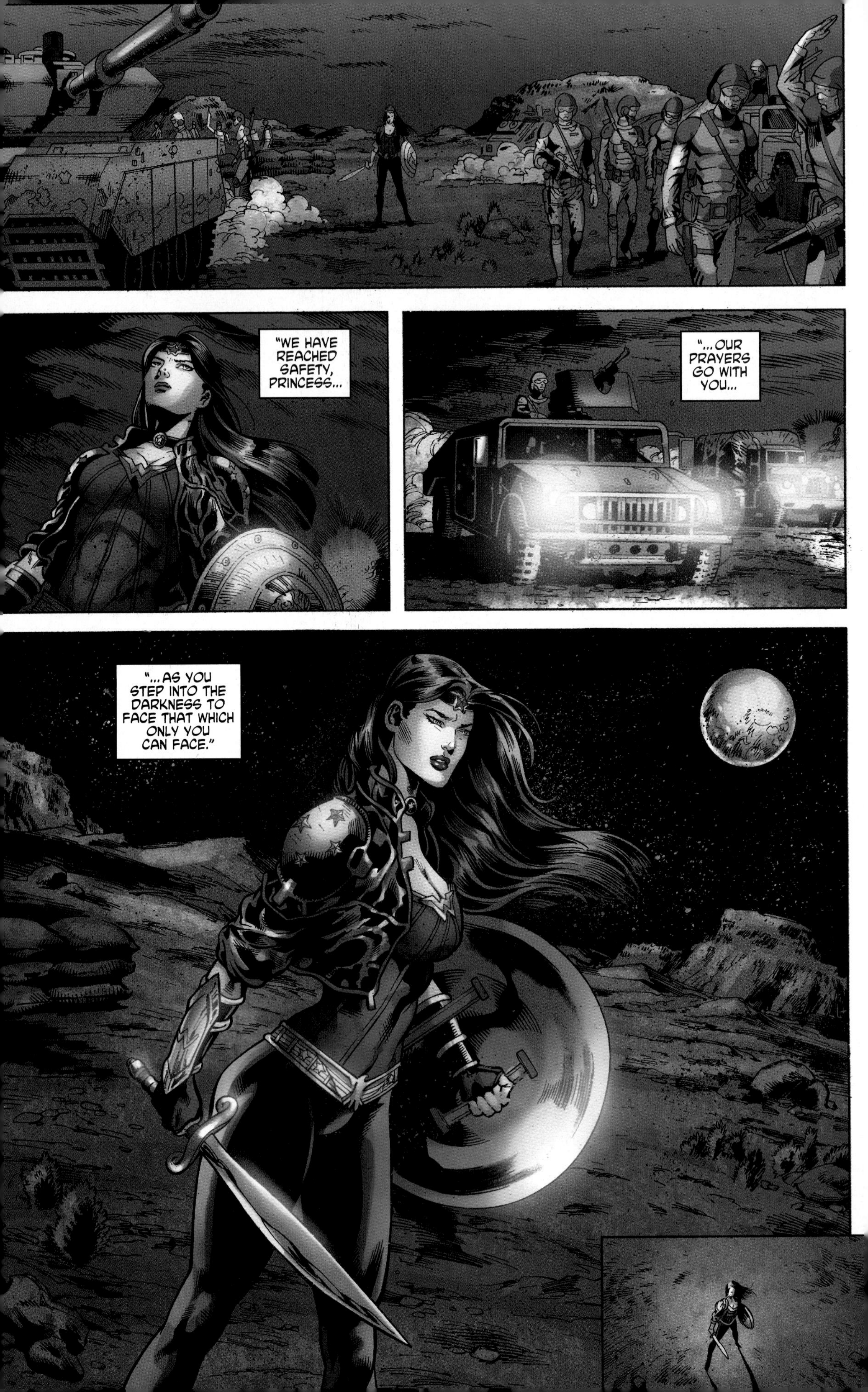
"WE HAVE REACHED SAFETY, PRINCESS...
"...OUR PRAYERS GO WITH YOU...
"...AS YOU STEP INTO THE DARKNESS TO FACE THAT WHICH ONLY YOU CAN FACE."

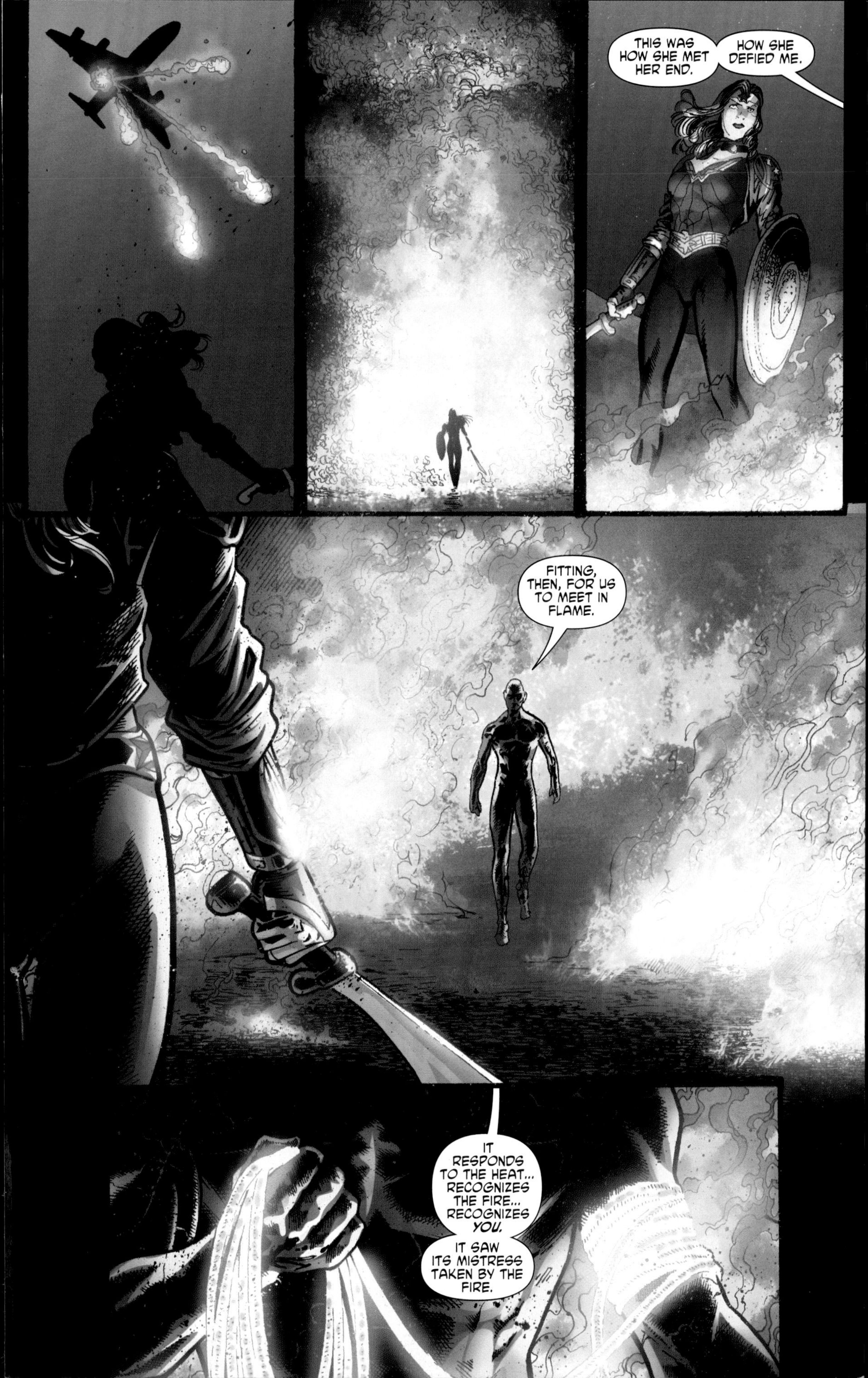
THIS WAS HOW SHE MET HER END.
HOW SHE DEFIED ME.
FITTING, THEN, FOR US TO MEET IN FLAME.
IT RESPONDS TO THE HEAT... RECOGNIZES THE FIRE... RECOGNIZES *YOU.*
IT SAW ITS MISTRESS TAKEN BY THE FIRE.

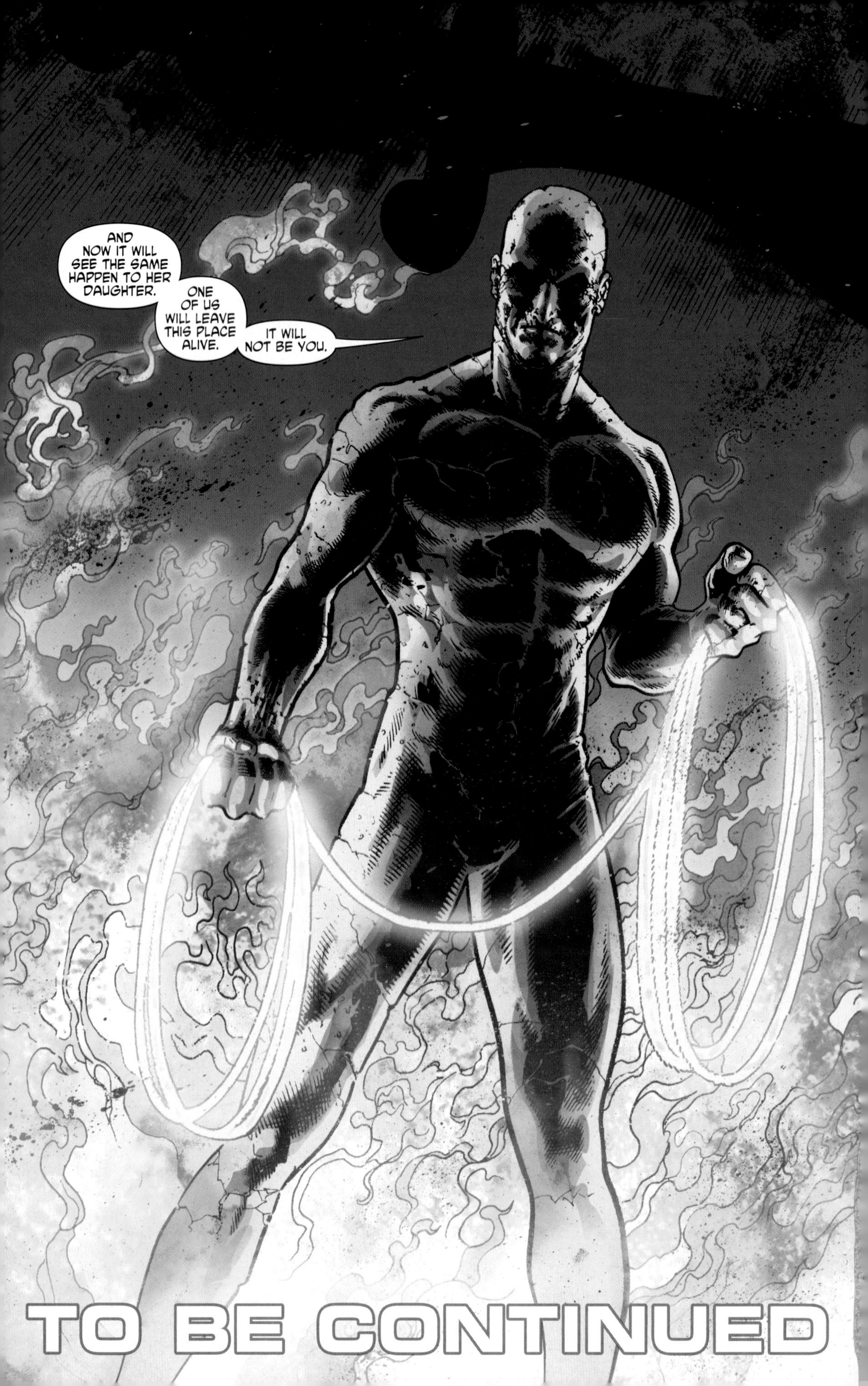
AND NOW IT WILL SEE THE SAME HAPPEN TO HER DAUGHTER.
ONE OF US WILL LEAVE THIS PLACE ALIVE.
IT WILL NOT BE YOU.
TO BE CONTINUED

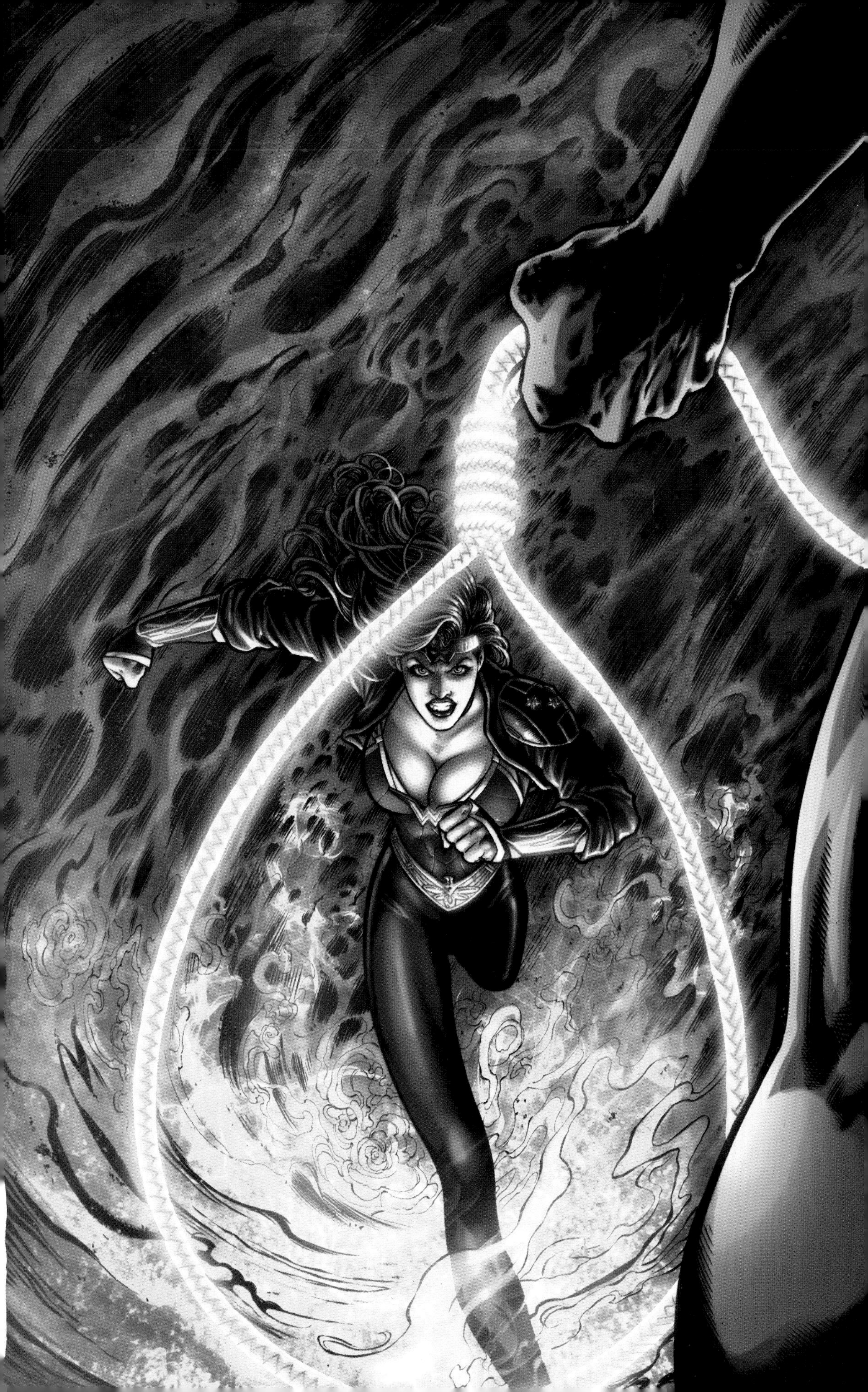

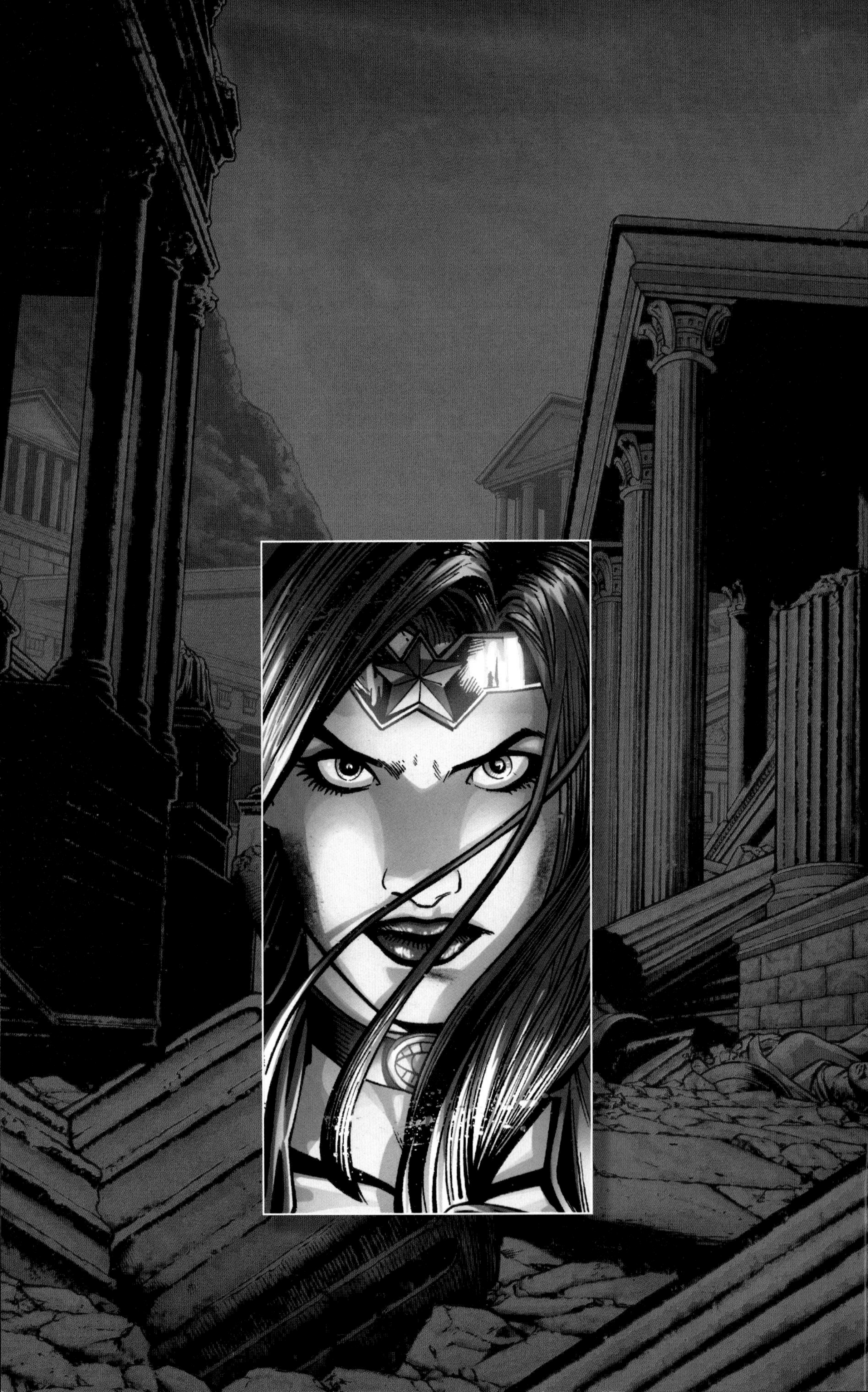

ODYSSEY: PART FOUR

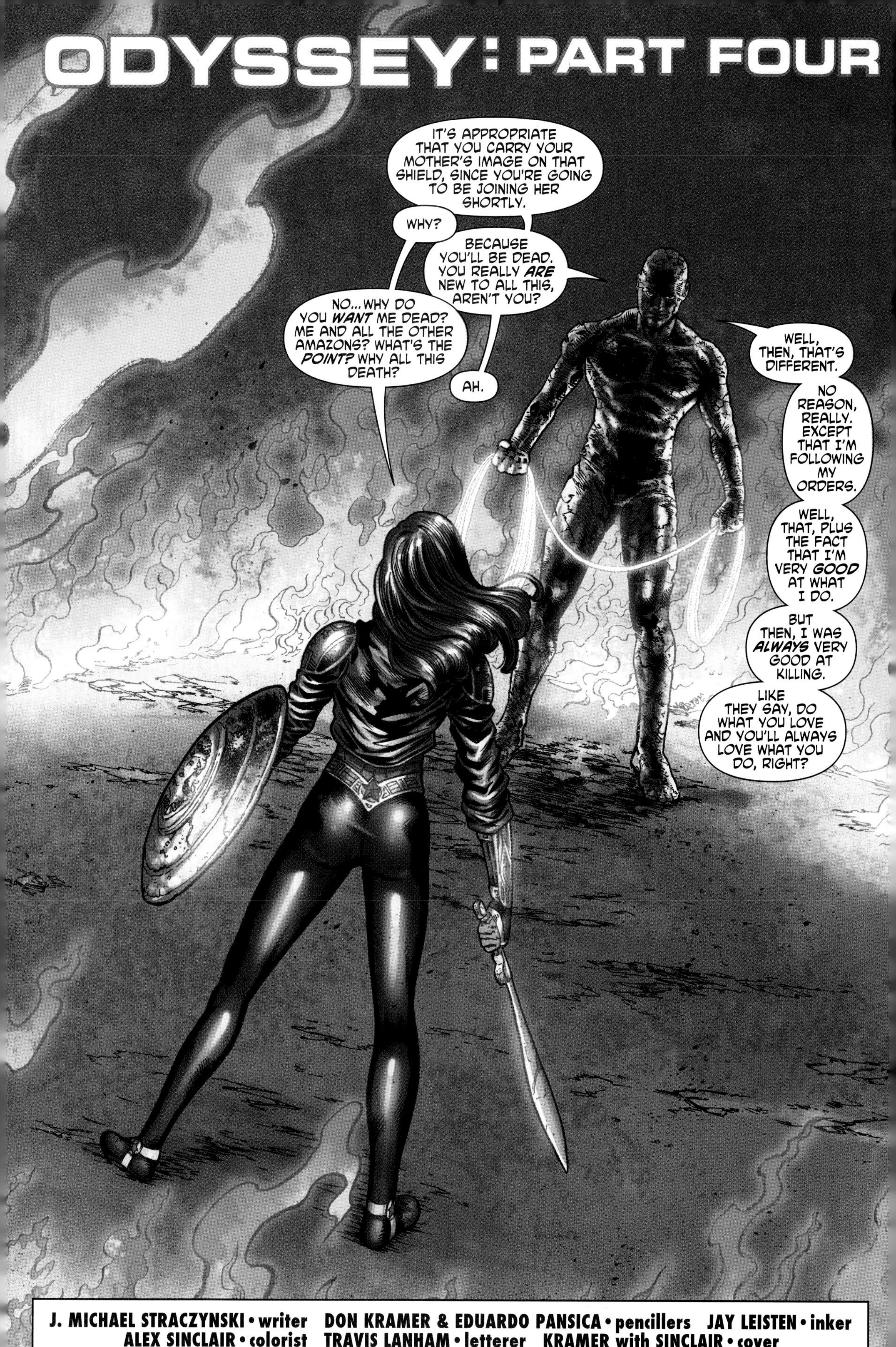

IT'S APPROPRIATE THAT YOU CARRY YOUR MOTHER'S IMAGE ON THAT SHIELD, SINCE YOU'RE GOING TO BE JOINING HER SHORTLY.
WHY?
BECAUSE YOU'LL BE DEAD. YOU REALLY ARE NEW TO ALL THIS, AREN'T YOU?
NO...WHY DO YOU WANT ME DEAD? ME AND ALL THE OTHER AMAZONS? WHAT'S THE POINT? WHY ALL THIS DEATH?
AH.
WELL, THEN, THAT'S DIFFERENT.
NO REASON, REALLY. EXCEPT THAT I'M FOLLOWING MY ORDERS.
WELL, THAT, PLUS THE FACT THAT I'M VERY GOOD AT WHAT I DO.
BUT THEN, I WAS ALWAYS VERY GOOD AT KILLING.
LIKE THEY SAY, DO WHAT YOU LOVE AND YOU'LL ALWAYS LOVE WHAT YOU DO, RIGHT?

J. MICHAEL STRACZYNSKI • writer DON KRAMER & EDUARDO PANSICA • pencillers JAY LEISTEN • inker
ALEX SINCLAIR • colorist TRAVIS LANHAM • letterer KRAMER with SINCLAIR • cover
ALEX GARNER • variant cover SEAN RYAN • associate editor BRIAN CUNNINGHAM • editor
WONDER WOMAN created by WILLIAM MOULTON MARSTON

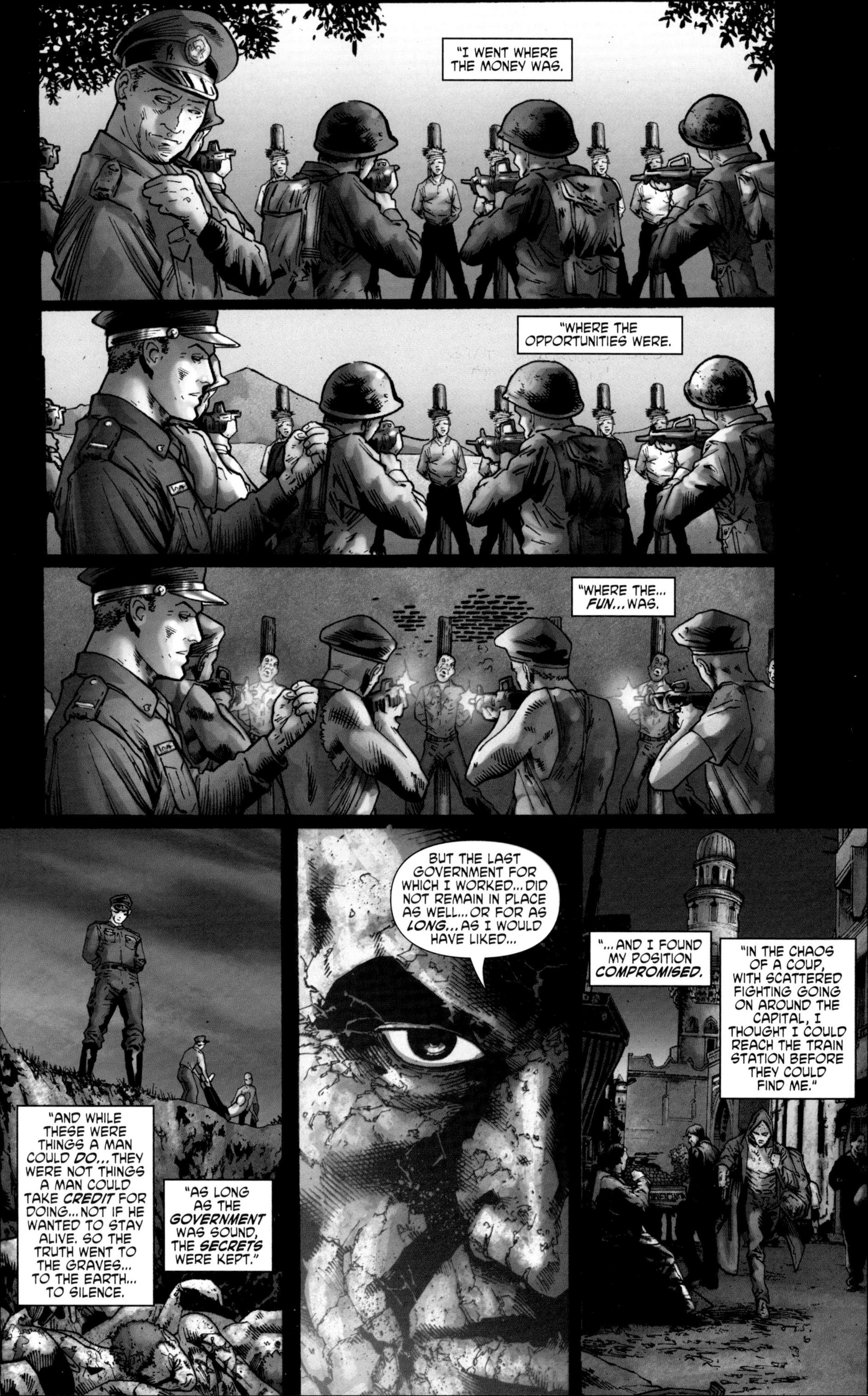
"I WENT WHERE THE MONEY WAS.
"WHERE THE OPPORTUNITIES WERE.
"WHERE THE... FUN... WAS.
"AND WHILE THESE WERE THINGS A MAN COULD DO... THEY WERE NOT THINGS A MAN COULD TAKE CREDIT FOR DOING... NOT IF HE WANTED TO STAY ALIVE. SO THE TRUTH WENT TO THE GRAVES... TO THE EARTH... TO SILENCE.
"AS LONG AS THE GOVERNMENT WAS SOUND, THE SECRETS WERE KEPT."
BUT THE LAST GOVERNMENT FOR WHICH I WORKED... DID NOT REMAIN IN PLACE AS WELL... OR FOR AS LONG... AS I WOULD HAVE LIKED...
"...AND I FOUND MY POSITION COMPROMISED.
"IN THE CHAOS OF A COUP, WITH SCATTERED FIGHTING GOING ON AROUND THE CAPITAL, I THOUGHT I COULD REACH THE TRAIN STATION BEFORE THEY COULD FIND ME."

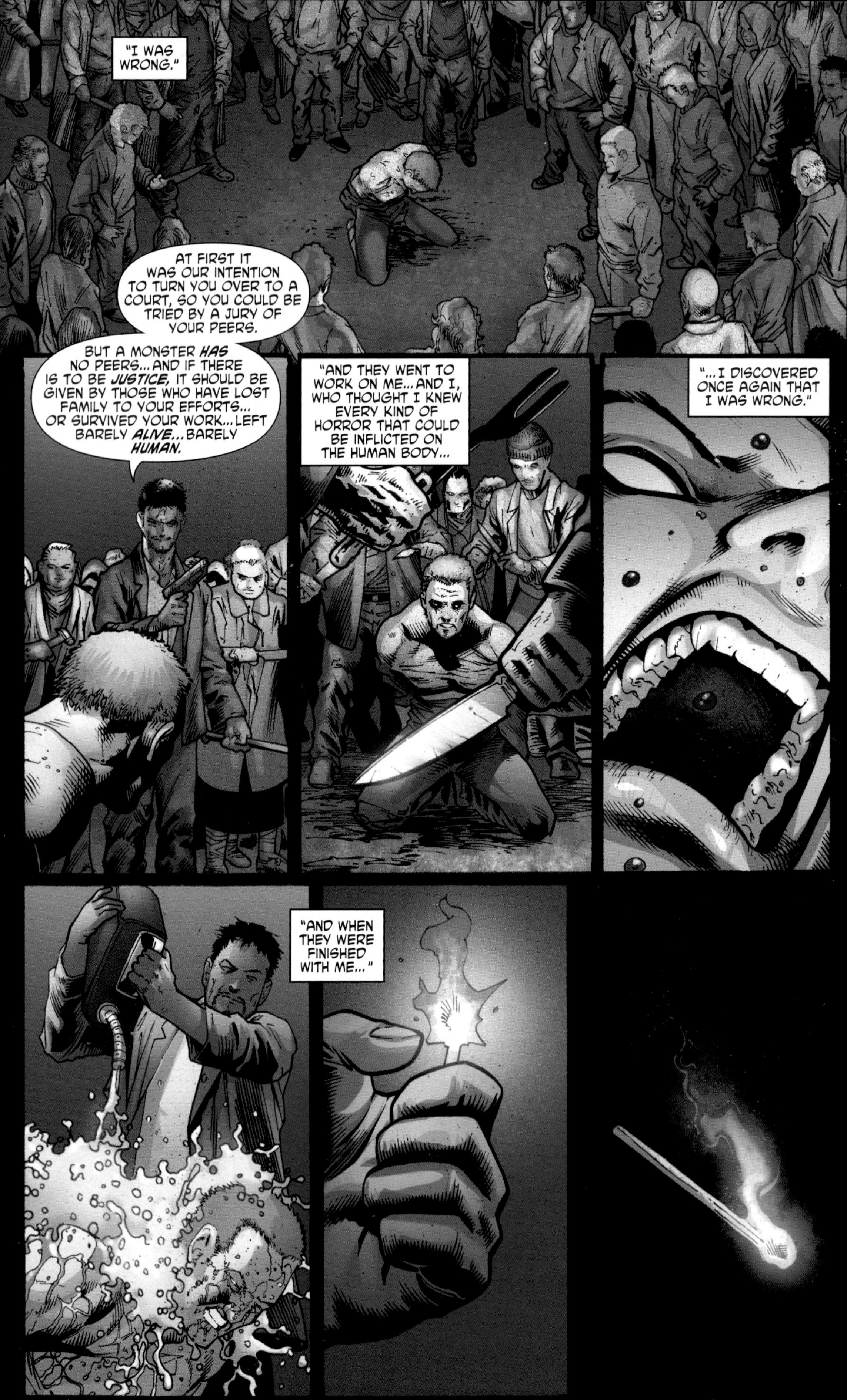
"I WAS WRONG."
AT FIRST IT WAS OUR INTENTION TO TURN YOU OVER TO A COURT, SO YOU COULD BE TRIED BY A JURY OF YOUR PEERS.
BUT A MONSTER *HAS* NO PEERS... AND IF THERE IS TO BE *JUSTICE,* IT SHOULD BE GIVEN BY THOSE WHO HAVE LOST FAMILY TO YOUR EFFORTS... OR SURVIVED YOUR WORK... LEFT BARELY *ALIVE*... BARELY *HUMAN.*
"AND THEY WENT TO WORK ON ME... AND I, WHO THOUGHT I KNEW EVERY KIND OF HORROR THAT COULD BE INFLICTED ON THE HUMAN BODY...
"...I DISCOVERED ONCE AGAIN THAT I WAS WRONG."
"AND WHEN THEY WERE FINISHED WITH ME..."

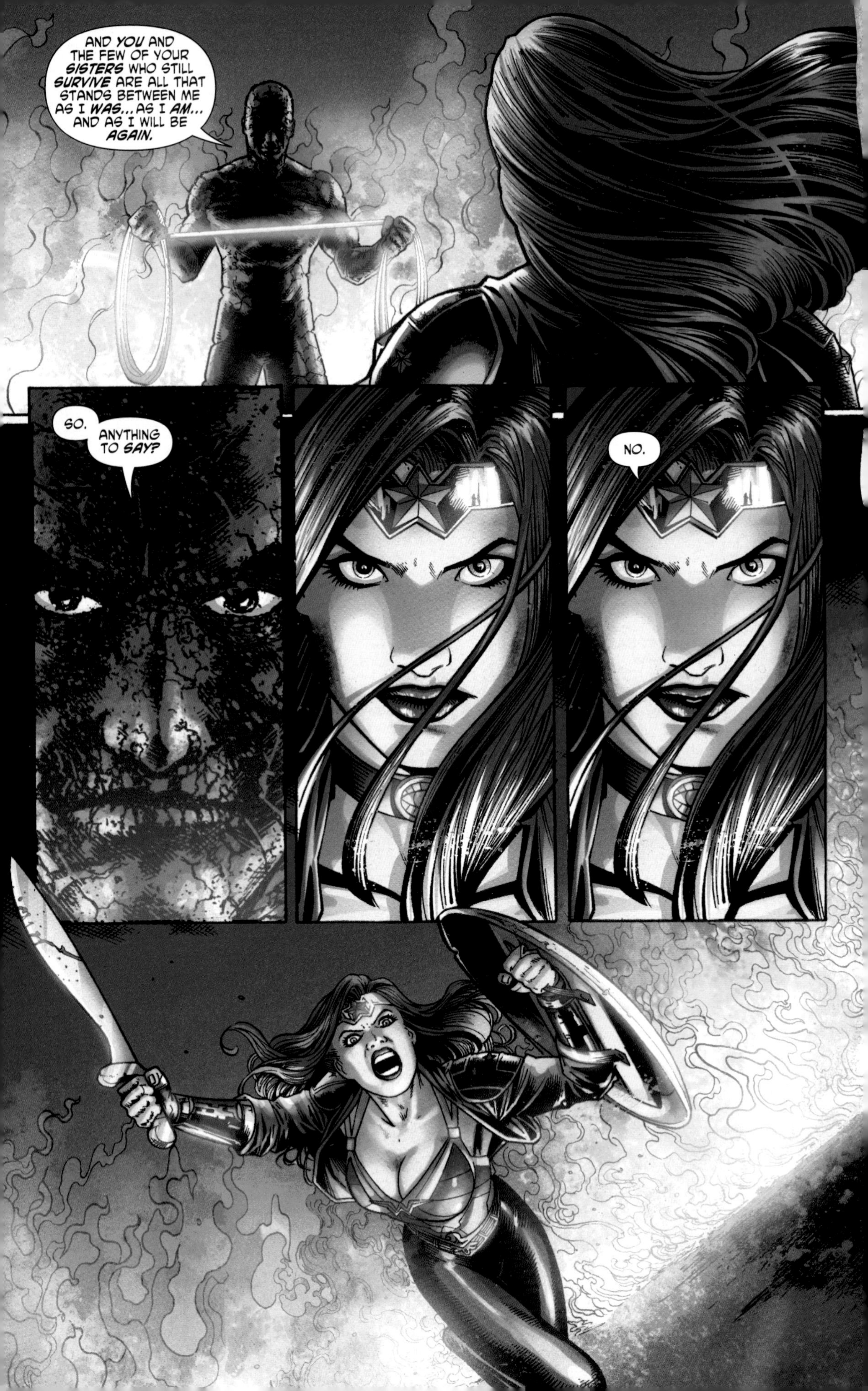
AND YOU AND THE FEW OF YOUR SISTERS WHO STILL SURVIVE ARE ALL THAT STANDS BETWEEN ME AS I WAS... AS I AM... AND AS I WILL BE AGAIN.
SO.
ANYTHING TO SAY?
NO.

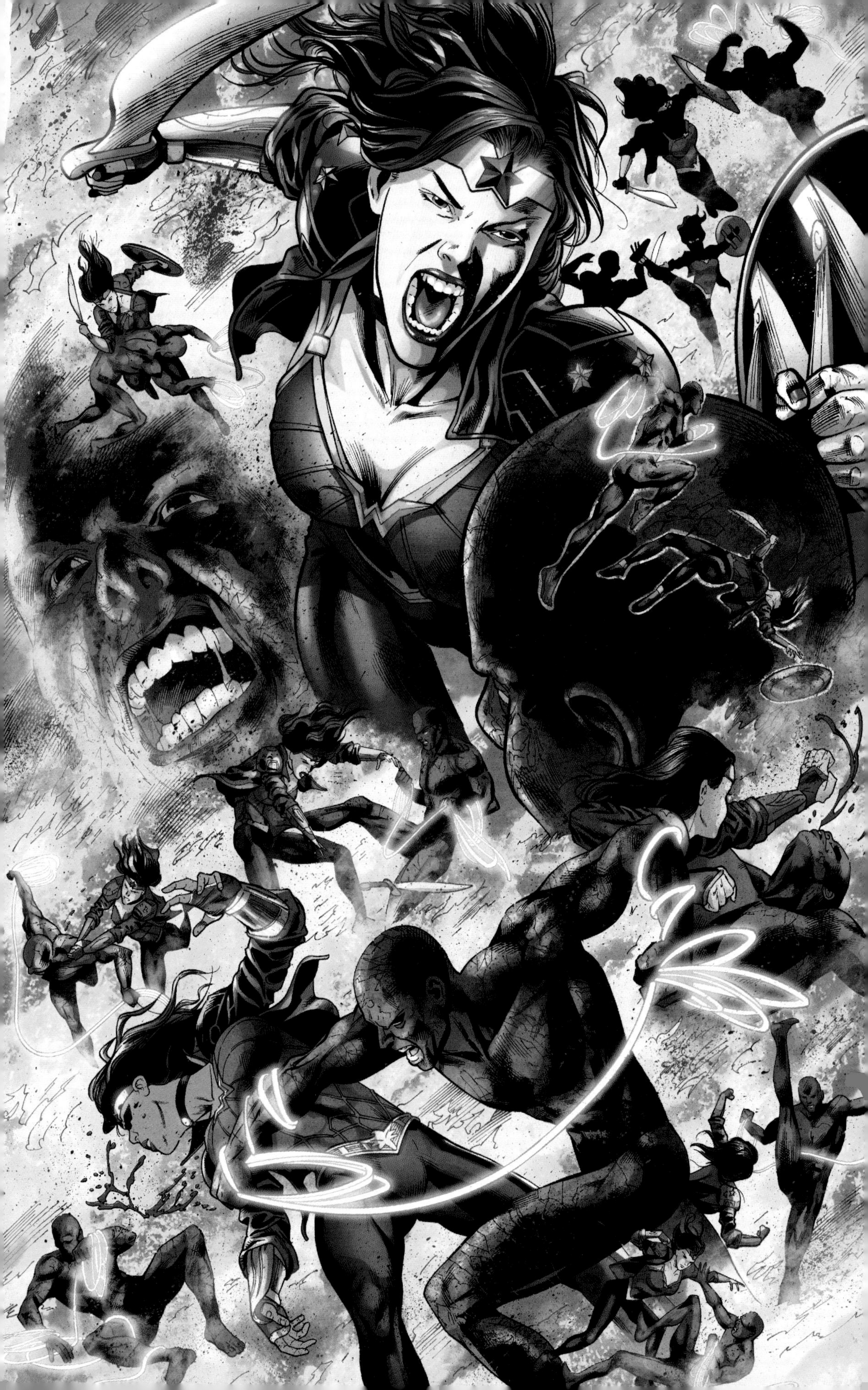

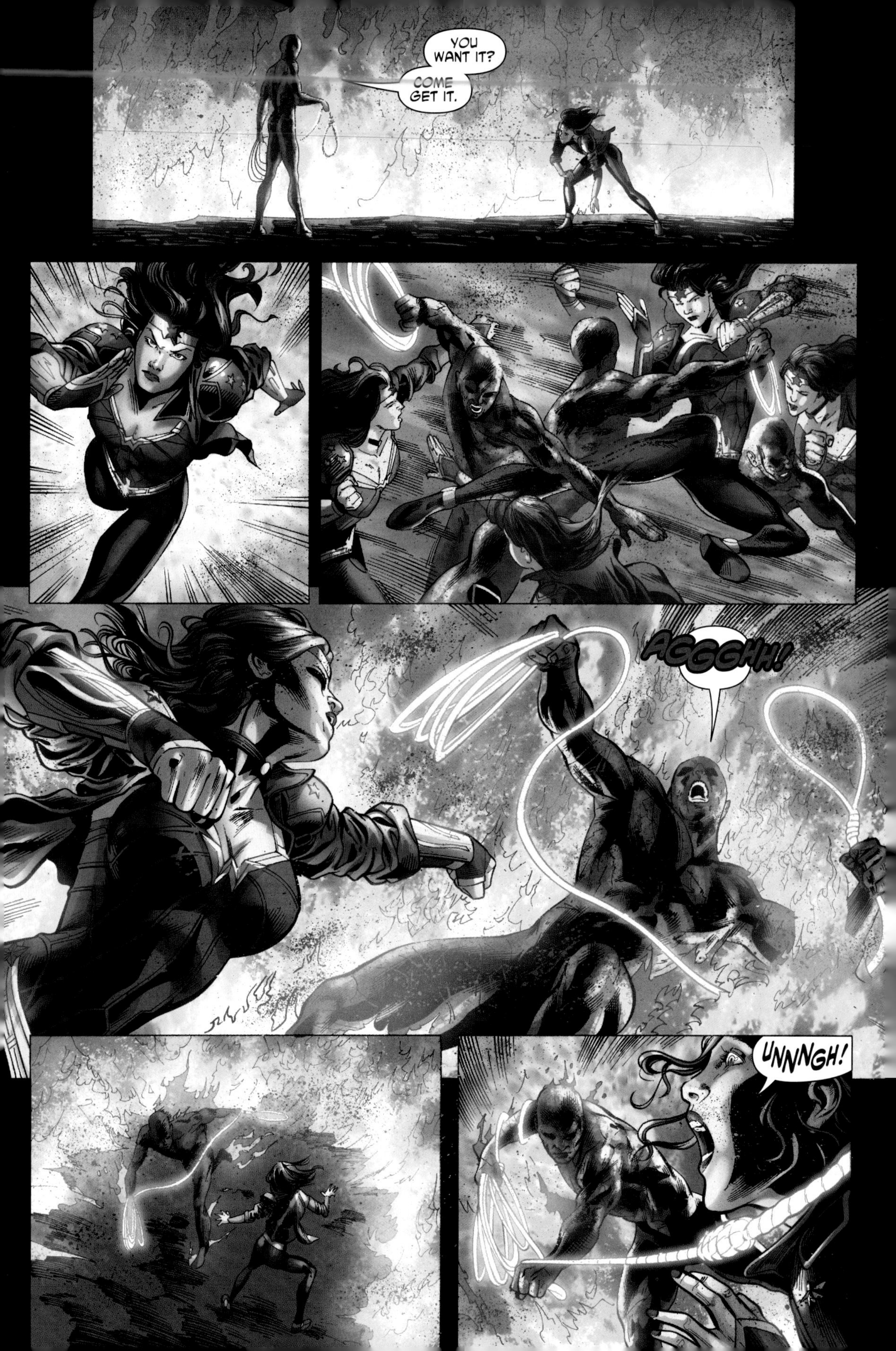
YOU WANT IT?
COME GET IT.
AGGGHH!
UNNNGH!

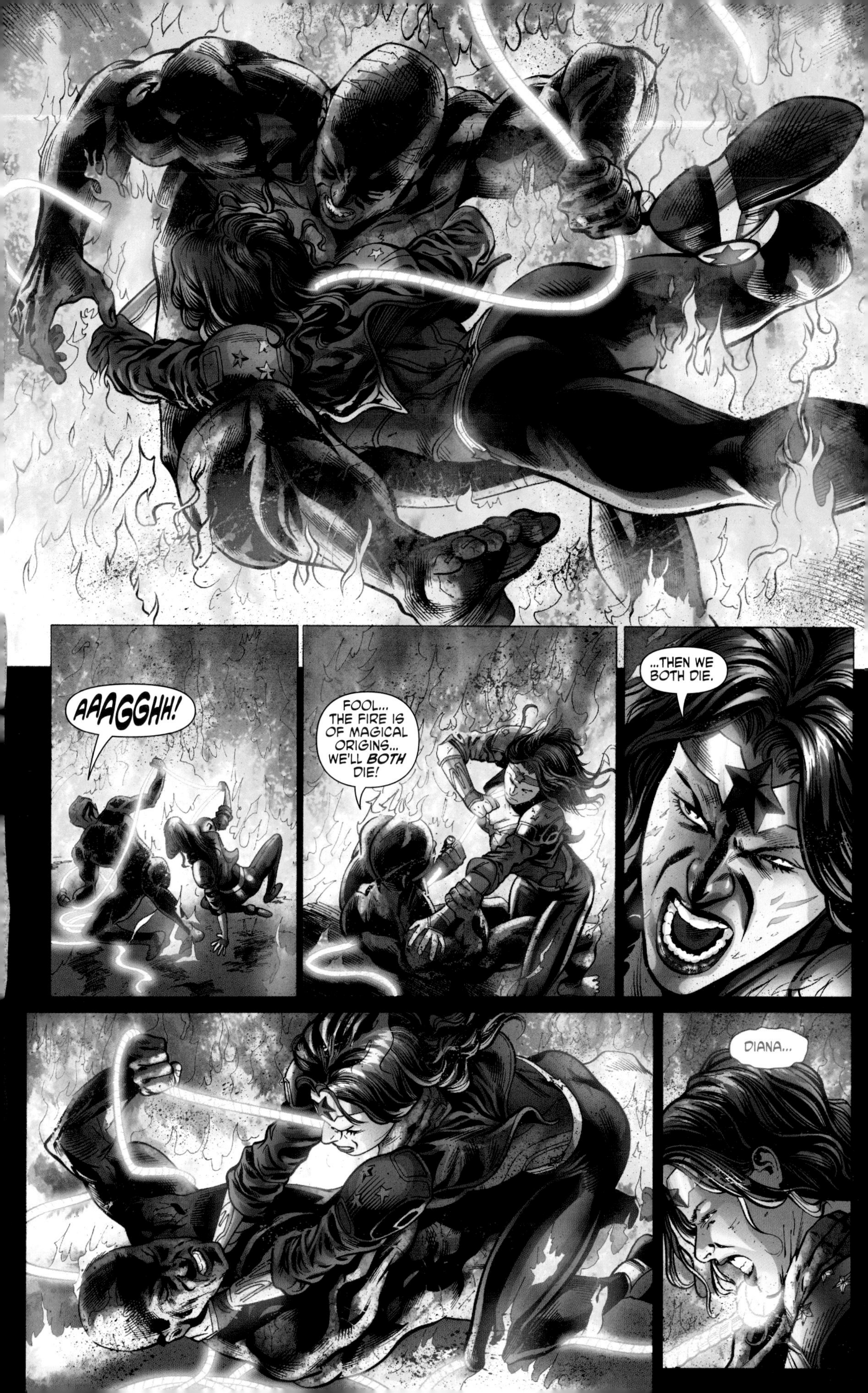
AAAGGHH!
FOOL... THE FIRE IS OF MAGICAL ORIGINS... WE'LL *BOTH* DIE!
...THEN WE BOTH DIE.
DIANA...

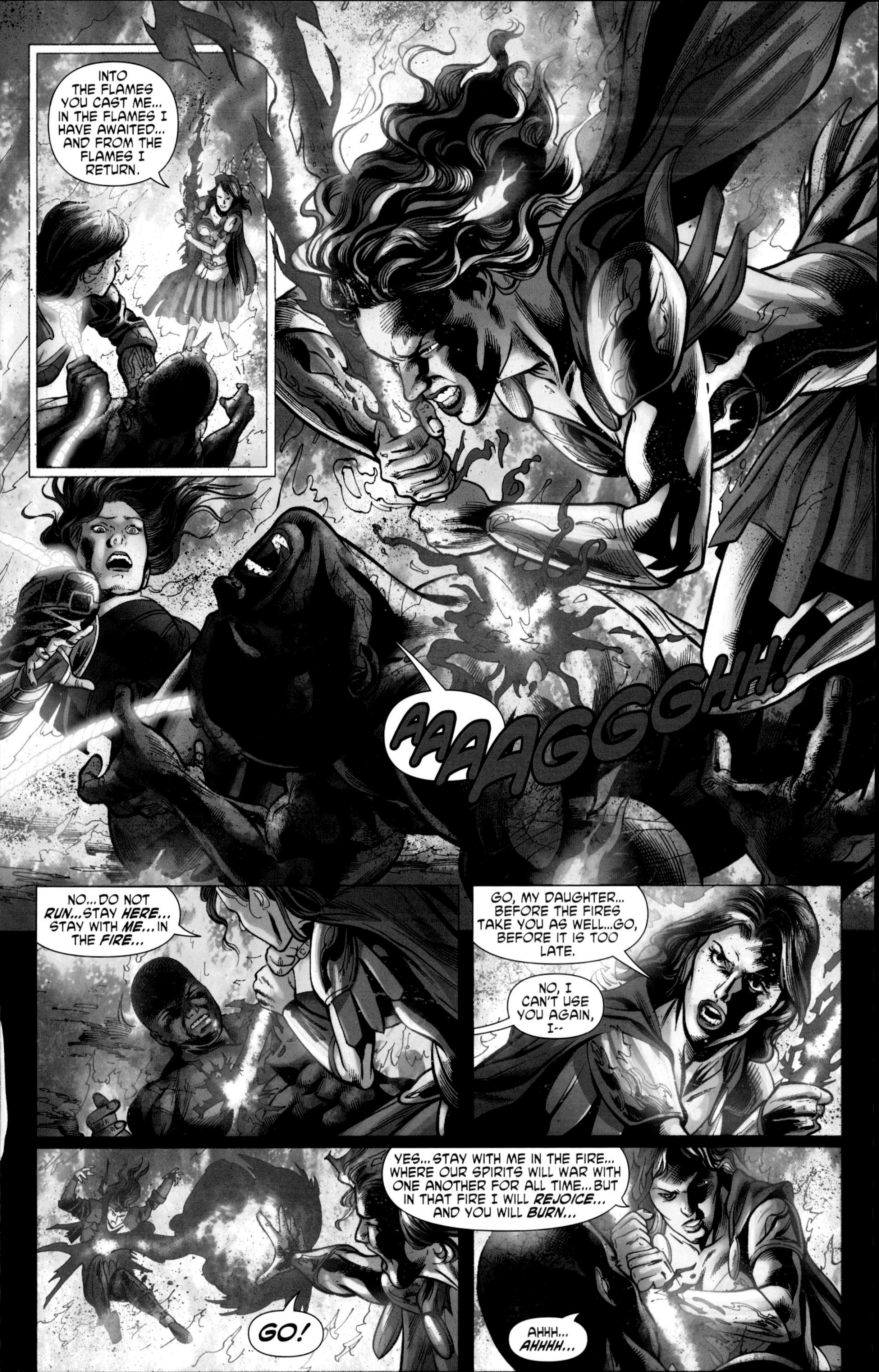
INTO THE FLAMES YOU CAST ME... IN THE FLAMES I HAVE AWAITED... AND FROM THE FLAMES I RETURN.
AAAAGGGGHH!
NO...DO NOT RUN...STAY HERE... STAY WITH ME...IN THE FIRE...
GO, MY DAUGHTER... BEFORE THE FIRES TAKE YOU AS WELL...GO, BEFORE IT IS TOO LATE.
NO, I CAN'T USE YOU AGAIN, I--
YES...STAY WITH ME IN THE FIRE... WHERE OUR SPIRITS WILL WAR WITH ONE ANOTHER FOR ALL TIME...BUT IN THAT FIRE I WILL REJOICE... AND YOU WILL BURN...
GO!
AHHH... AHHHH...

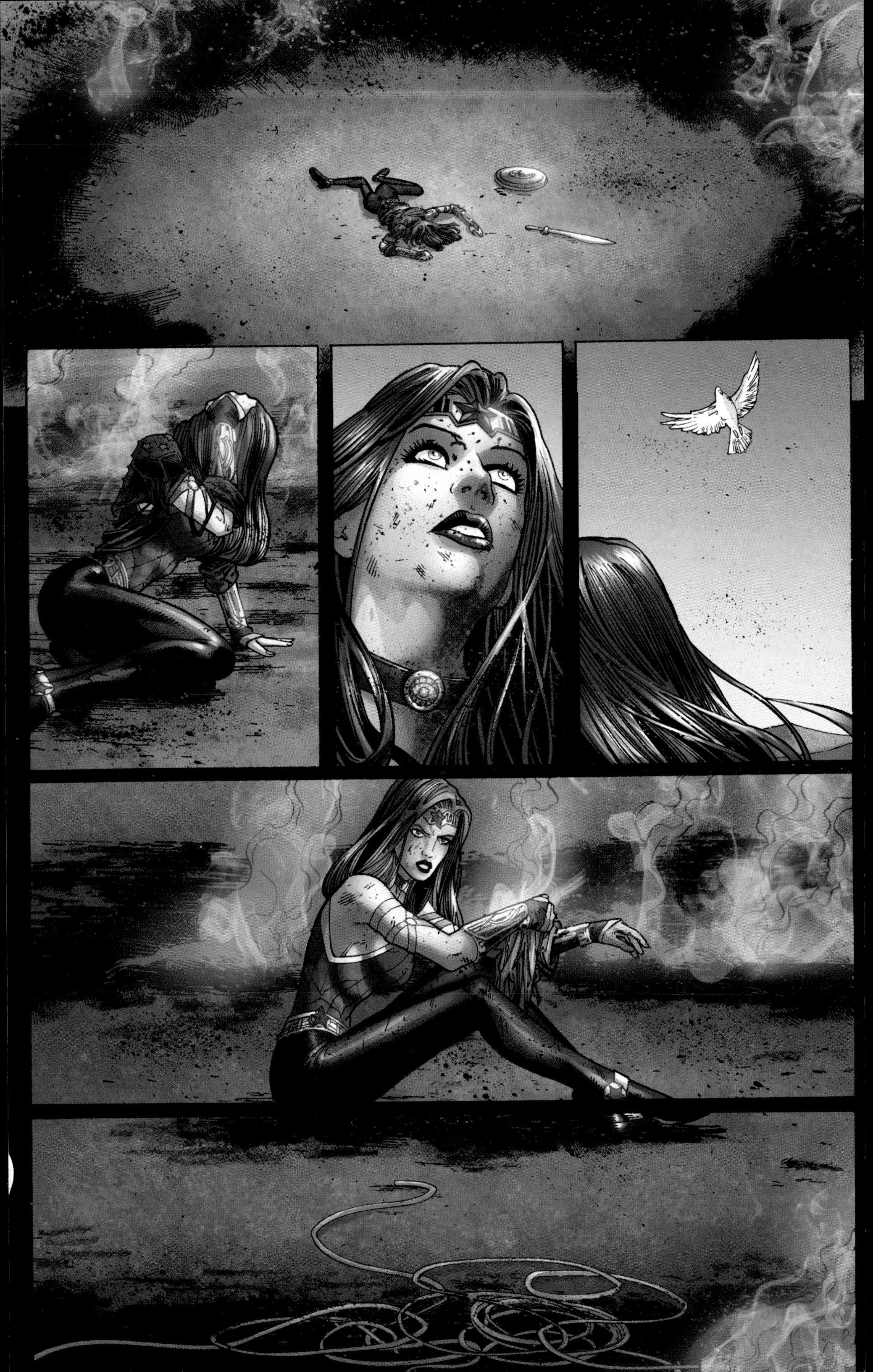

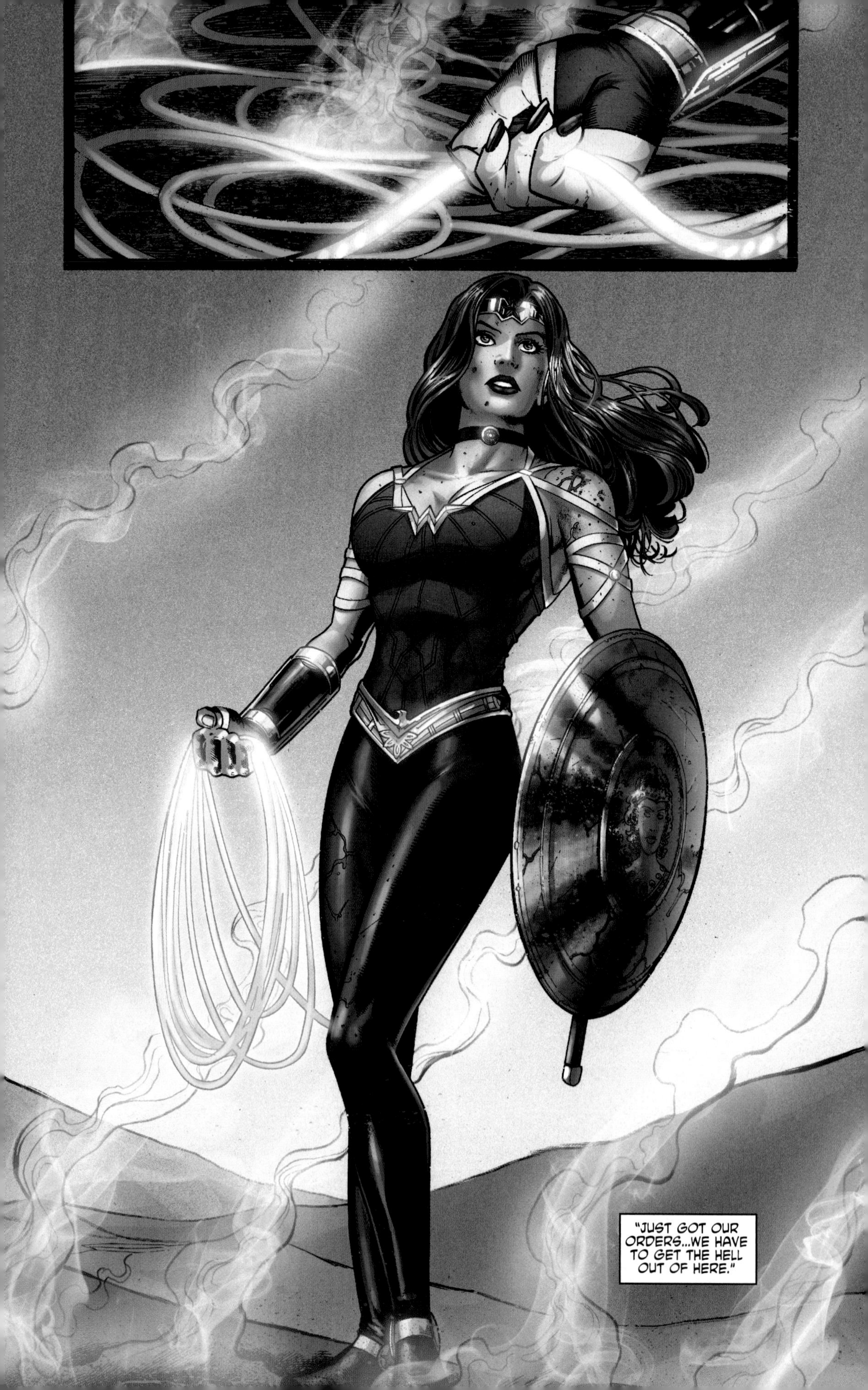
"JUST GOT OUR ORDERS...WE HAVE TO GET THE HELL OUT OF HERE."

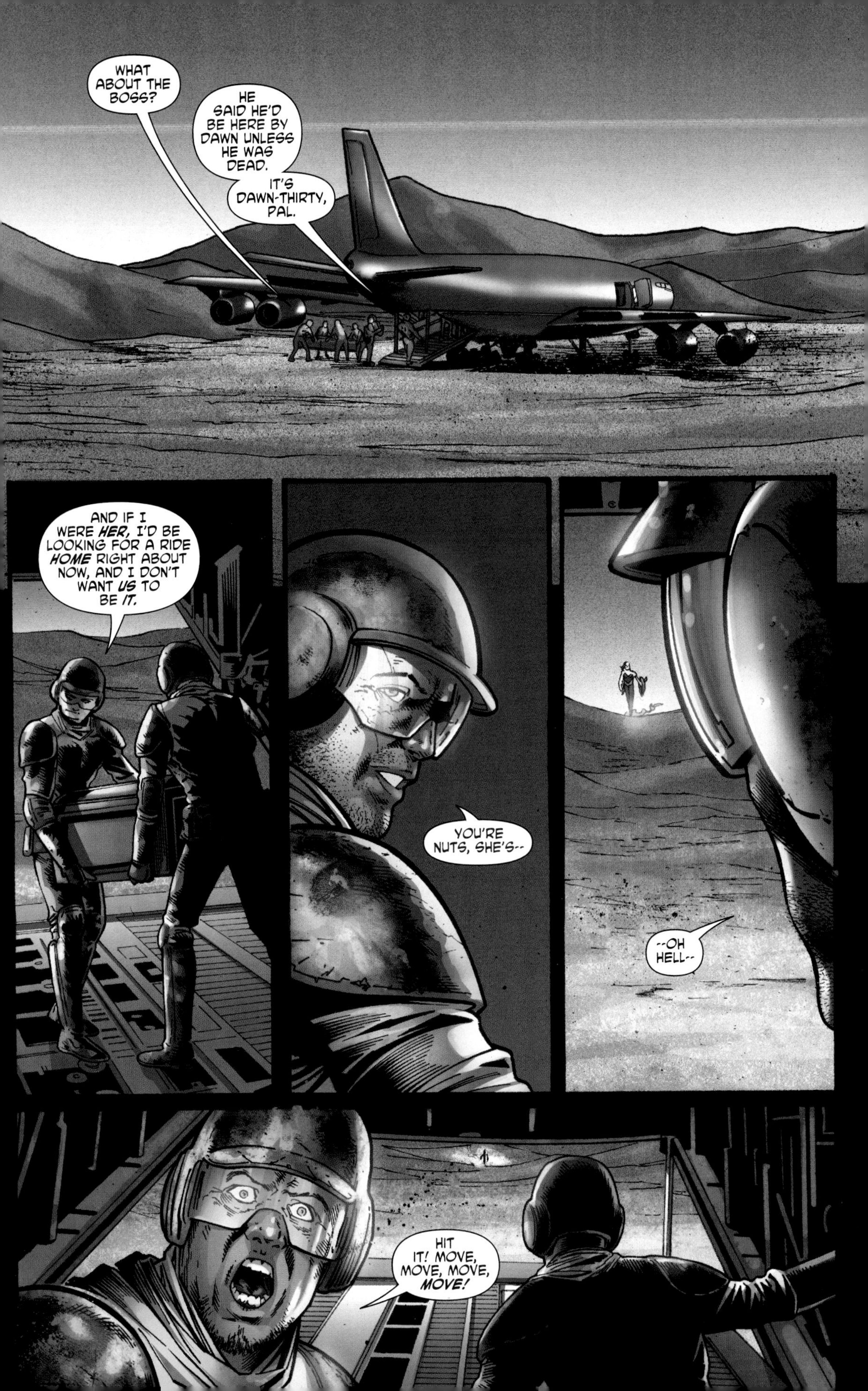
WHAT ABOUT THE BOSS?
HE SAID HE'D BE HERE BY DAWN UNLESS HE WAS DEAD.
IT'S DAWN-THIRTY, PAL.
AND IF I WERE ***HER***, I'D BE LOOKING FOR A RIDE ***HOME*** RIGHT ABOUT NOW, AND I DON'T WANT ***US*** TO BE ***IT.***
YOU'RE NUTS, SHE'S--
--OH HELL--
HIT IT! MOVE, MOVE, MOVE, ***MOVE!***

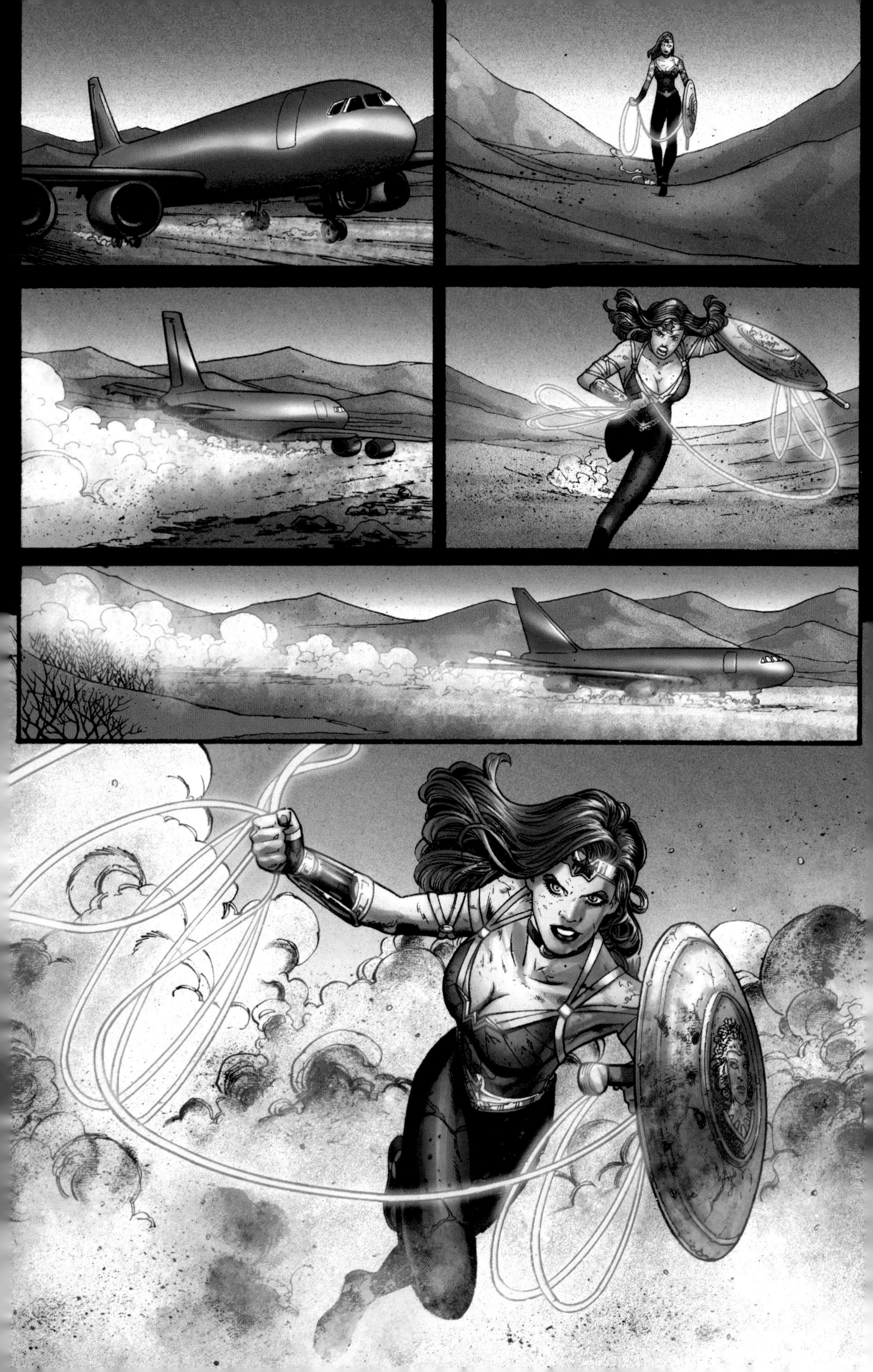

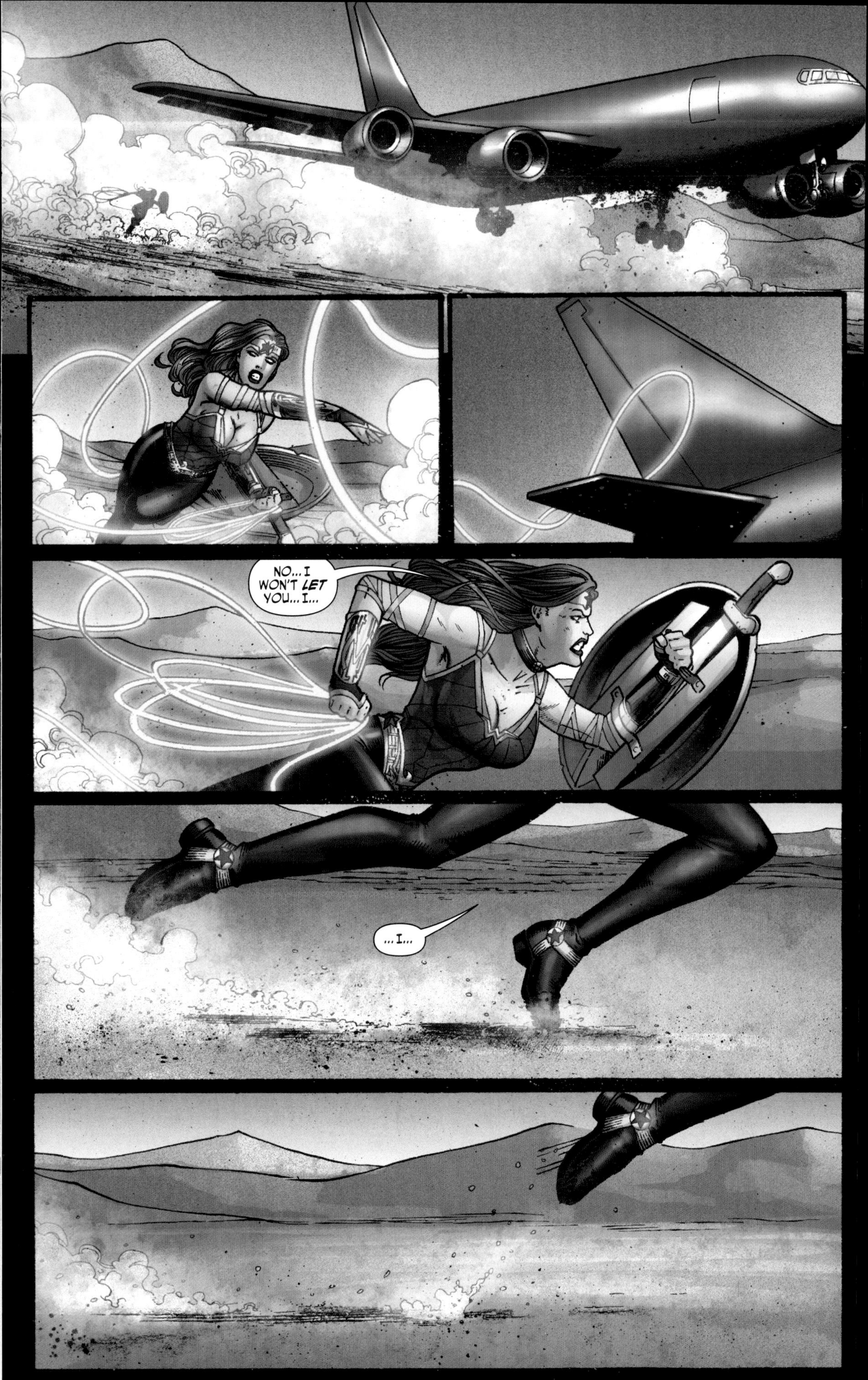
NO... I WON'T LET YOU... I...
...I...

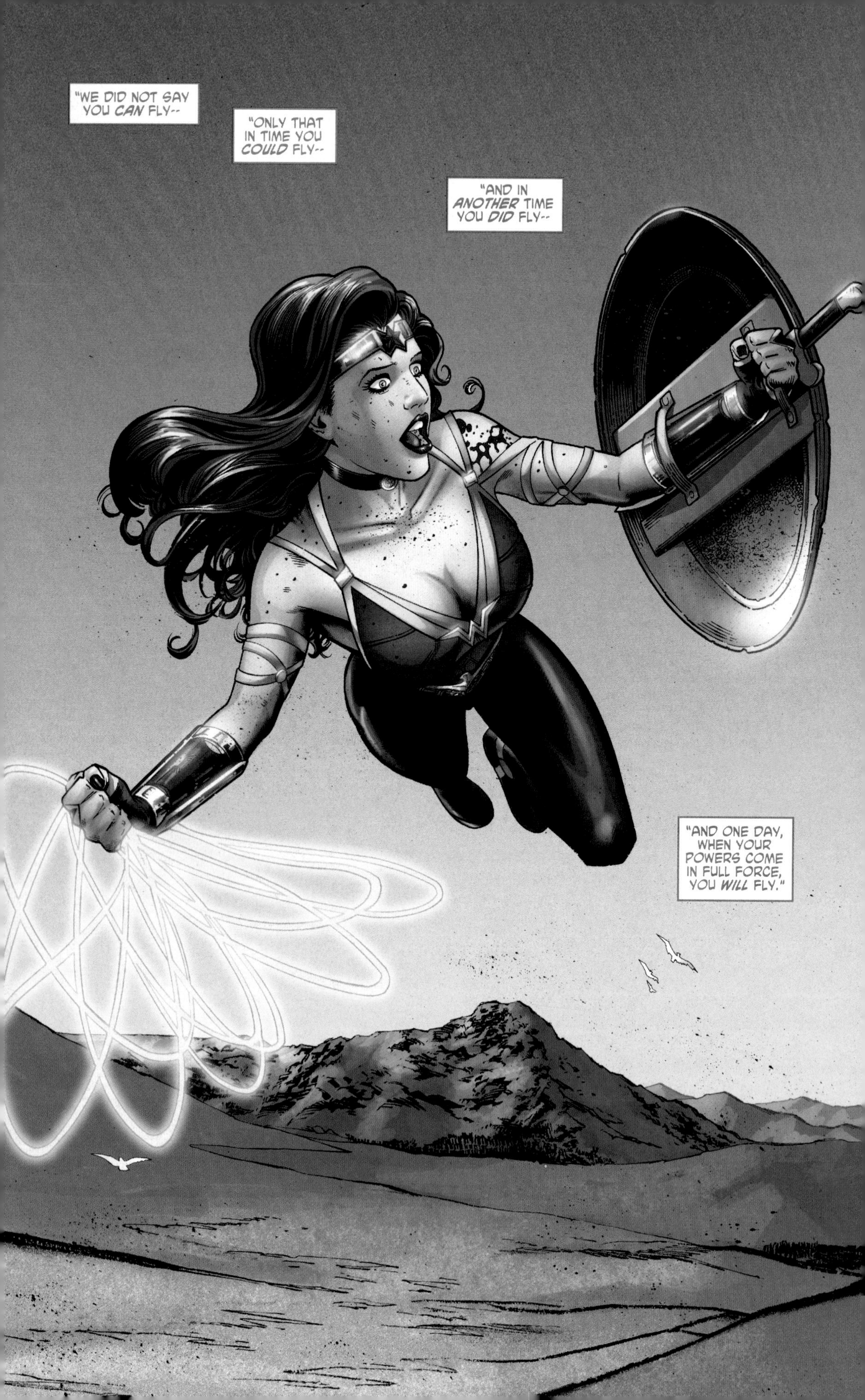
"WE DID NOT SAY YOU CAN FLY--
"ONLY THAT IN TIME YOU COULD FLY--
"AND IN ANOTHER TIME YOU DID FLY--
"AND ONE DAY, WHEN YOUR POWERS COME IN FULL FORCE, YOU WILL FLY."

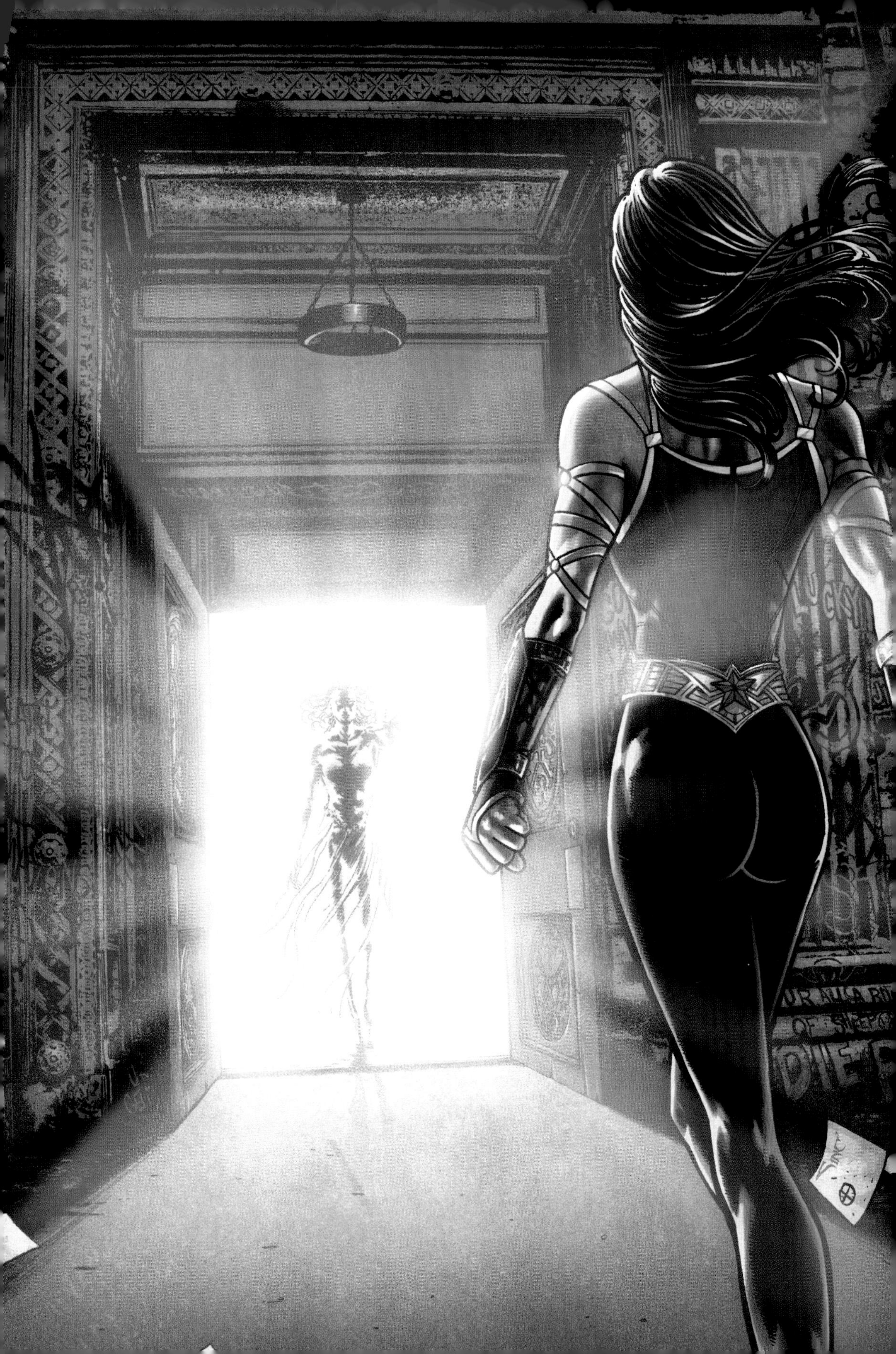

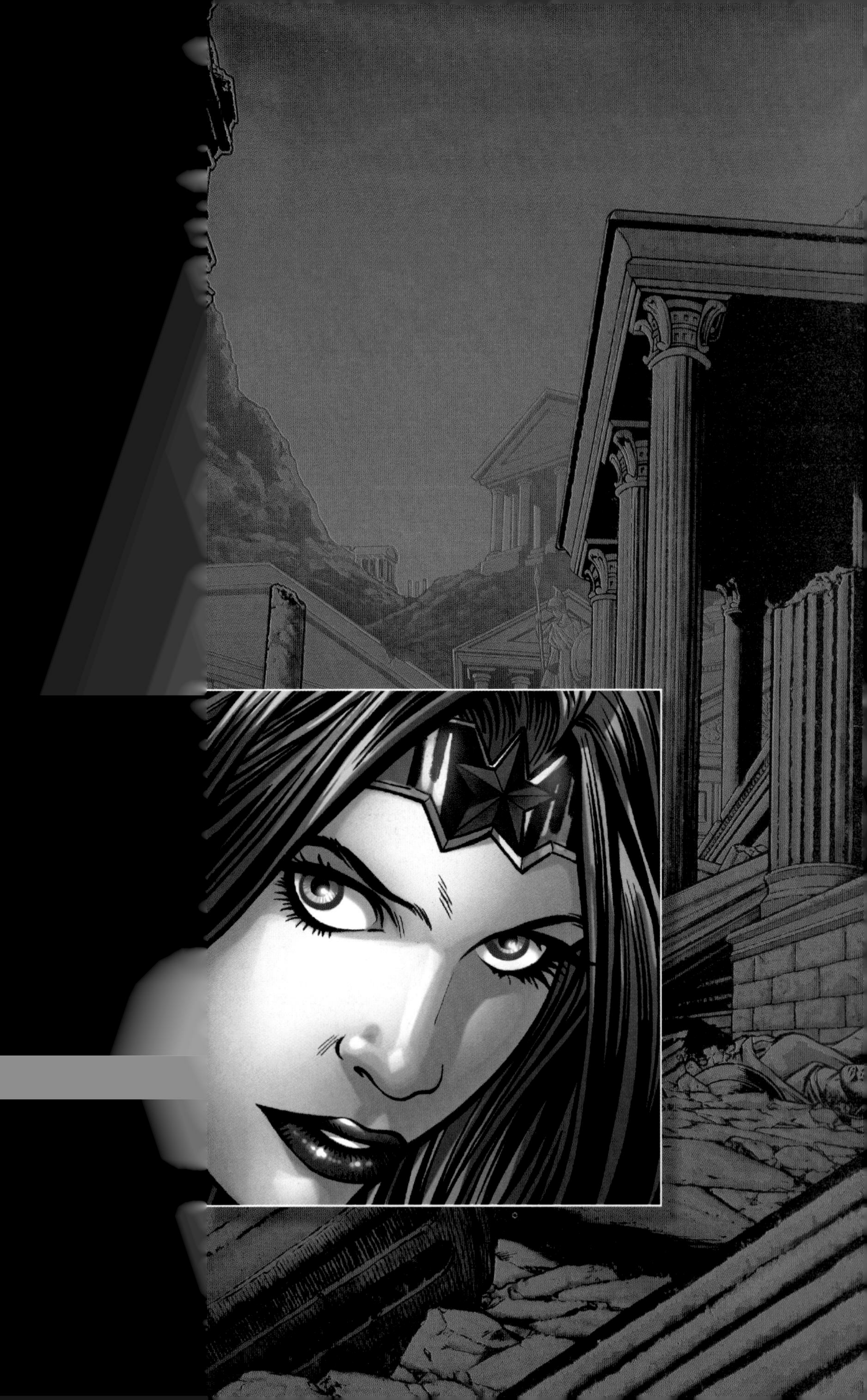

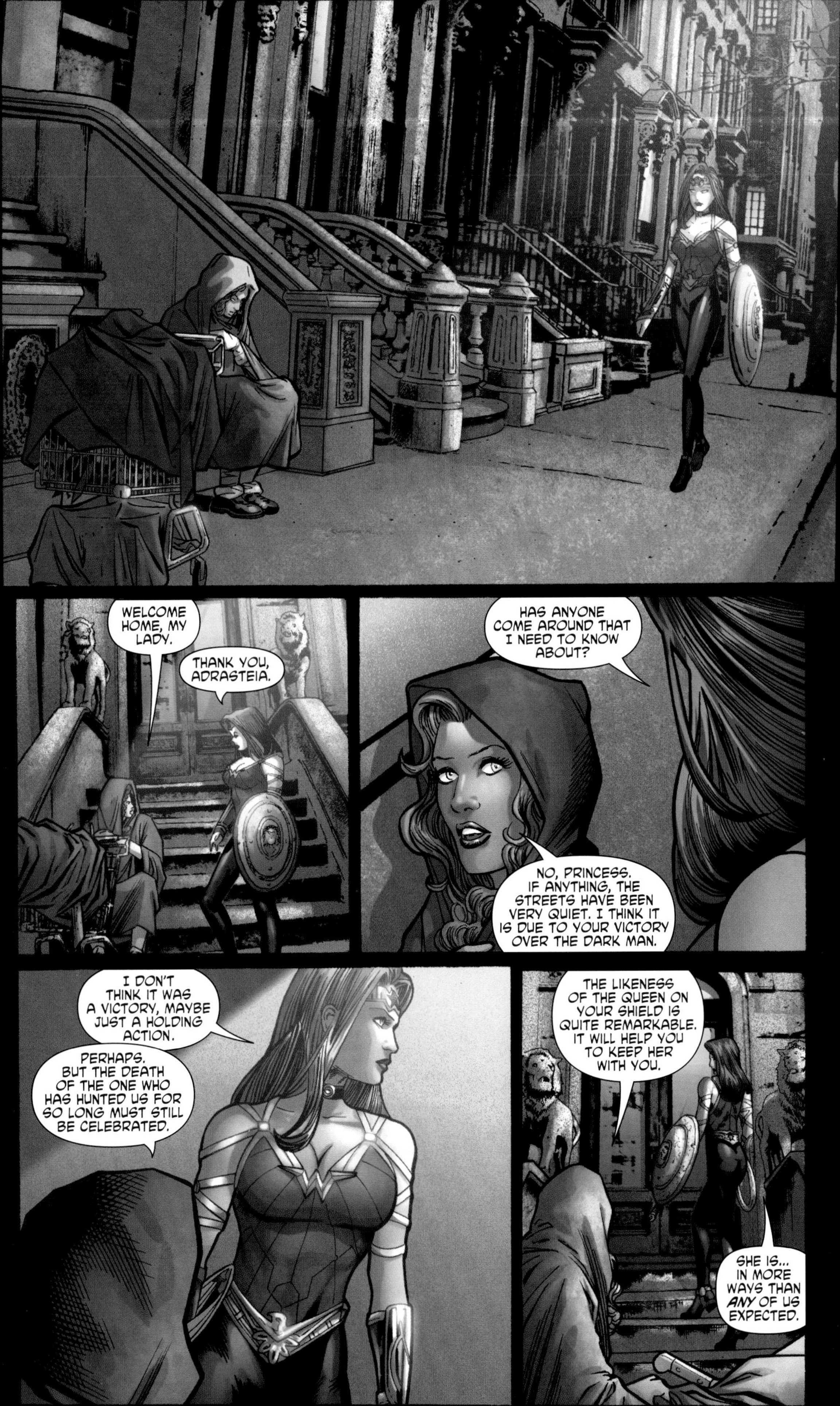
WELCOME HOME, MY LADY.
THANK YOU, ADRASTEIA.
HAS ANYONE COME AROUND THAT I NEED TO KNOW ABOUT?
NO, PRINCESS. IF ANYTHING, THE STREETS HAVE BEEN VERY QUIET. I THINK IT IS DUE TO YOUR VICTORY OVER THE DARK MAN.
I DON'T THINK IT WAS A VICTORY, MAYBE JUST A HOLDING ACTION.
PERHAPS. BUT THE DEATH OF THE ONE WHO HAS HUNTED US FOR SO LONG MUST STILL BE CELEBRATED.
THE LIKENESS OF THE QUEEN ON YOUR SHIELD IS QUITE REMARKABLE. IT WILL HELP YOU TO KEEP HER WITH YOU.
SHE IS... IN MORE WAYS THAN *ANY* OF US EXPECTED.

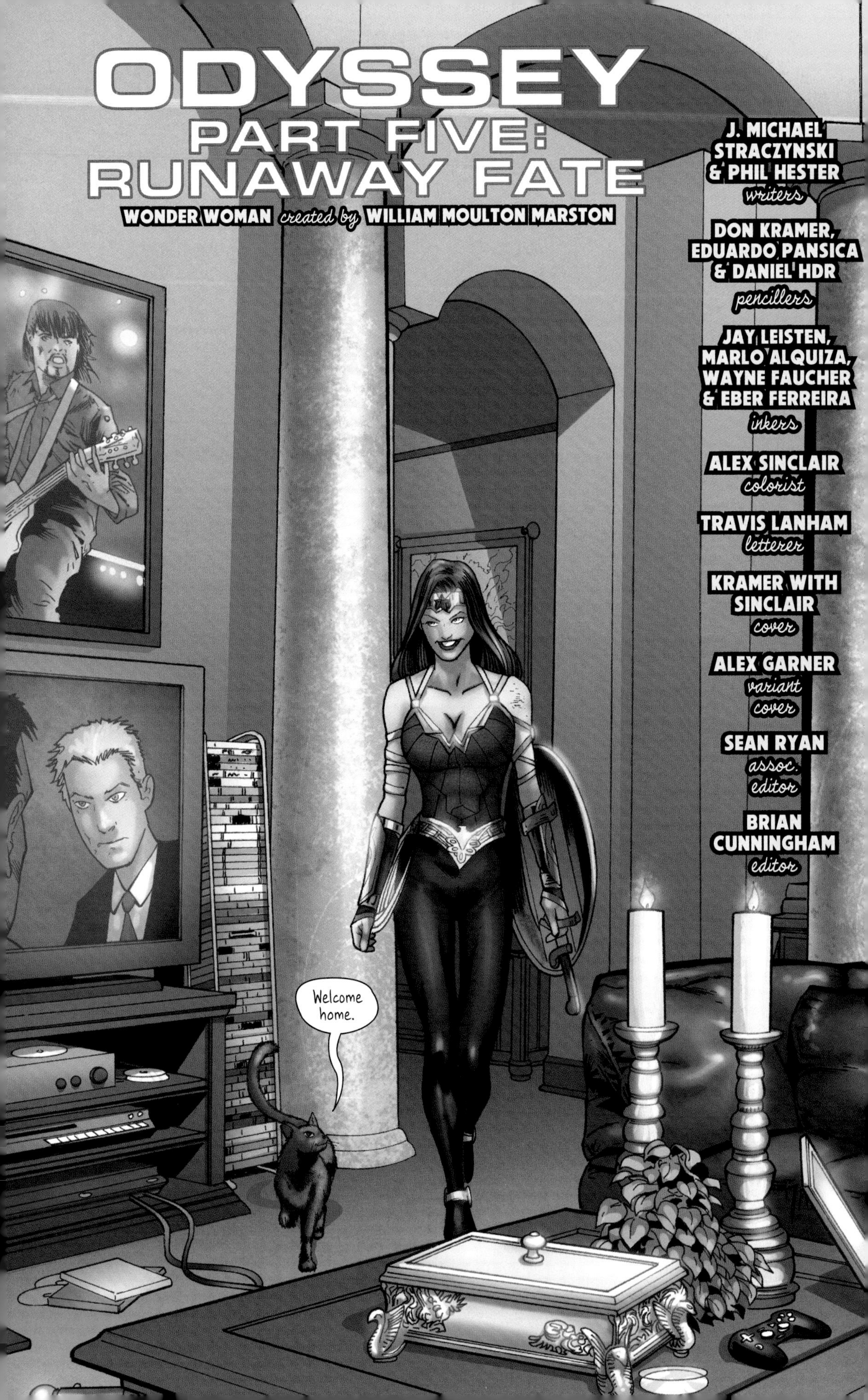
ODYSSEY
PART FIVE: RUNAWAY FATE
WONDER WOMAN created by WILLIAM MOULTON MARSTON
J. MICHAEL STRACZYNSKI & PHIL HESTER writers
DON KRAMER, EDUARDO PANSICA & DANIEL HDR pencillers
JAY LEISTEN, MARLO ALQUIZA, WAYNE FAUCHER & EBER FERREIRA inkers
ALEX SINCLAIR colorist
TRAVIS LANHAM letterer
KRAMER WITH SINCLAIR cover
ALEX GARNER variant cover
SEAN RYAN assoc. editor
BRIAN CUNNINGHAM editor
Welcome home.

EXCUSE ME!

SORRY, GALENTHIAS.

himself would hide every head from that countenance.

FOOTBALL, GAL. YOU SHOULD MAKE AN EFFORT TO STAY CURRENT, YOU KNOW.

SORRY, SISTER. IT'S JUST THAT THE KNIGHTS ARE DRIVING ON THE METEORS LATE IN THE FOURTH, AND ONE OF OUR SCOUTS JUST CALLED FOR EMERGENCY BACK-UP.

I'll never understand your fascination with man's world, sister. The slowest among us could outrun the swiftest man on any team.

Meteors? The Fourth?

These boys can barely tackle one another without collapsing in pain.

MAYBE THAT'S WHY I LIKE IT. THEY PUT THEIR MORTAL BODIES AT RISK FOR NOTHING BUT VALOR. WHILE WE'VE BEEN FIGHTING SO LONG... JUST TO SURVIVE.

You long to PLAY as they do.

CHILDISH, I KNOW, SPECIALLY FOR THE CAPTAIN OF THE GUARD.

REGARDLESS, THERESTRA BELIEVES SHE'S FOUND THE REMAINS OF A TEMPLE IN THE SOUTH BRONX. ONE MUCH LIKE OURS, YET NOT OURS.

TROUBLING.

ALMOST AS TROUBLING AS THAT CATERWAULING FROM DIANA'S QUARTERS.

♪ I HAVE ♪ YOUR ♪♪ HEAD

"It's that awful mortal music of hers. PAN HIMSELF would stop up his ears.

"But if I know that girl, she's already sleeping like a lamb."

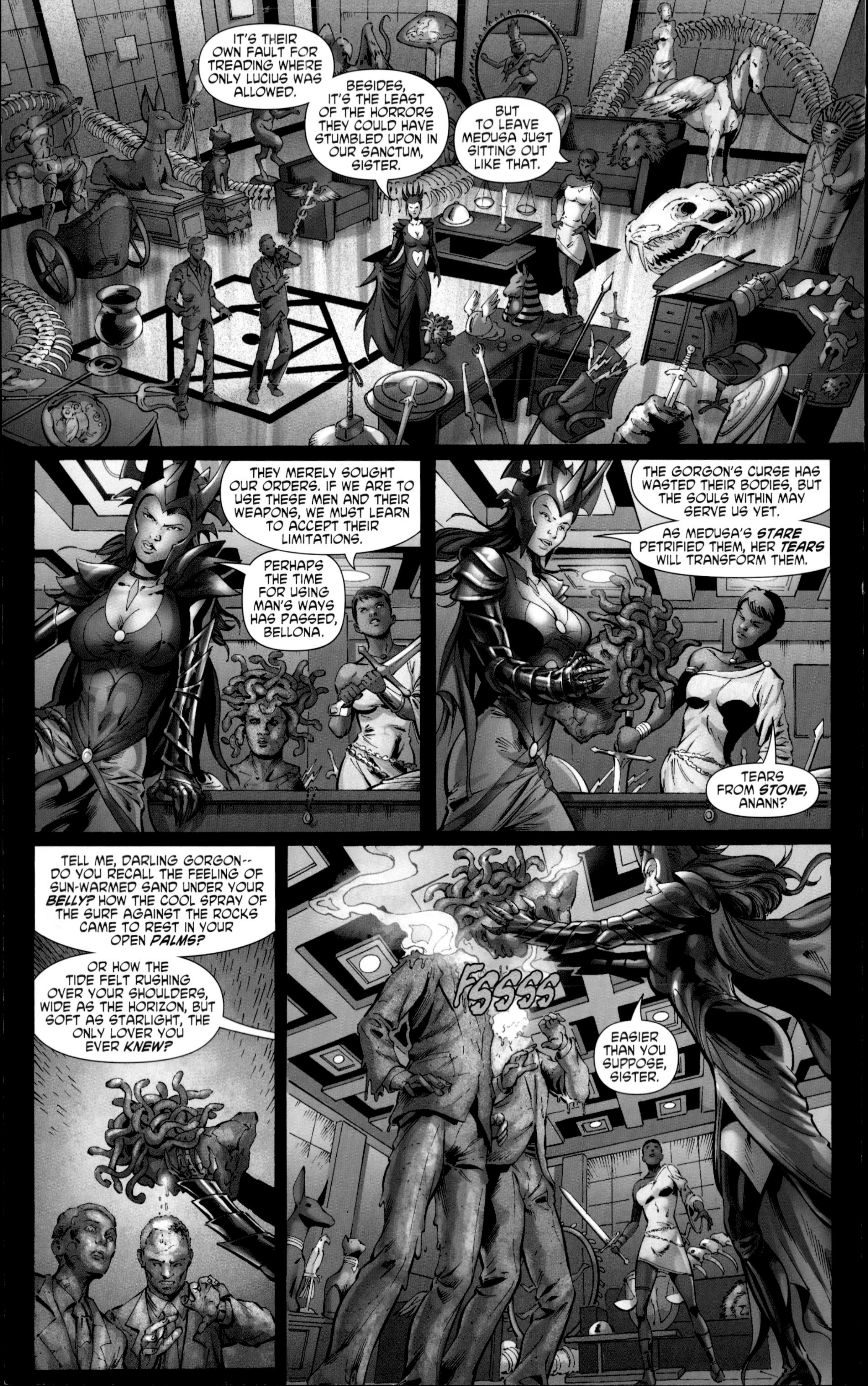
IT'S THEIR OWN FAULT FOR TREADING WHERE ONLY LUCIUS WAS ALLOWED.
BESIDES, IT'S THE LEAST OF THE HORRORS THEY COULD HAVE STUMBLED UPON IN OUR SANCTUM, SISTER.
BUT TO LEAVE MEDUSA JUST SITTING OUT LIKE THAT.
THEY MERELY SOUGHT OUR ORDERS. IF WE ARE TO USE THESE MEN AND THEIR WEAPONS, WE MUST LEARN TO ACCEPT THEIR LIMITATIONS.
PERHAPS THE TIME FOR USING MAN'S WAYS HAS PASSED, BELLONA.
THE GORGON'S CURSE HAS WASTED THEIR BODIES, BUT THE SOULS WITHIN MAY SERVE US YET.
AS MEDUSA'S STARE PETRIFIED THEM, HER TEARS WILL TRANSFORM THEM.
TEARS FROM STONE, ANANN?
TELL ME, DARLING GORGON-- DO YOU RECALL THE FEELING OF SUN-WARMED SAND UNDER YOUR BELLY? HOW THE COOL SPRAY OF THE SURF AGAINST THE ROCKS CAME TO REST IN YOUR OPEN PALMS?
OR HOW THE TIDE FELT RUSHING OVER YOUR SHOULDERS, WIDE AS THE HORIZON, BUT SOFT AS STARLIGHT, THE ONLY LOVER YOU EVER KNEW?
FSSSS
EASIER THAN YOU SUPPOSE, SISTER.

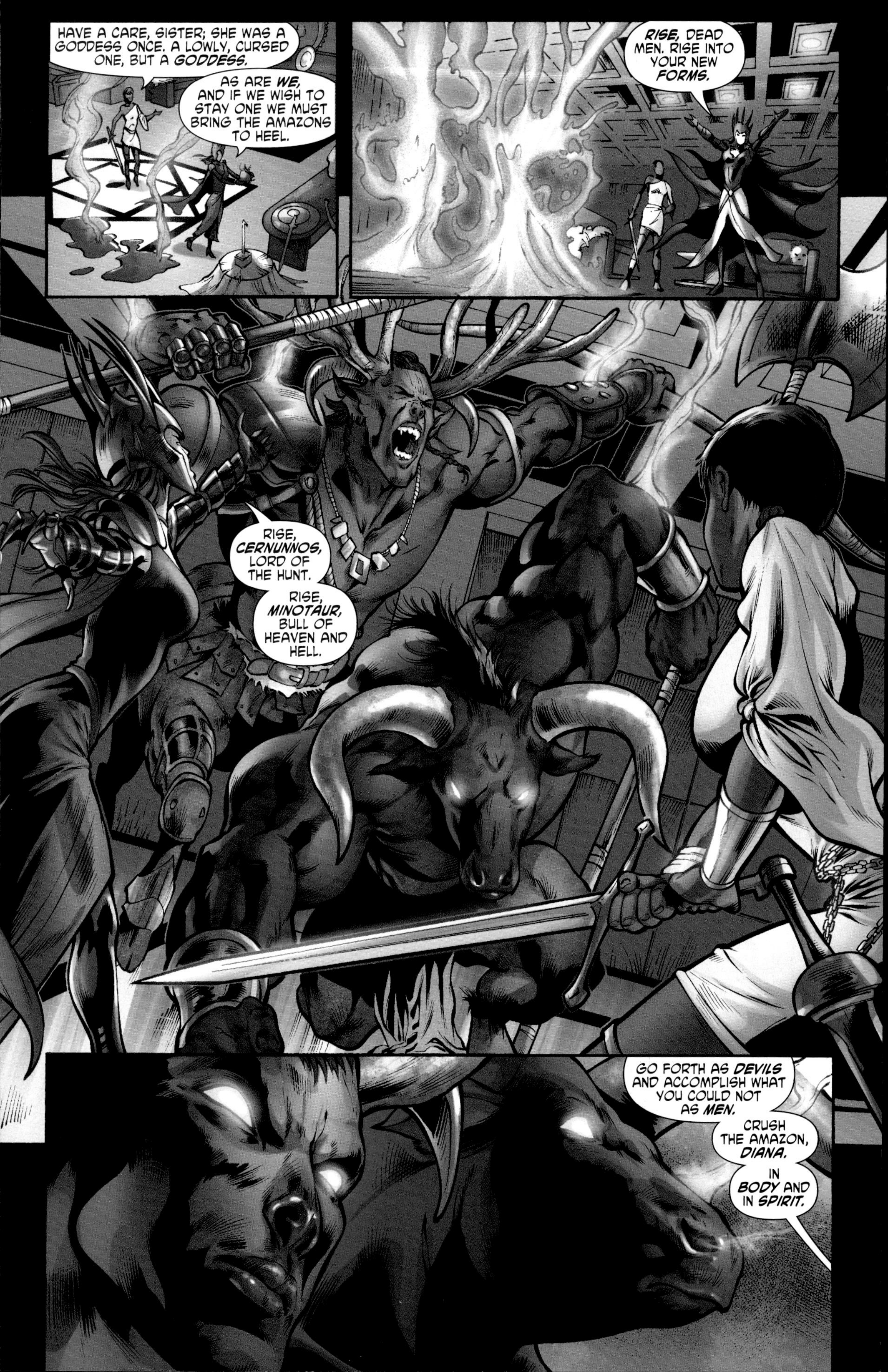
HAVE A CARE, SISTER; SHE WAS A GODDESS ONCE. A LOWLY, CURSED ONE, BUT A *GODDESS.*
AS ARE *WE,* AND IF WE WISH TO STAY ONE WE MUST BRING THE AMAZONS TO HEEL.
RISE, DEAD MEN. RISE INTO YOUR NEW *FORMS.*
RISE, *CERNUNNOS,* LORD OF THE HUNT.
RISE, *MINOTAUR,* BULL OF HEAVEN AND HELL.
GO FORTH AS *DEVILS* AND ACCOMPLISH WHAT YOU COULD NOT AS *MEN.*
CRUSH THE AMAZON, *DIANA.*
IN *BODY* AND IN *SPIRIT.*

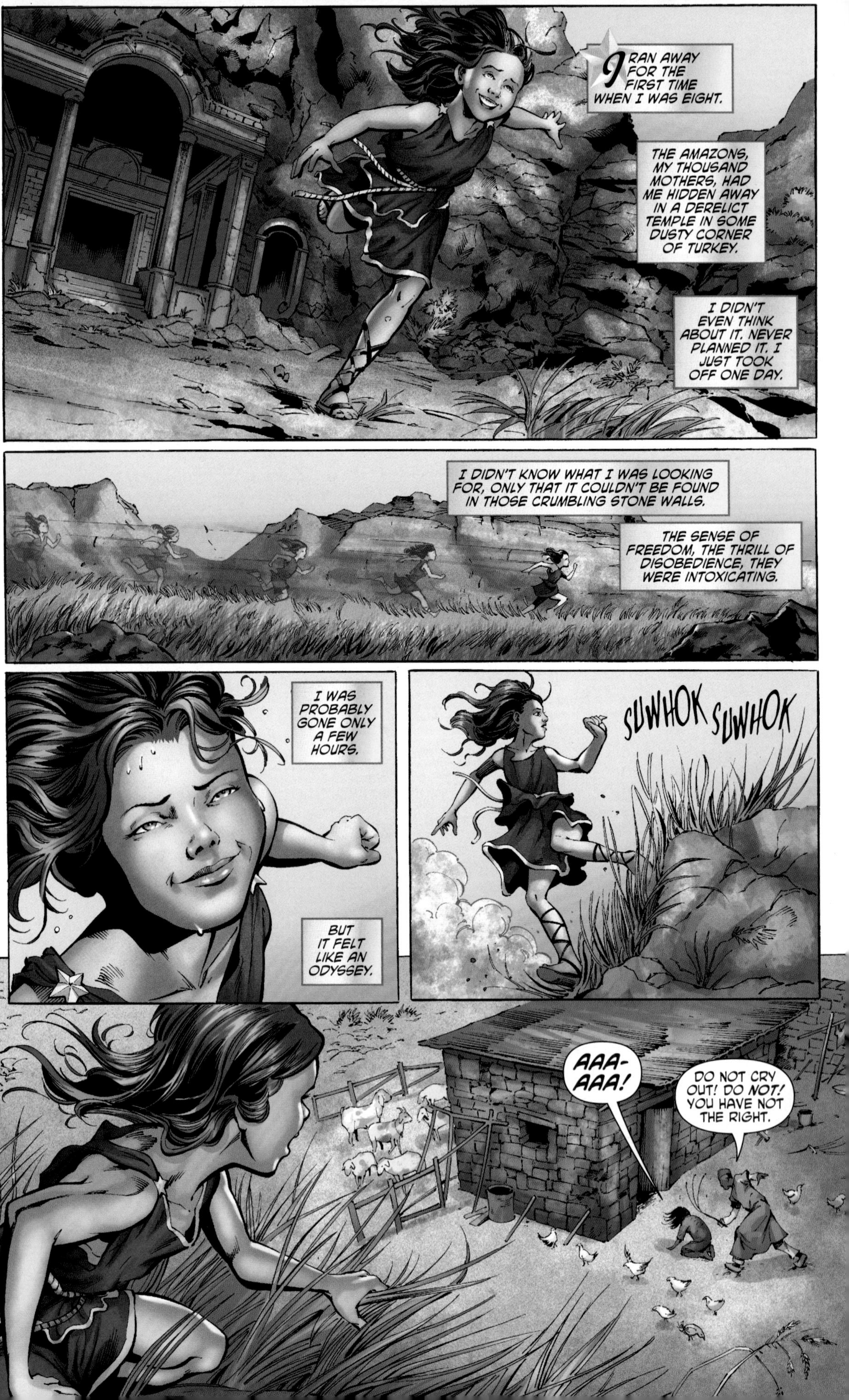
I RAN AWAY FOR THE FIRST TIME WHEN I WAS EIGHT.
THE AMAZONS, MY THOUSAND MOTHERS, HAD ME HIDDEN AWAY IN A DERELICT TEMPLE IN SOME DUSTY CORNER OF TURKEY.
I DIDN'T EVEN THINK ABOUT IT. NEVER PLANNED IT. I JUST TOOK OFF ONE DAY.
I DIDN'T KNOW WHAT I WAS LOOKING FOR, ONLY THAT IT COULDN'T BE FOUND IN THOSE CRUMBLING STONE WALLS.
THE SENSE OF FREEDOM, THE THRILL OF DISOBEDIENCE, THEY WERE INTOXICATING.
I WAS PROBABLY GONE ONLY A FEW HOURS.
BUT IT FELT LIKE AN ODYSSEY.
SUWHOK SUWHOK
AAA-AAA!
DO NOT CRY OUT! DO NOT! YOU HAVE NOT THE RIGHT.

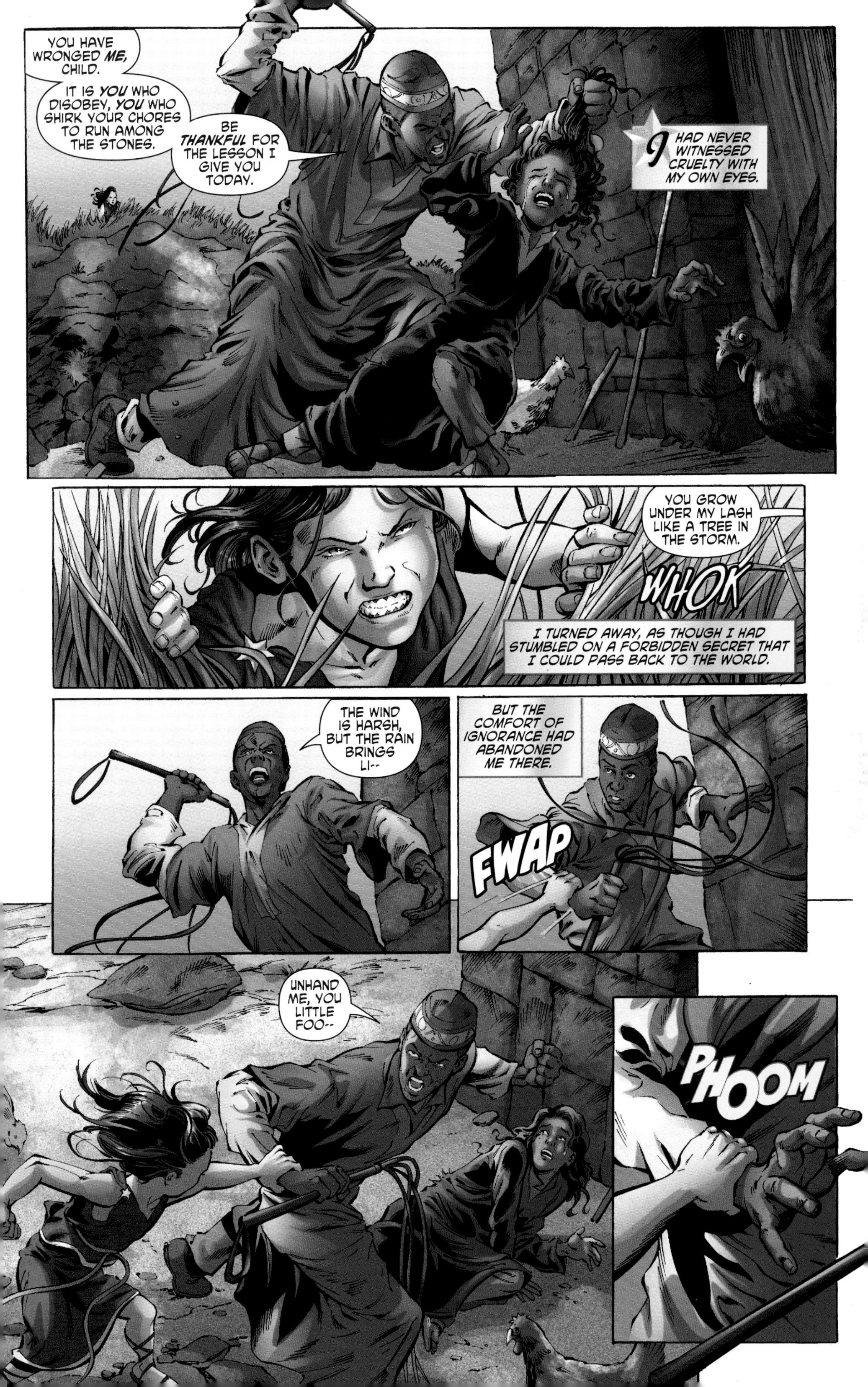

YOU HAVE WRONGED *ME*, CHILD.
IT IS *YOU* WHO DISOBEY, *YOU* WHO SHIRK YOUR CHORES TO RUN AMONG THE STONES.
BE *THANKFUL* FOR THE LESSON I GIVE YOU TODAY.
I HAD NEVER WITNESSED CRUELTY WITH MY OWN EYES.
YOU GROW UNDER MY LASH LIKE A TREE IN THE STORM.
WHOK
I TURNED AWAY, AS THOUGH I HAD STUMBLED ON A FORBIDDEN SECRET THAT I COULD PASS BACK TO THE WORLD.
THE WIND IS HARSH, BUT THE RAIN BRINGS LI--
BUT THE COMFORT OF IGNORANCE HAD ABANDONED ME THERE.
FWAP
UNHAND ME, YOU LITTLE FOO--
PHOOM

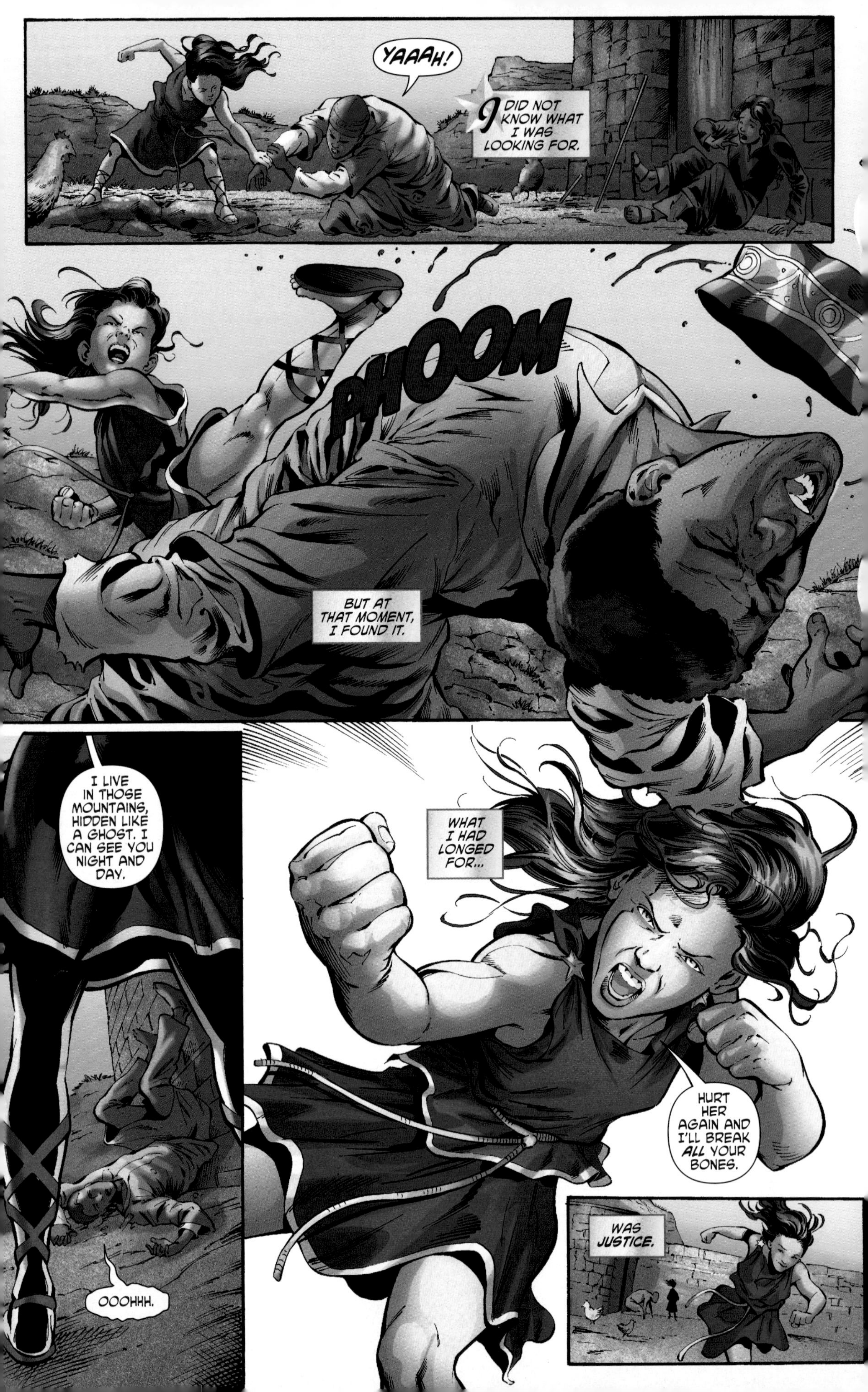
YAAAH!
I DID NOT KNOW WHAT I WAS LOOKING FOR.
PHOOM
BUT AT THAT MOMENT, I FOUND IT.
I LIVE IN THOSE MOUNTAINS, HIDDEN LIKE A GHOST. I CAN SEE YOU NIGHT AND DAY.
OOOHHH.
WHAT I HAD LONGED FOR...
HURT HER AGAIN AND I'LL BREAK ALL YOUR BONES.
WAS JUSTICE.

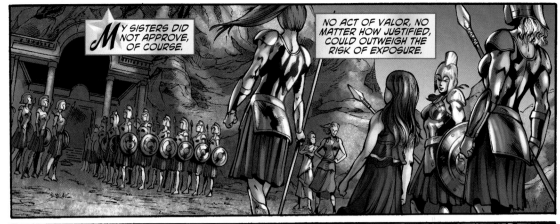

MY SISTERS DID NOT APPROVE, OF COURSE.

NO ACT OF VALOR, NO MATTER HOW JUSTIFIED, COULD OUTWEIGH THE RISK OF EXPOSURE.

BUT EVEN AT THAT AGE, I COULD DETECT THE ADMIRATION BEHIND THEIR ANGER.

AND EVERYWHERE OUR DIASPORA WOULD COME TO REST AROUND THE WORLD, I FOUND INJUSTICE.

AND WENT TO WAR AGAINST IT.

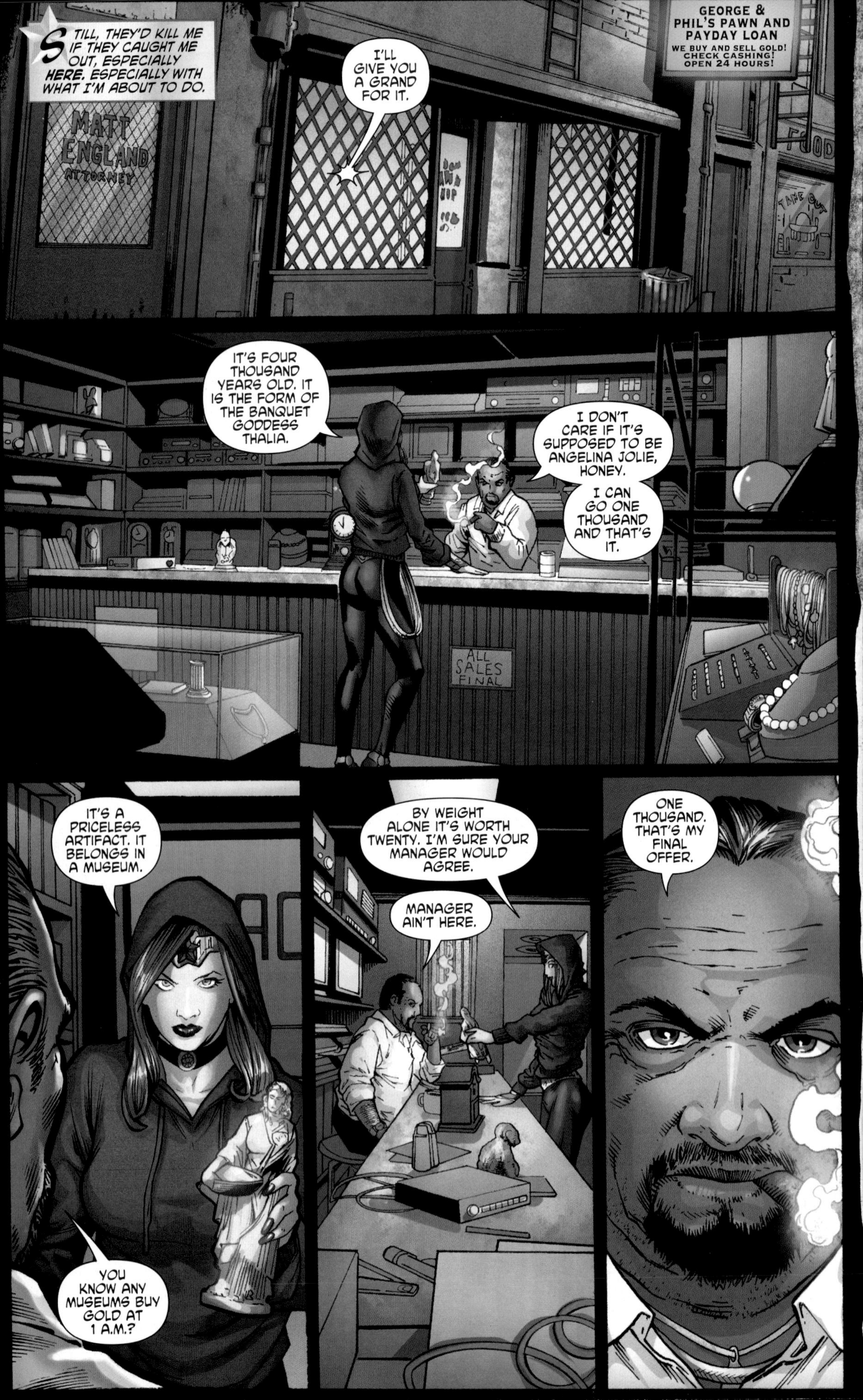
STILL, THEY'D KILL ME IF THEY CAUGHT ME OUT, ESPECIALLY HERE. ESPECIALLY WITH WHAT I'M ABOUT TO DO.
GEORGE & PHIL'S PAWN AND PAYDAY LOAN
WE BUY AND SELL GOLD! CHECK CASHING! OPEN 24 HOURS!
MATT ENGLAND ATTORNEY
I'LL GIVE YOU A GRAND FOR IT.
TAKE OUT
IT'S FOUR THOUSAND YEARS OLD. IT IS THE FORM OF THE BANQUET GODDESS THALIA.
I DON'T CARE IF IT'S SUPPOSED TO BE ANGELINA JOLIE, HONEY.
I CAN GO ONE THOUSAND AND THAT'S IT.
ALL SALES FINAL
IT'S A PRICELESS ARTIFACT. IT BELONGS IN A MUSEUM.
YOU KNOW ANY MUSEUMS BUY GOLD AT 1 A.M.?
BY WEIGHT ALONE IT'S WORTH TWENTY. I'M SURE YOUR MANAGER WOULD AGREE.
MANAGER AIN'T HERE.
ONE THOUSAND. THAT'S MY FINAL OFFER.

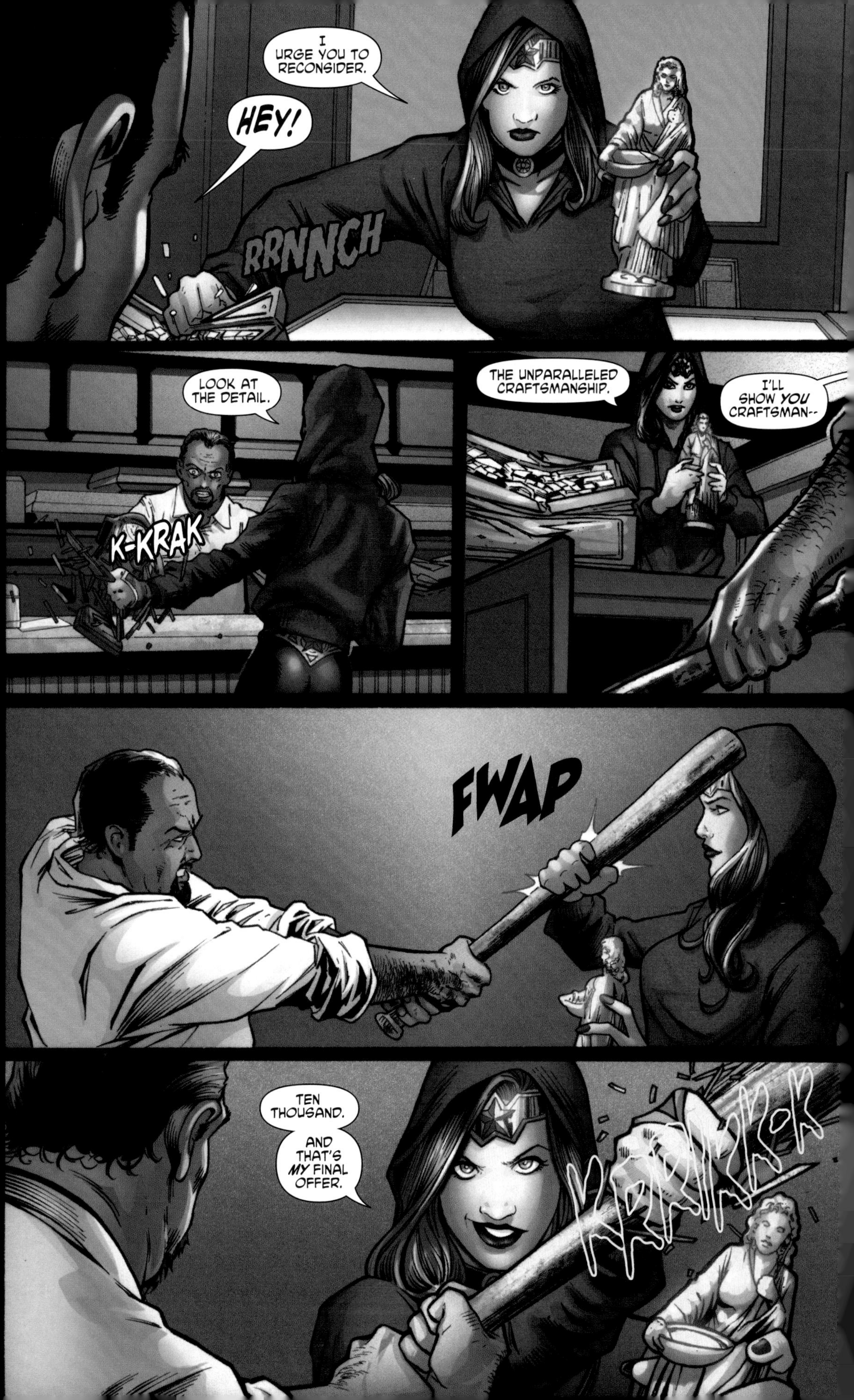
I URGE YOU TO RECONSIDER.
HEY!
RRNNCH
LOOK AT THE DETAIL.
K-KRAK
THE UNPARALLELED CRAFTSMANSHIP.
I'LL SHOW *YOU* CRAFTSMAN--
FWAP
TEN THOUSAND.
AND THAT'S *MY* FINAL OFFER.

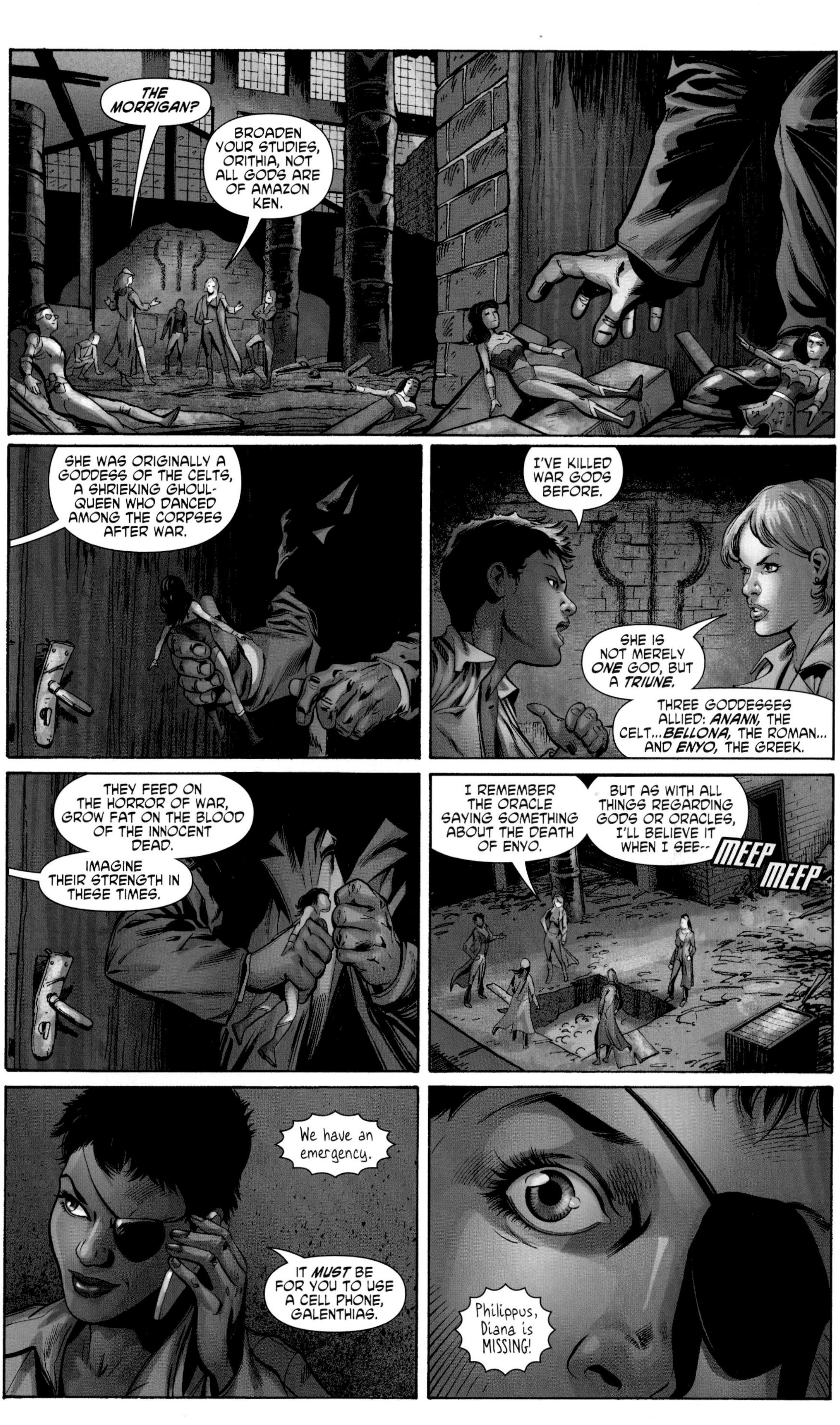
THE MORRIGAN?
BROADEN YOUR STUDIES, ORITHIA, NOT ALL GODS ARE OF AMAZON KEN.
SHE WAS ORIGINALLY A GODDESS OF THE CELTS, A SHRIEKING GHOUL-QUEEN WHO DANCED AMONG THE CORPSES AFTER WAR.
I'VE KILLED WAR GODS BEFORE.
SHE IS NOT MERELY ONE GOD, BUT A TRIUNE.
THREE GODDESSES ALLIED: ANANN, THE CELT...BELLONA, THE ROMAN... AND ENYO, THE GREEK.
THEY FEED ON THE HORROR OF WAR, GROW FAT ON THE BLOOD OF THE INNOCENT DEAD.
IMAGINE THEIR STRENGTH IN THESE TIMES.
I REMEMBER THE ORACLE SAYING SOMETHING ABOUT THE DEATH OF ENYO.
BUT AS WITH ALL THINGS REGARDING GODS OR ORACLES, I'LL BELIEVE IT WHEN I SEE--
MEEP MEEP
We have an emergency.
IT MUST BE FOR YOU TO USE A CELL PHONE, GALENTHIAS.
Philippus, Diana is MISSING!

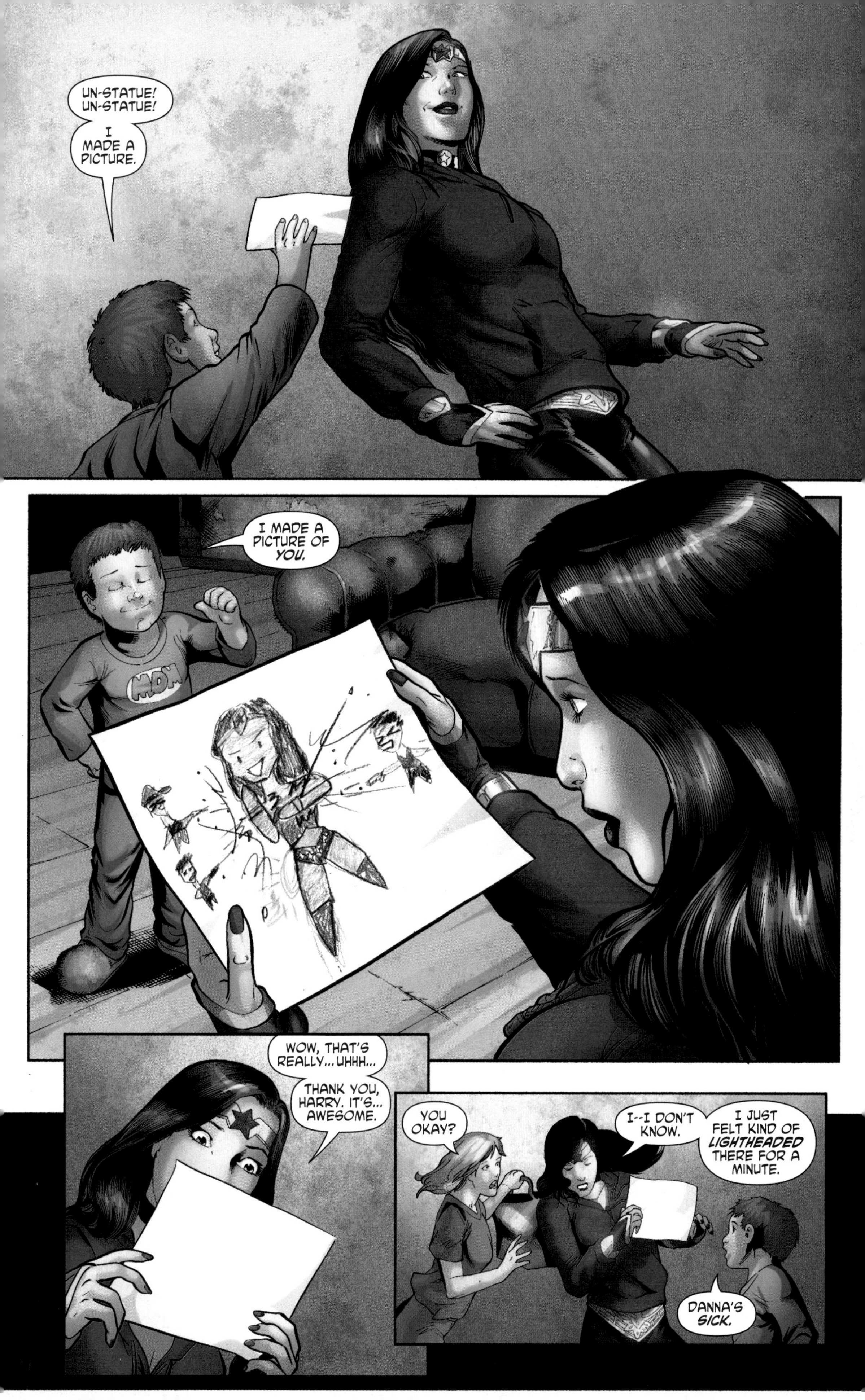
UN-STATUE! UN-STATUE!
I MADE A PICTURE.
I MADE A PICTURE OF *YOU.*
WOW, THAT'S REALLY... UHHH...
THANK YOU, HARRY. IT'S... AWESOME.
YOU OKAY?
I--I DON'T KNOW.
I JUST FELT KIND OF *LIGHTHEADED* THERE FOR A MINUTE.
DANNA'S *SICK.*

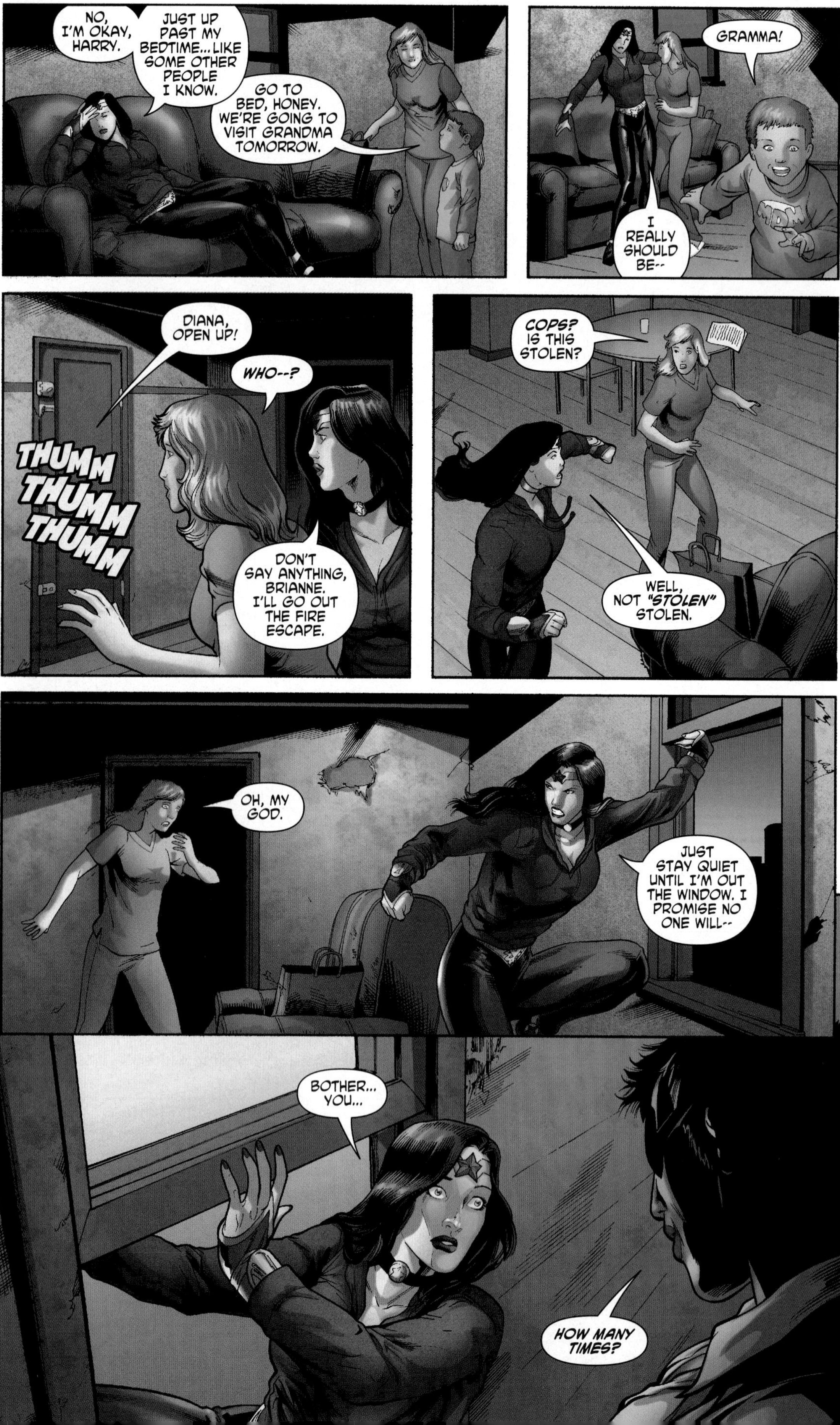
NO, I'M OKAY, HARRY.
JUST UP PAST MY BEDTIME... LIKE SOME OTHER PEOPLE I KNOW.
GO TO BED, HONEY. WE'RE GOING TO VISIT GRANDMA TOMORROW.
GRAMMA!
I REALLY SHOULD BE--
DIANA, OPEN UP!
WHO--?
THUMM THUMM THUMM
DON'T SAY ANYTHING, BRIANNE. I'LL GO OUT THE FIRE ESCAPE.
COPS? IS THIS STOLEN?
WELL, NOT "STOLEN" STOLEN.
OH, MY GOD.
JUST STAY QUIET UNTIL I'M OUT THE WINDOW. I PROMISE NO ONE WILL--
BOTHER... YOU...
HOW MANY TIMES?

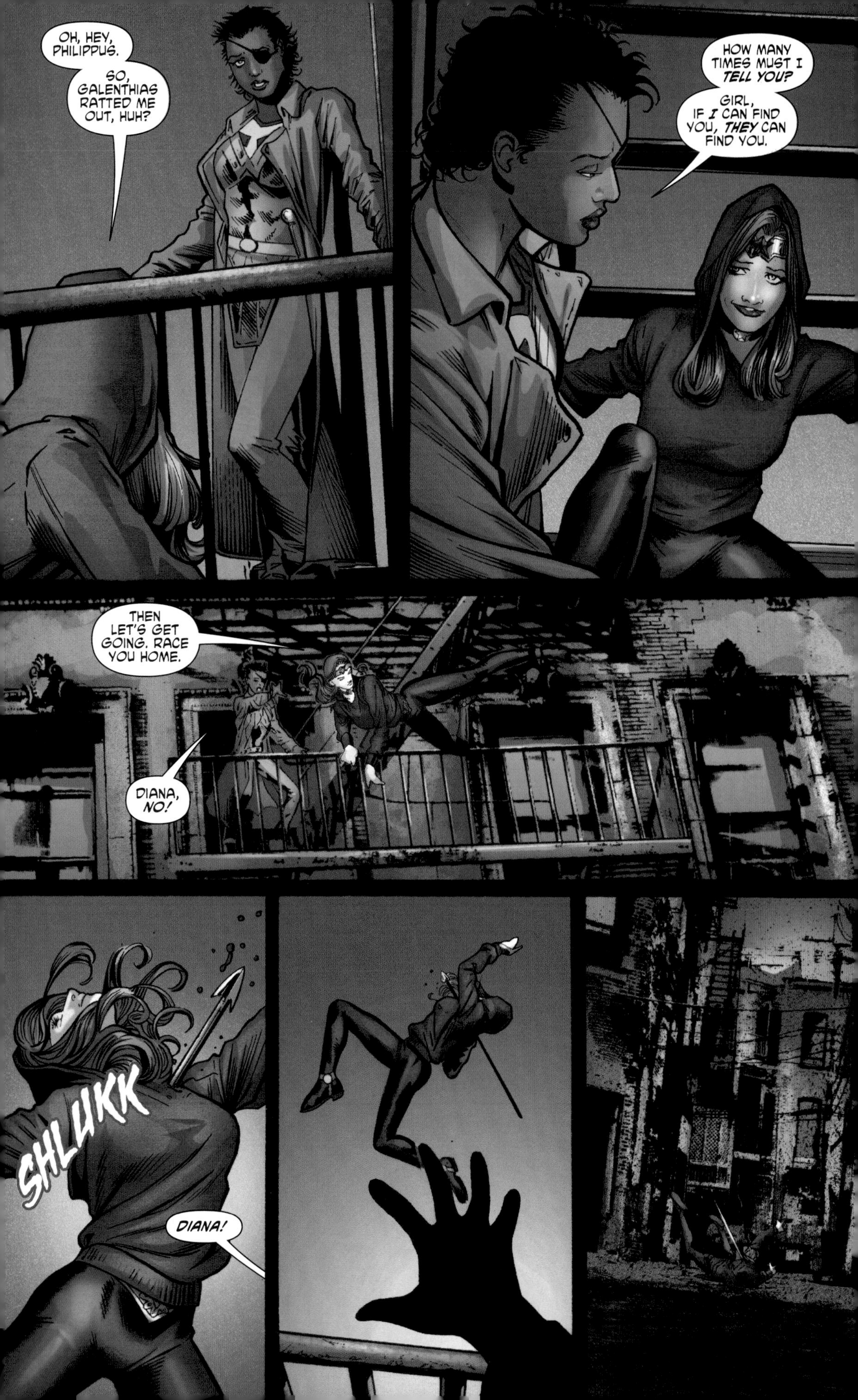

OH, HEY, PHILIPPUS.
SO, GALENTHIAS RATTED ME OUT, HUH?
HOW MANY TIMES MUST I *TELL YOU?*
GIRL, IF *I* CAN FIND YOU, *THEY* CAN FIND YOU.
THEN LET'S GET GOING. RACE YOU HOME.
DIANA, *NO!*
SHLUKK
DIANA!

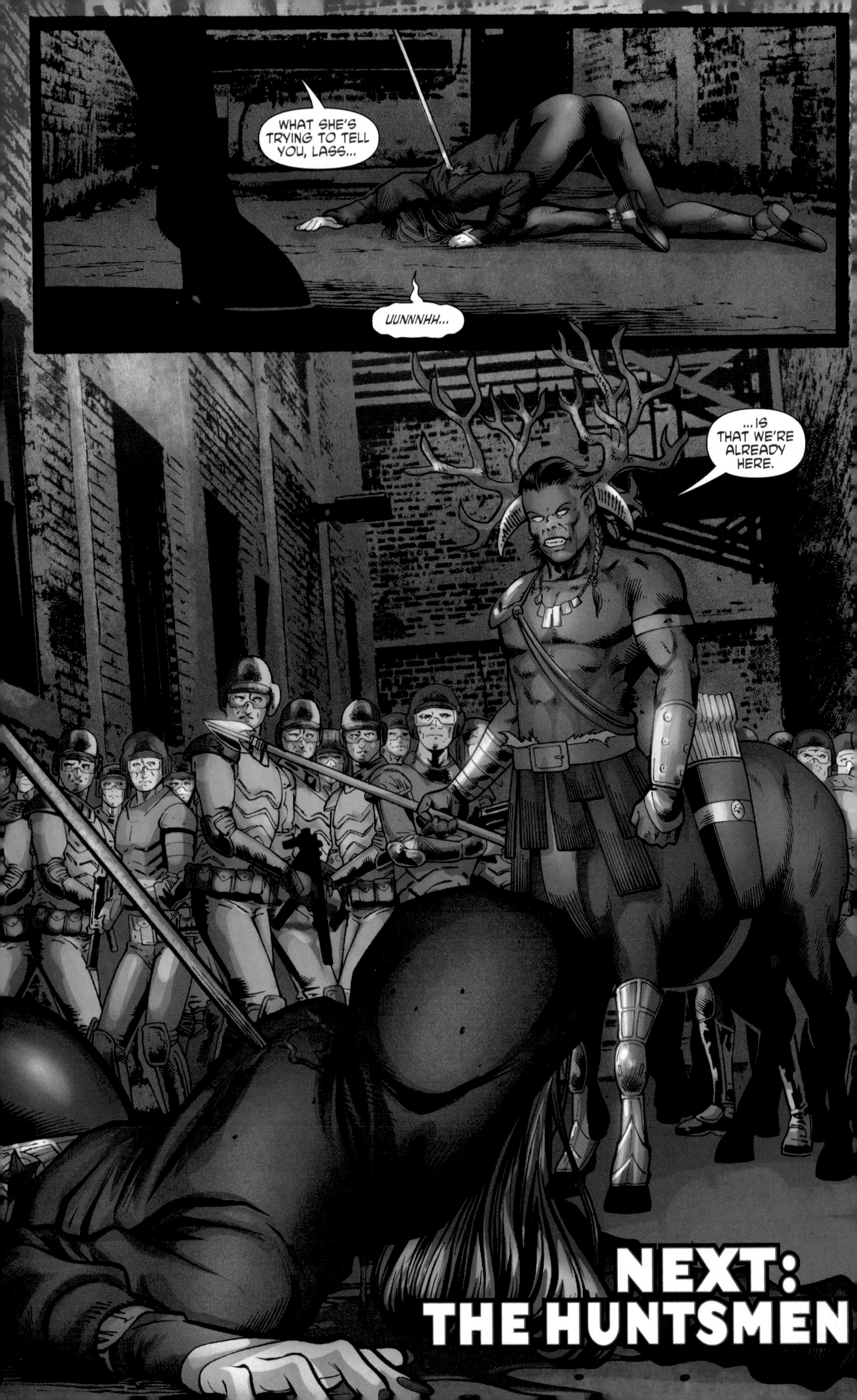
WHAT SHE'S TRYING TO TELL YOU, LASS...
UUNNNHH...
...IS THAT WE'RE ALREADY HERE.
NEXT: THE HUNTSMEN

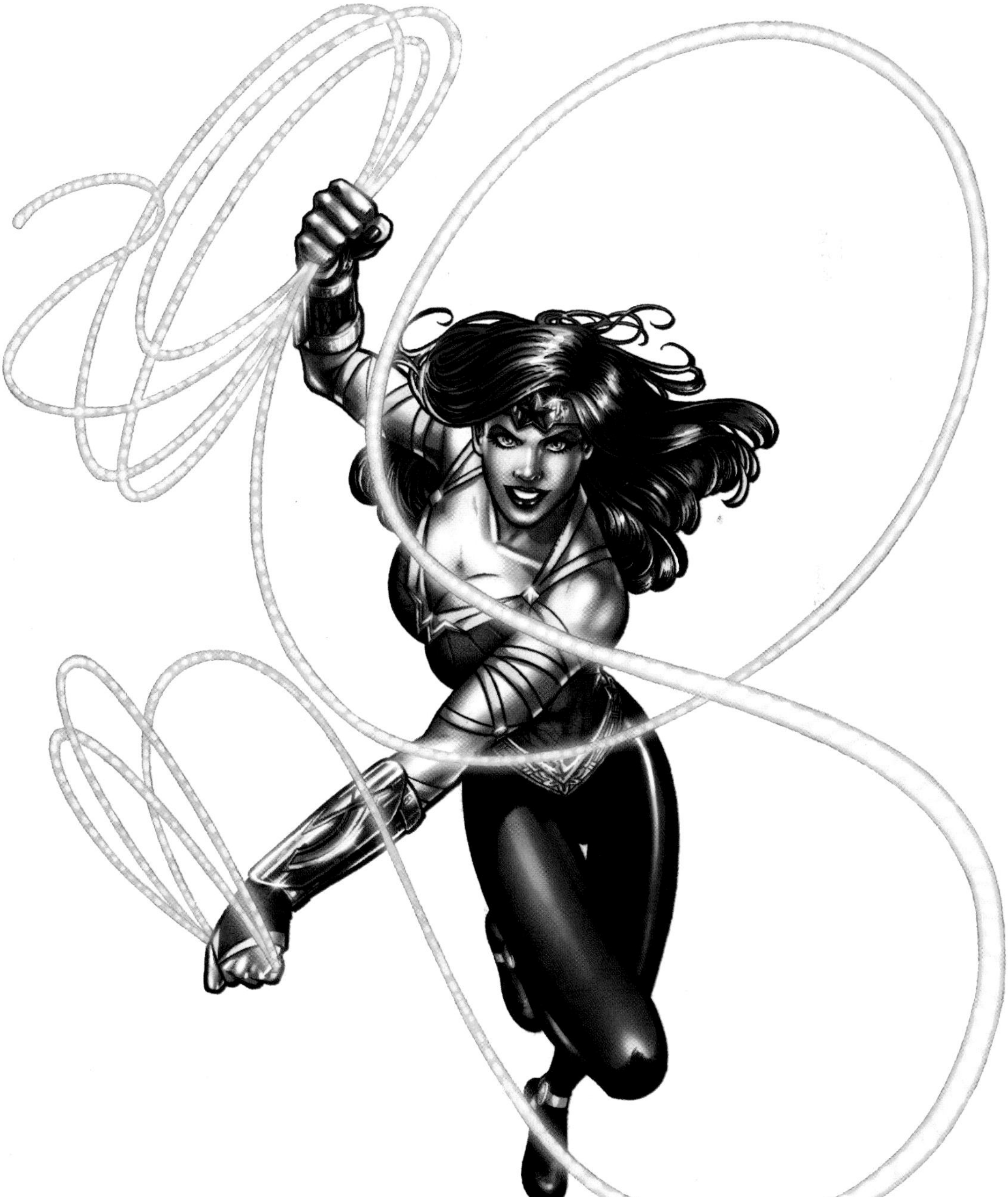

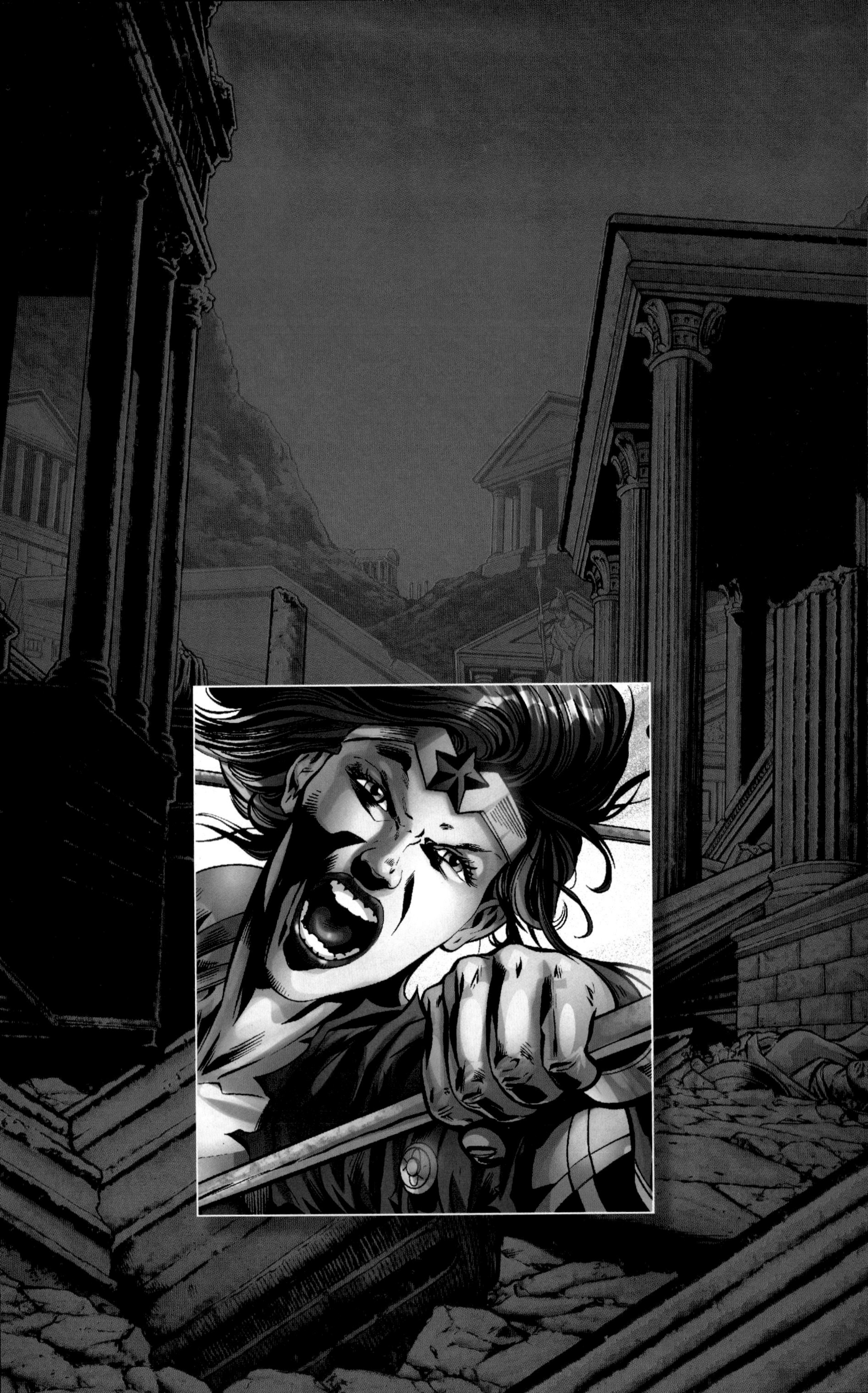

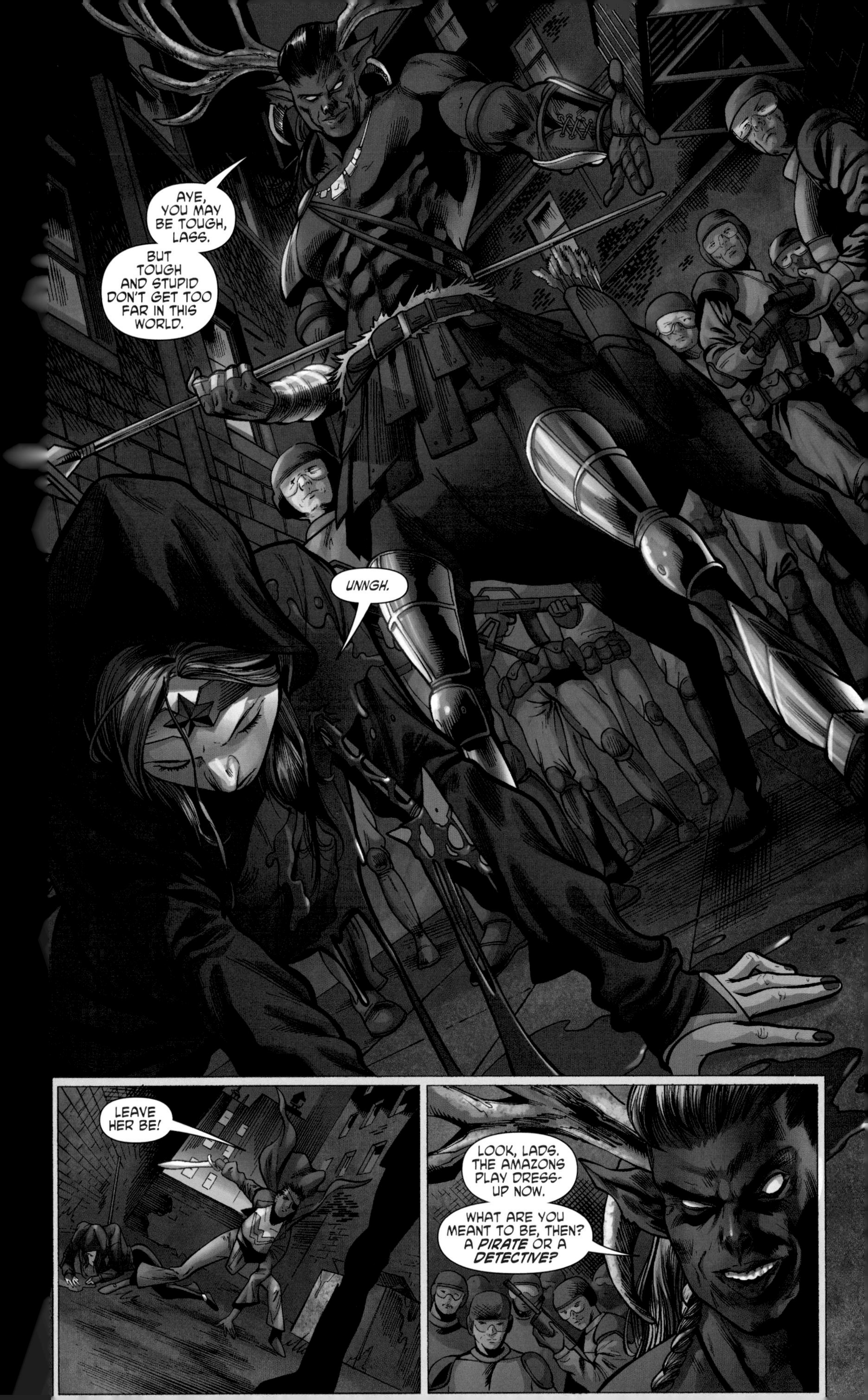
AYE, YOU MAY BE TOUGH, LASS.
BUT TOUGH AND STUPID DON'T GET TOO FAR IN THIS WORLD.
UNNGH.
LEAVE HER BE!
LOOK, LADS. THE AMAZONS PLAY DRESS-UP NOW.
WHAT ARE YOU MEANT TO BE, THEN? A *PIRATE* OR A *DETECTIVE?*

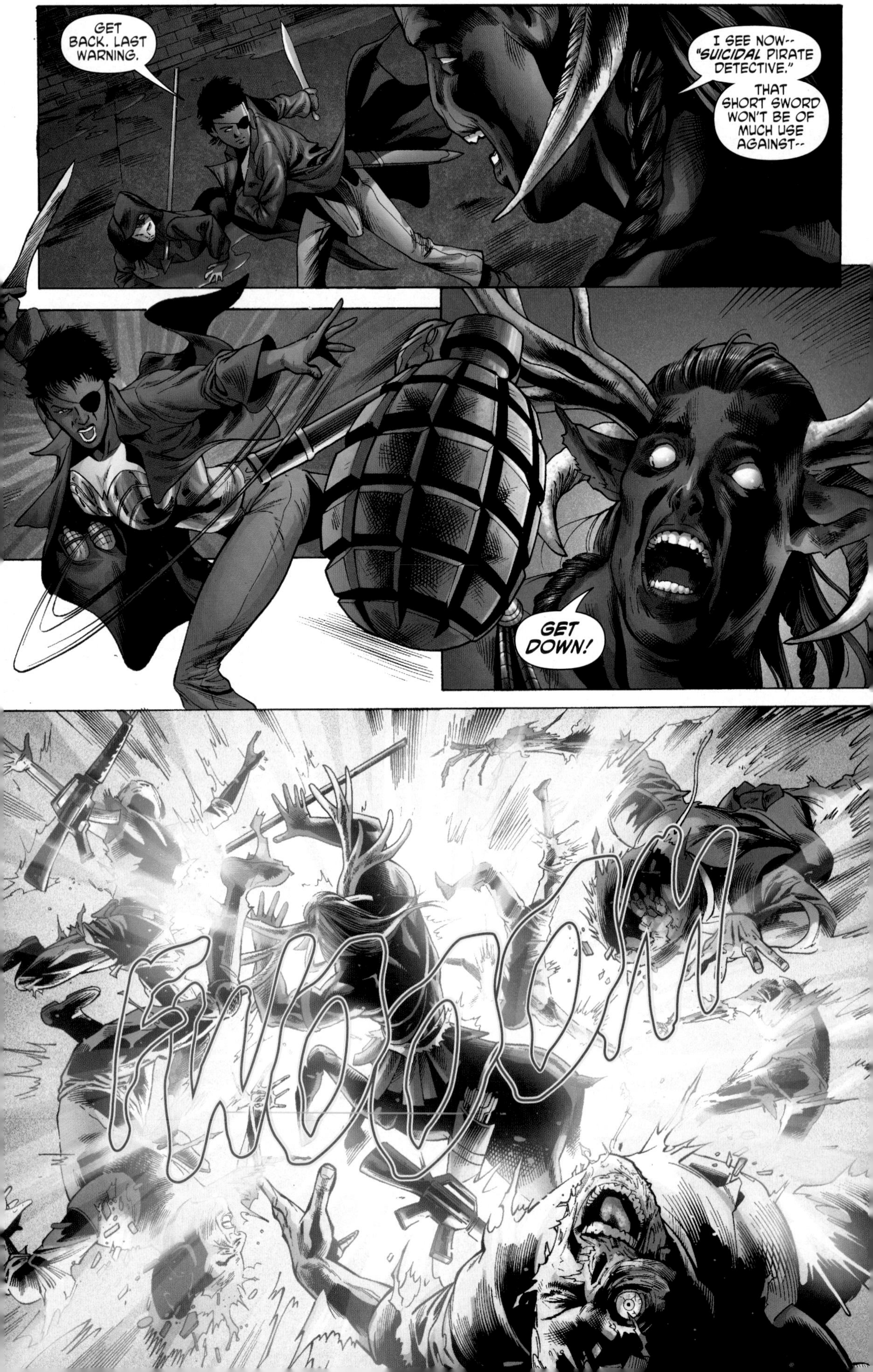
GET BACK. LAST WARNING.
I SEE NOW-- "SUICIDAL PIRATE DETECTIVE."
THAT SHORT SWORD WON'T BE OF MUCH USE AGAINST--
GET DOWN!
FWOOOOM

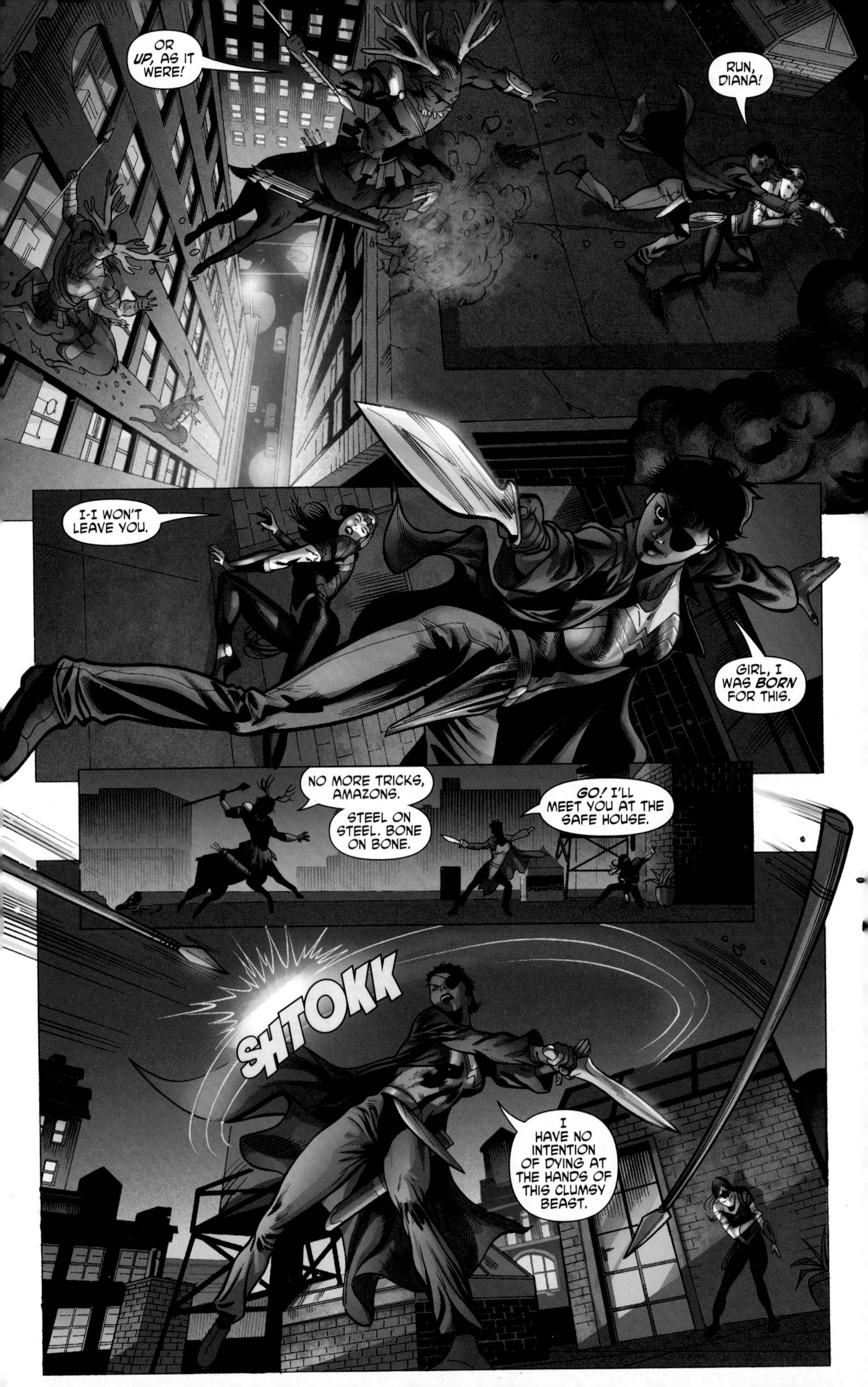
OR *UP*, AS IT WERE!
RUN, DIANA!
I-I WON'T LEAVE YOU.
GIRL, I WAS *BORN* FOR THIS.
NO MORE TRICKS, AMAZONS.
STEEL ON STEEL. BONE ON BONE.
GO! I'LL MEET YOU AT THE SAFE HOUSE.
SHTOKK
I HAVE NO INTENTION OF DYING AT THE HANDS OF THIS CLUMSY BEAST.

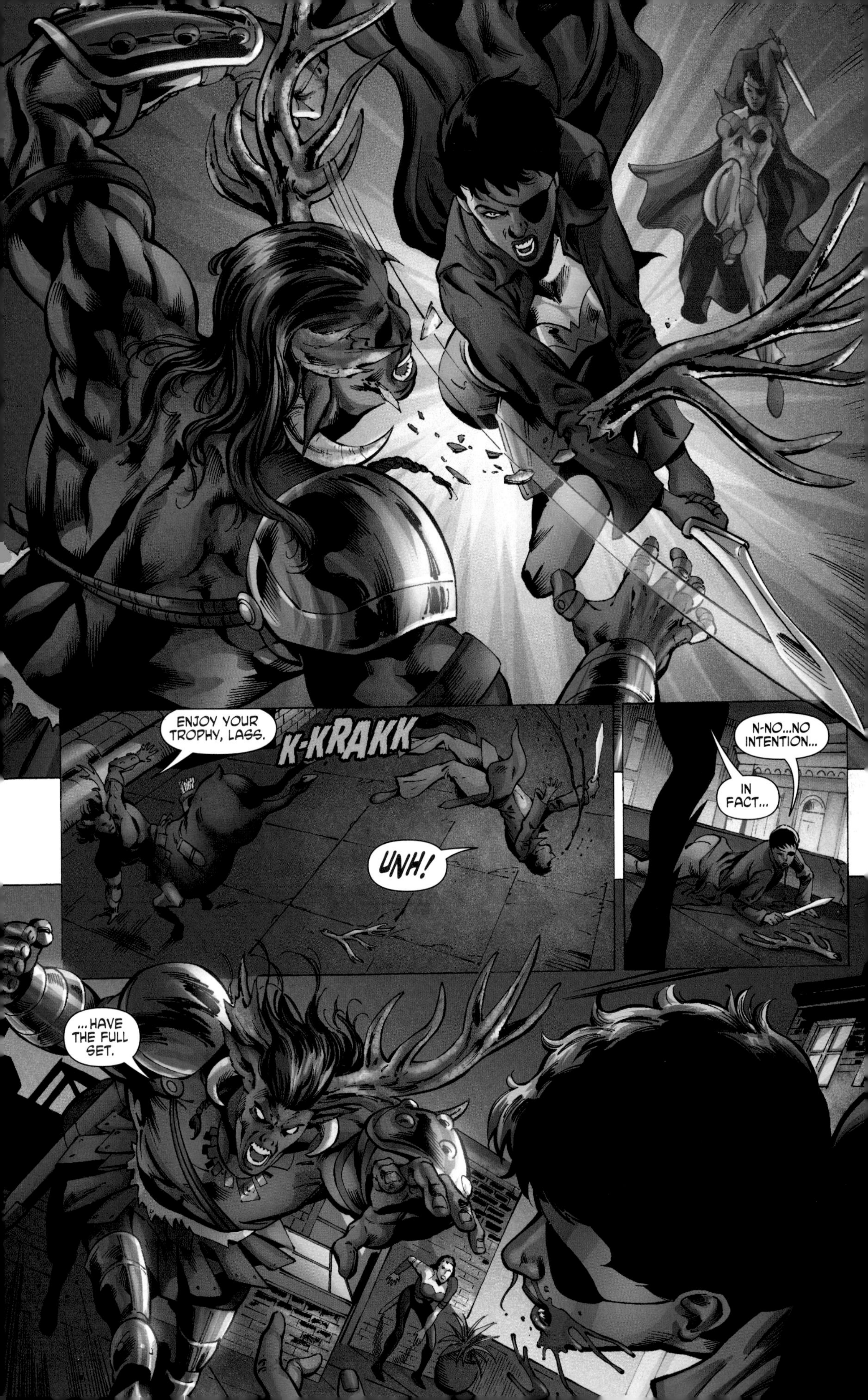
ENJOY YOUR TROPHY, LASS.
K-KRAKK
UNH!
N-NO...NO INTENTION...
IN FACT...
...HAVE THE FULL SET.

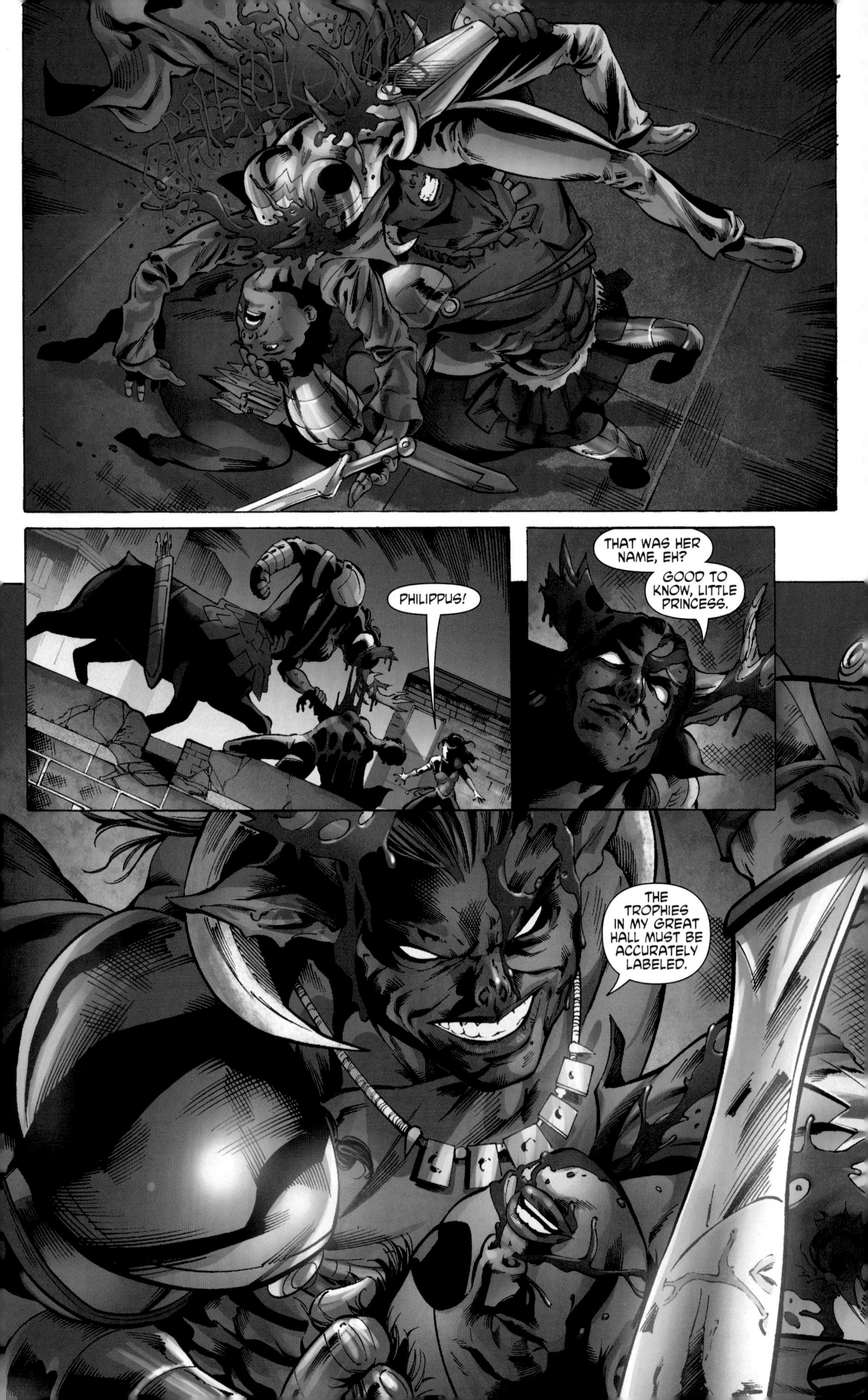
PHILIPPUS!
THAT WAS HER NAME, EH?
GOOD TO KNOW, LITTLE PRINCESS.
THE TROPHIES IN MY GREAT HALL MUST BE ACCURATELY LABELED.

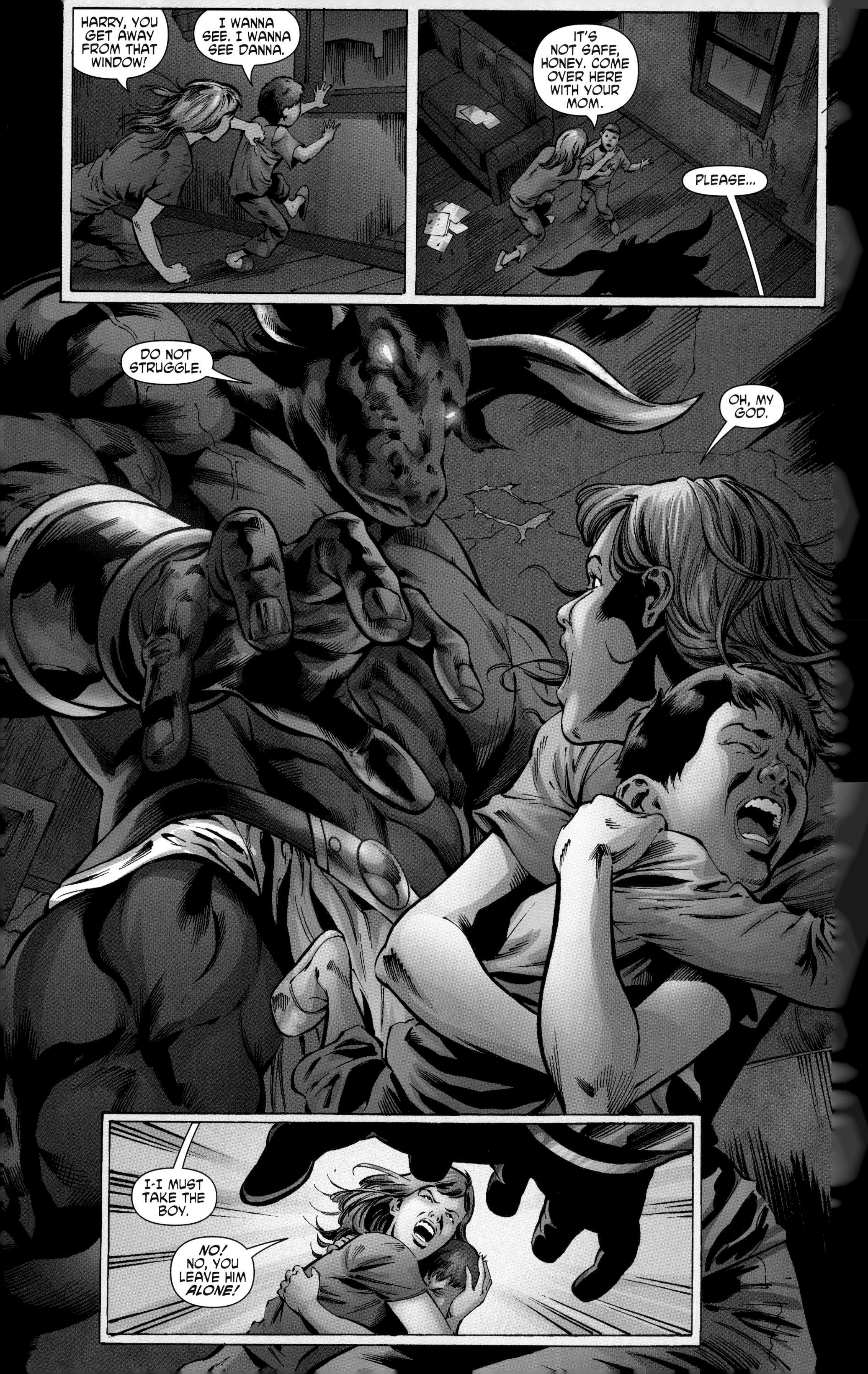
HARRY, YOU GET AWAY FROM THAT WINDOW!
I WANNA SEE. I WANNA SEE DANNA.
IT'S NOT SAFE, HONEY. COME OVER HERE WITH YOUR MOM.
PLEASE...
DO NOT STRUGGLE.
OH, MY GOD.
I-I MUST TAKE THE BOY.
NO! NO, YOU LEAVE HIM ALONE!

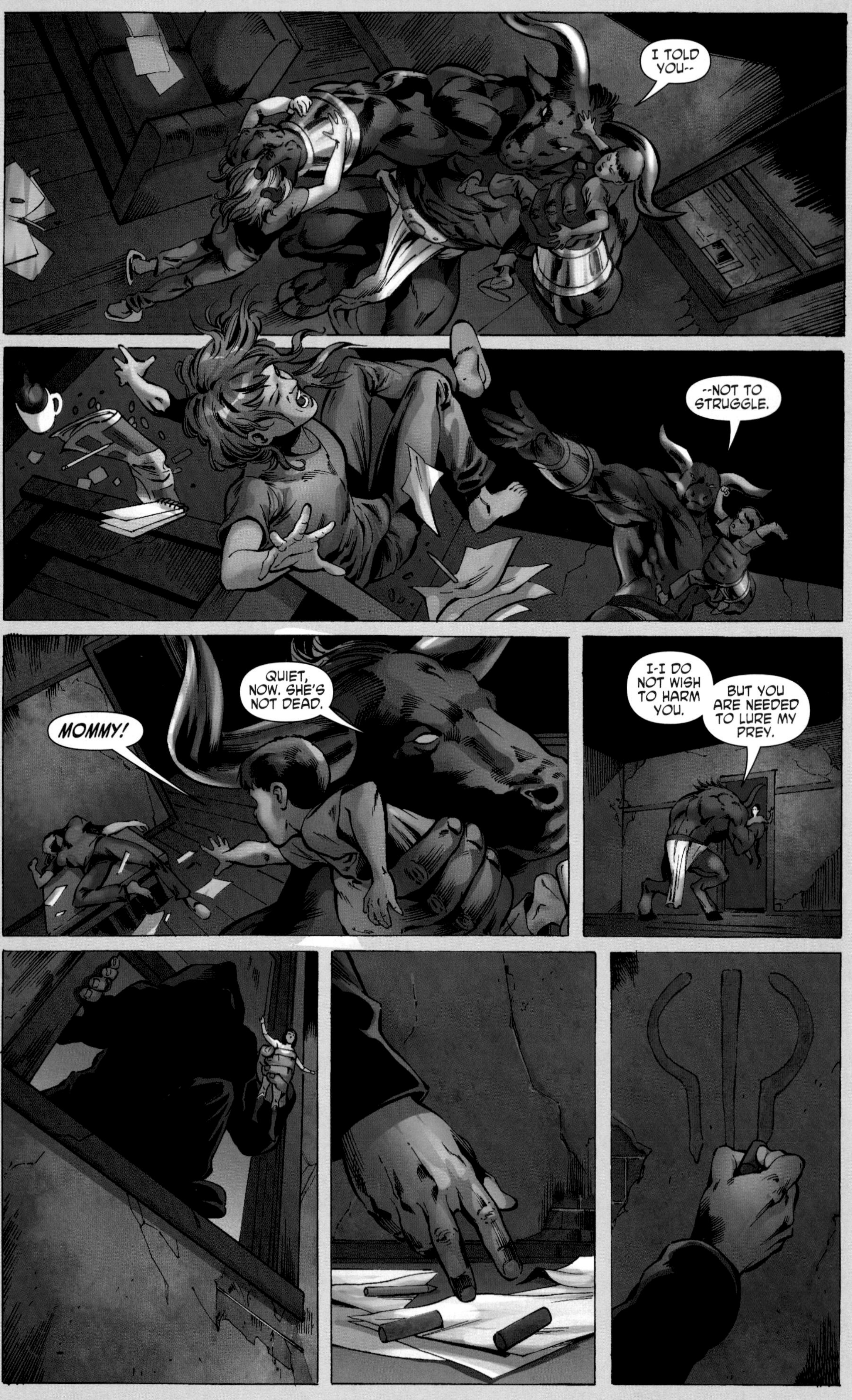
I TOLD YOU--
--NOT TO STRUGGLE.
MOMMY!
QUIET, NOW. SHE'S NOT DEAD.
I-I DO NOT WISH TO HARM YOU.
BUT YOU ARE NEEDED TO LURE MY PREY.

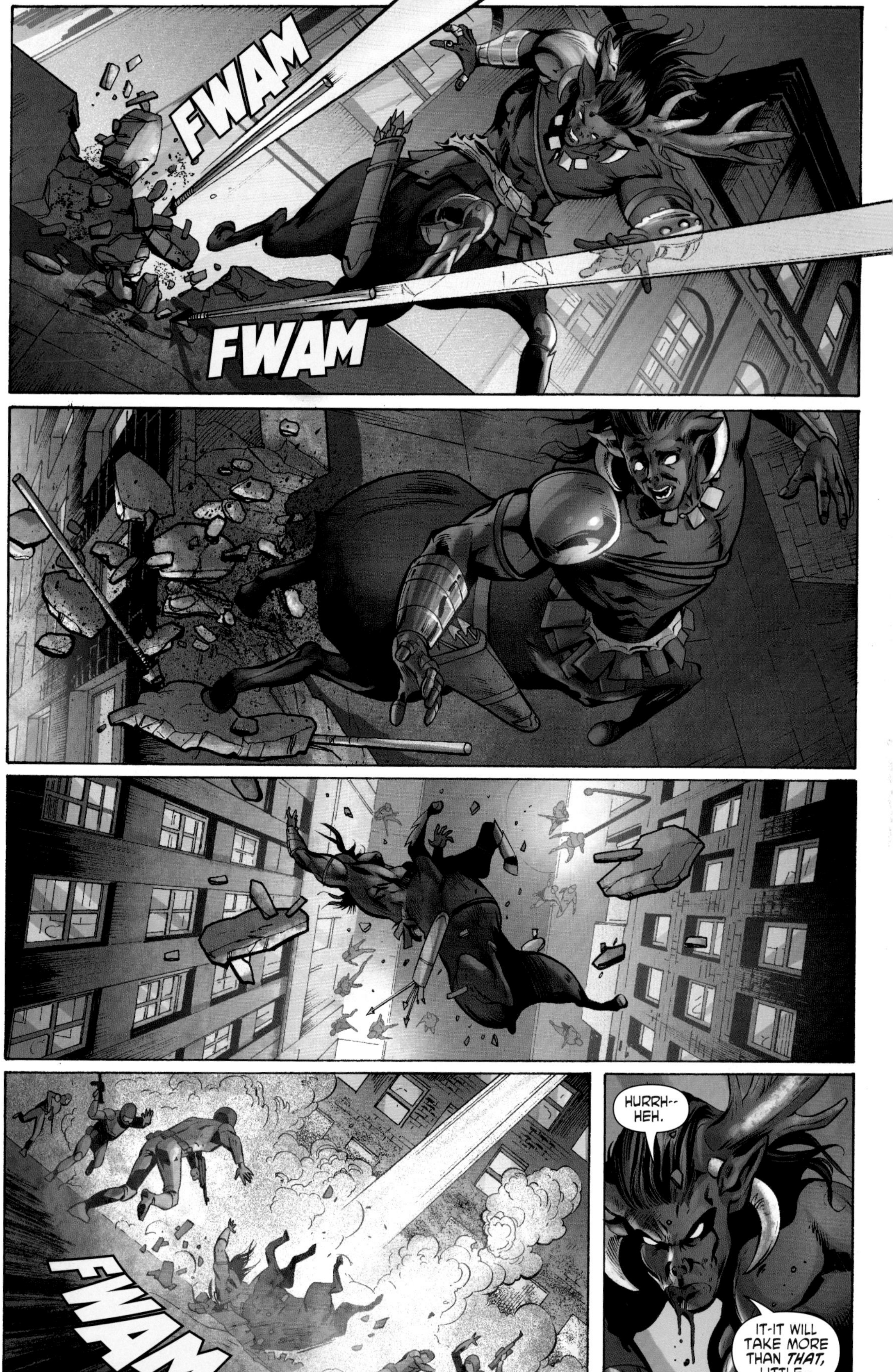
FWAM
FWAM
FWAM
HURRH--
HEH.
IT-IT WILL TAKE MORE THAN *THAT,* LITTLE--

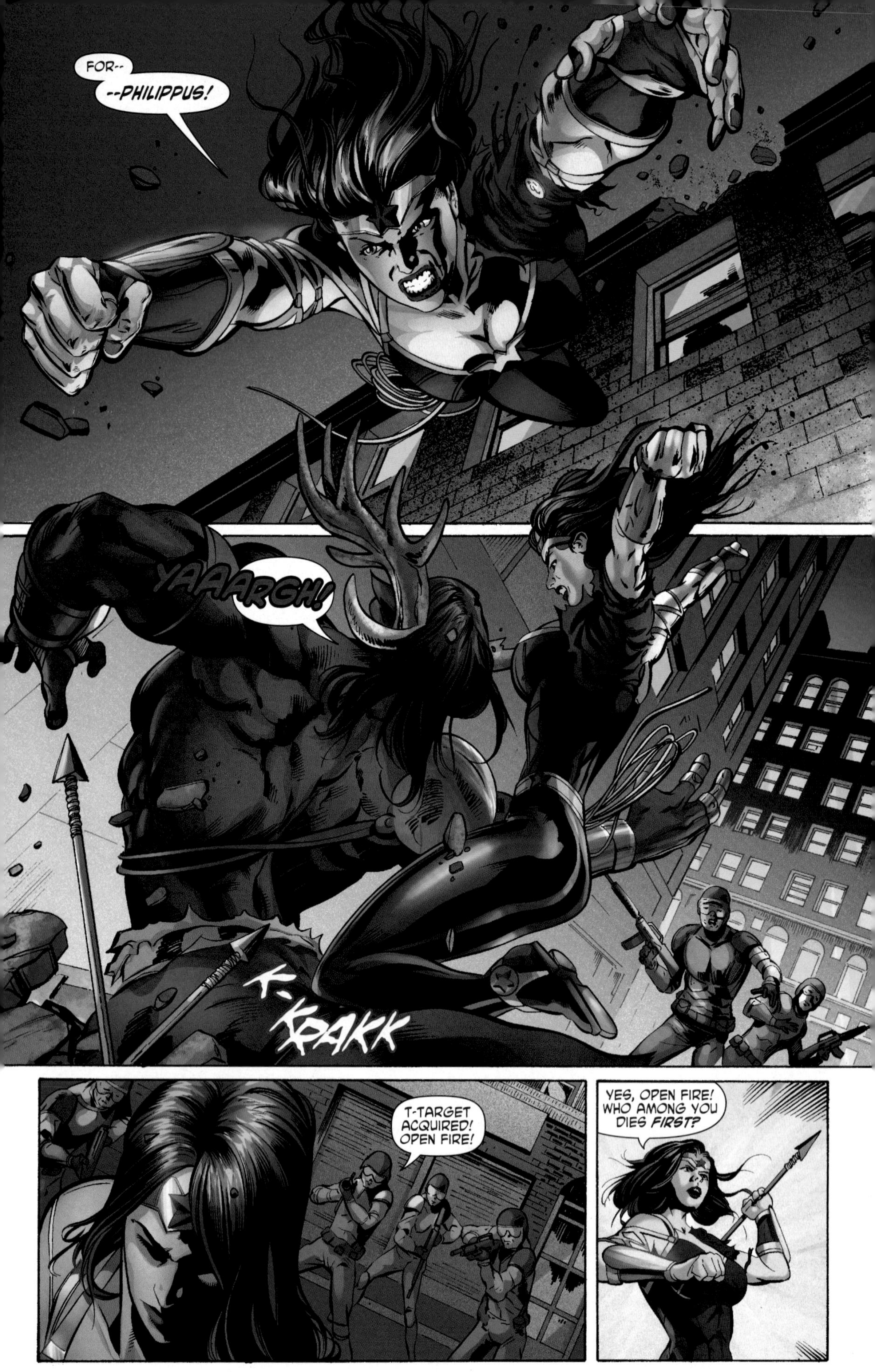
FOR--
--PHILIPPUS!
YAAAARGH!
K-KRAKK
T-TARGET ACQUIRED! OPEN FIRE!
YES, OPEN FIRE! WHO AMONG YOU DIES FIRST?

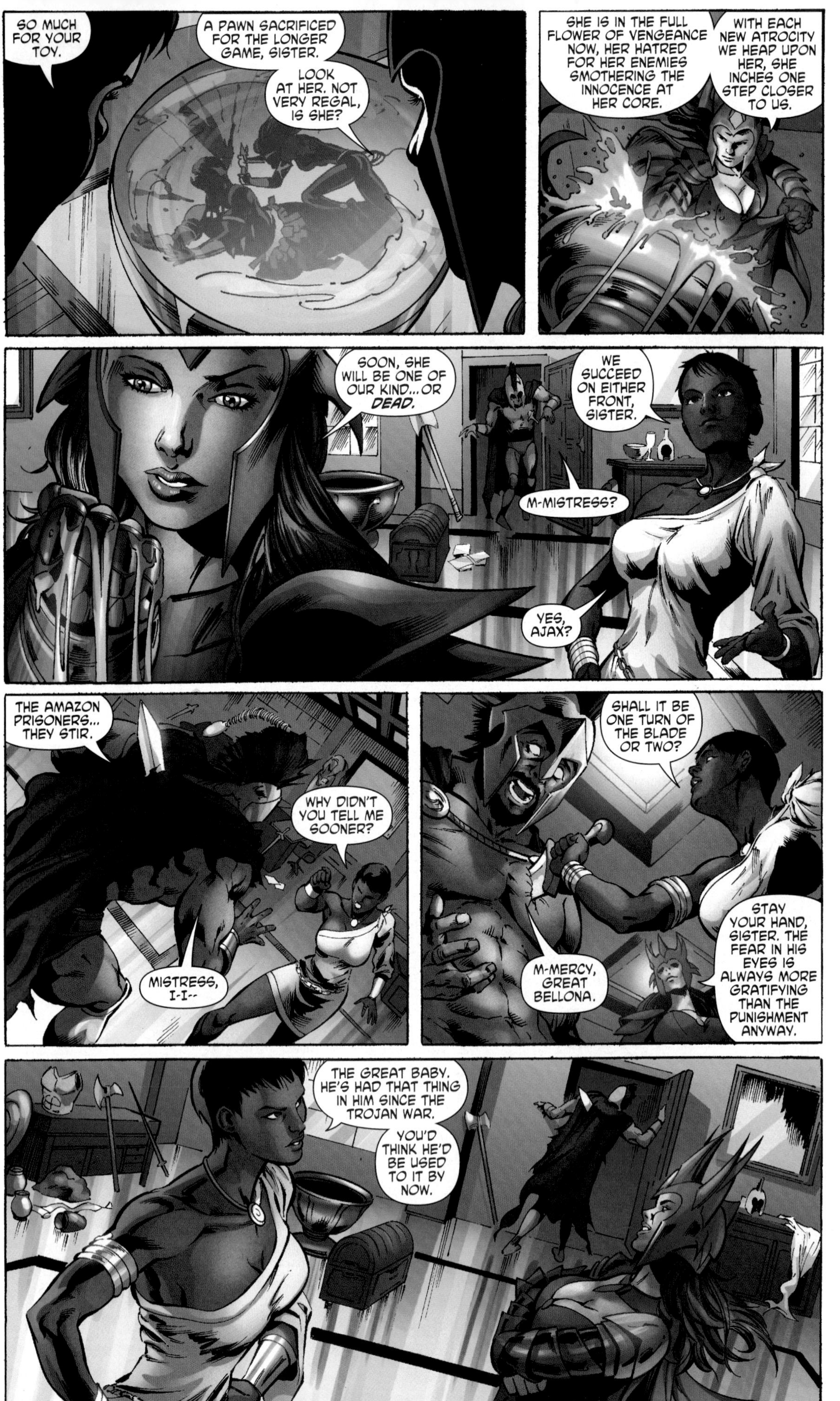
SO MUCH FOR YOUR TOY.
A PAWN SACRIFICED FOR THE LONGER GAME, SISTER.
LOOK AT HER. NOT VERY REGAL, IS SHE?
SHE IS IN THE FULL FLOWER OF VENGEANCE NOW, HER HATRED FOR HER ENEMIES SMOTHERING THE INNOCENCE AT HER CORE.
WITH EACH NEW ATROCITY WE HEAP UPON HER, SHE INCHES ONE STEP CLOSER TO US.
SOON, SHE WILL BE ONE OF OUR KIND...OR DEAD.
WE SUCCEED ON EITHER FRONT, SISTER.
M-MISTRESS?
YES, AJAX?
THE AMAZON PRISONERS... THEY STIR.
WHY DIDN'T YOU TELL ME SOONER?
MISTRESS, I-I--
SHALL IT BE ONE TURN OF THE BLADE OR TWO?
M-MERCY, GREAT BELLONA.
STAY YOUR HAND, SISTER. THE FEAR IN HIS EYES IS ALWAYS MORE GRATIFYING THAN THE PUNISHMENT ANYWAY.
THE GREAT BABY. HE'S HAD THAT THING IN HIM SINCE THE TROJAN WAR.
YOU'D THINK HE'D BE USED TO IT BY NOW.

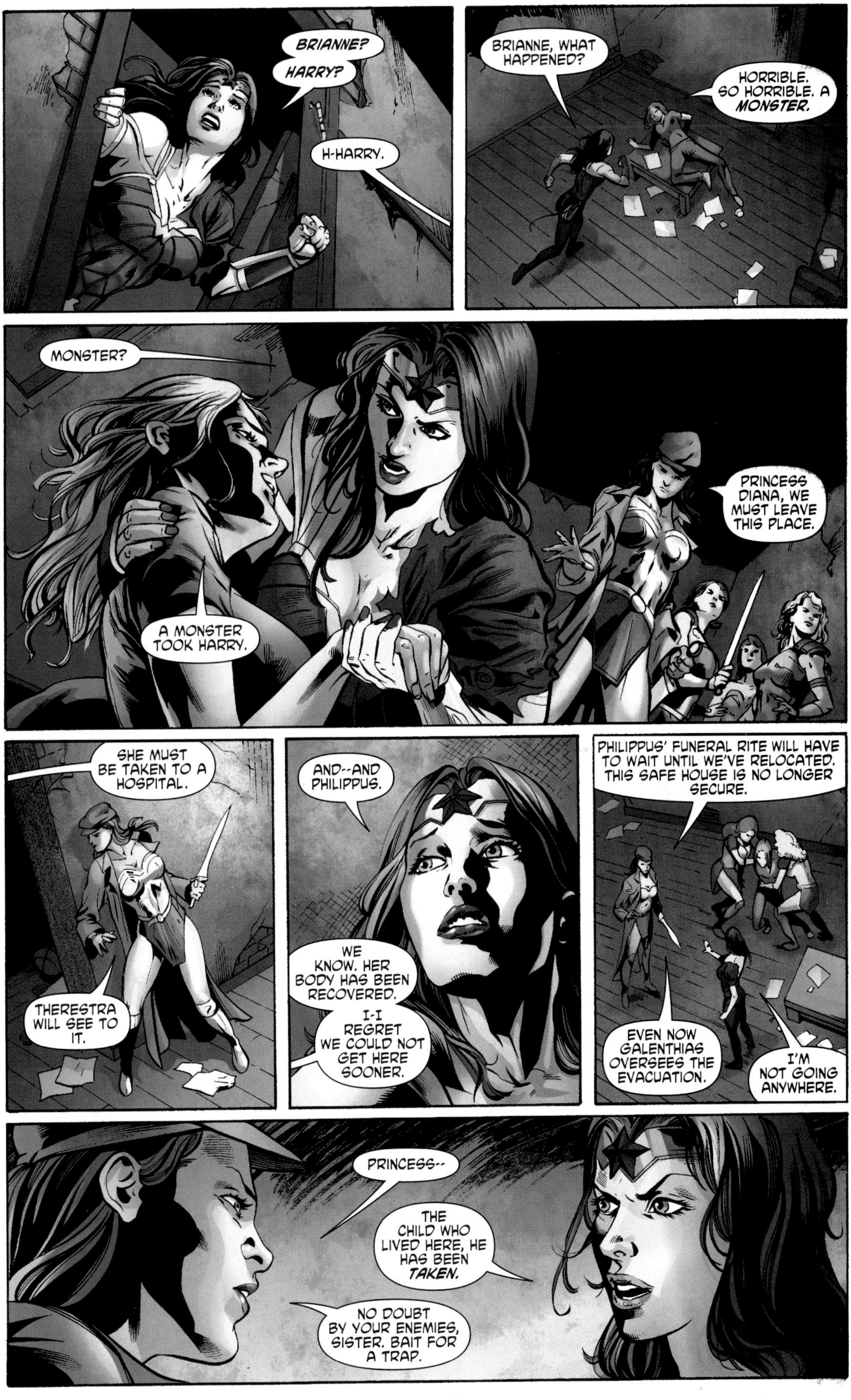
BRIANNE?
HARRY?
H-HARRY.
BRIANNE, WHAT HAPPENED?
HORRIBLE. SO HORRIBLE. A *MONSTER.*
MONSTER?
A MONSTER TOOK HARRY.
PRINCESS DIANA, WE MUST LEAVE THIS PLACE.
SHE MUST BE TAKEN TO A HOSPITAL.
THERESTRA WILL SEE TO IT.
AND--AND PHILIPPUS.
WE KNOW. HER BODY HAS BEEN RECOVERED.
I-I REGRET WE COULD NOT GET HERE SOONER.
PHILIPPUS' FUNERAL RITE WILL HAVE TO WAIT UNTIL WE'VE RELOCATED. THIS SAFE HOUSE IS NO LONGER SECURE.
EVEN NOW GALENTHIAS OVERSEES THE EVACUATION.
I'M NOT GOING ANYWHERE.
PRINCESS--
THE CHILD WHO LIVED HERE, HE HAS BEEN *TAKEN.*
NO DOUBT BY YOUR ENEMIES, SISTER. BAIT FOR A TRAP.

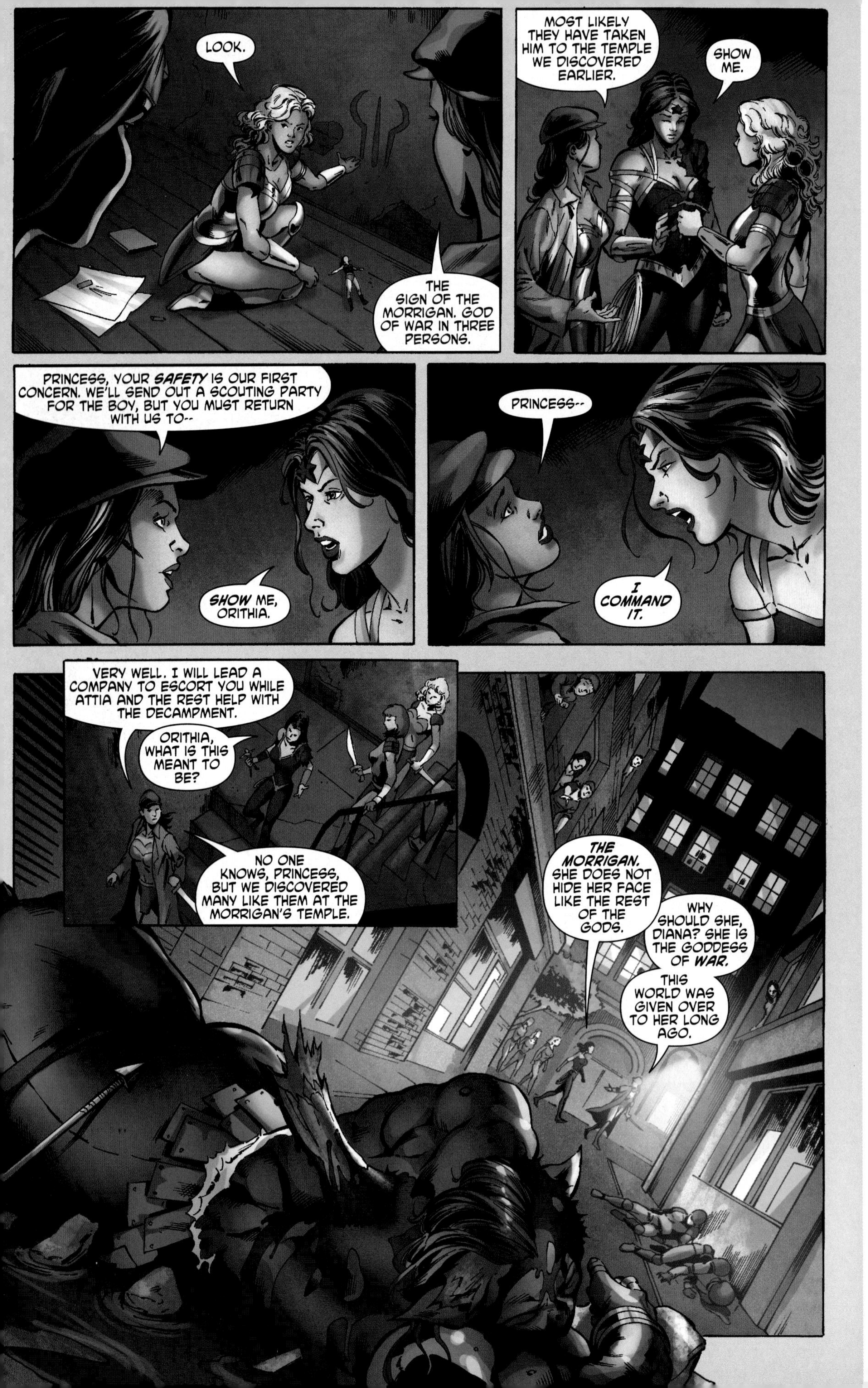
LOOK.
THE SIGN OF THE MORRIGAN. GOD OF WAR IN THREE PERSONS.
MOST LIKELY THEY HAVE TAKEN HIM TO THE TEMPLE WE DISCOVERED EARLIER.
SHOW ME.
PRINCESS, YOUR SAFETY IS OUR FIRST CONCERN. WE'LL SEND OUT A SCOUTING PARTY FOR THE BOY, BUT YOU MUST RETURN WITH US TO--
SHOW ME, ORITHIA.
PRINCESS--
I COMMAND IT.
VERY WELL. I WILL LEAD A COMPANY TO ESCORT YOU WHILE ATTIA AND THE REST HELP WITH THE DECAMPMENT.
ORITHIA, WHAT IS THIS MEANT TO BE?
NO ONE KNOWS, PRINCESS, BUT WE DISCOVERED MANY LIKE THEM AT THE MORRIGAN'S TEMPLE.
THE MORRIGAN. SHE DOES NOT HIDE HER FACE LIKE THE REST OF THE GODS.
WHY SHOULD SHE, DIANA? SHE IS THE GODDESS OF WAR.
THIS WORLD WAS GIVEN OVER TO HER LONG AGO.

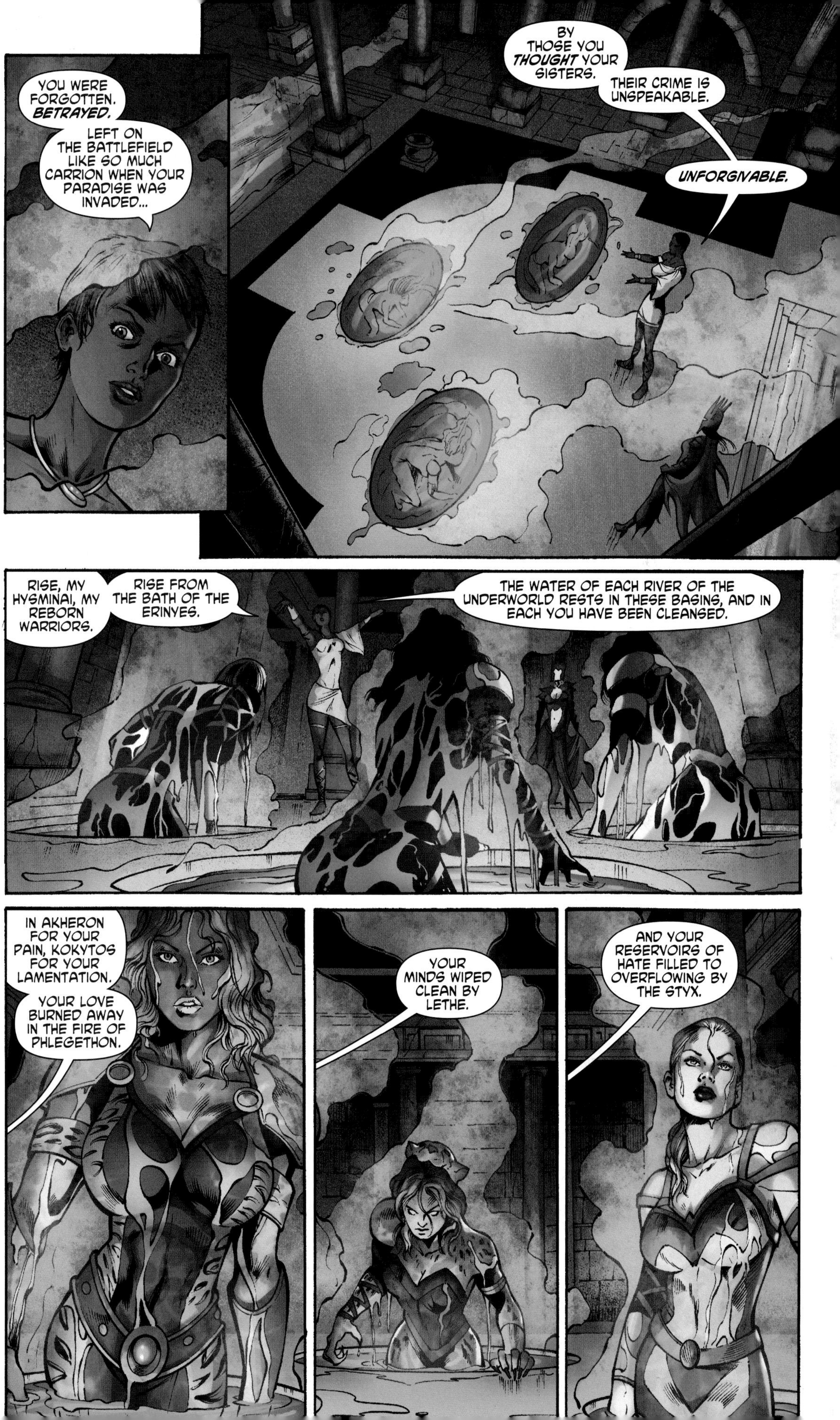
YOU WERE FORGOTTEN. BETRAYED.
LEFT ON THE BATTLEFIELD LIKE SO MUCH CARRION WHEN YOUR PARADISE WAS INVADED...
BY THOSE YOU THOUGHT YOUR SISTERS.
THEIR CRIME IS UNSPEAKABLE.
UNFORGIVABLE.
RISE, MY HYSMINAI, MY REBORN WARRIORS.
RISE FROM THE BATH OF THE ERINYES.
THE WATER OF EACH RIVER OF THE UNDERWORLD RESTS IN THESE BASINS, AND IN EACH YOU HAVE BEEN CLEANSED.
IN AKHERON FOR YOUR PAIN, KOKYTOS FOR YOUR LAMENTATION.
YOUR LOVE BURNED AWAY IN THE FIRE OF PHLEGETHON.
YOUR MINDS WIPED CLEAN BY LETHE.
AND YOUR RESERVOIRS OF HATE FILLED TO OVERFLOWING BY THE STYX.

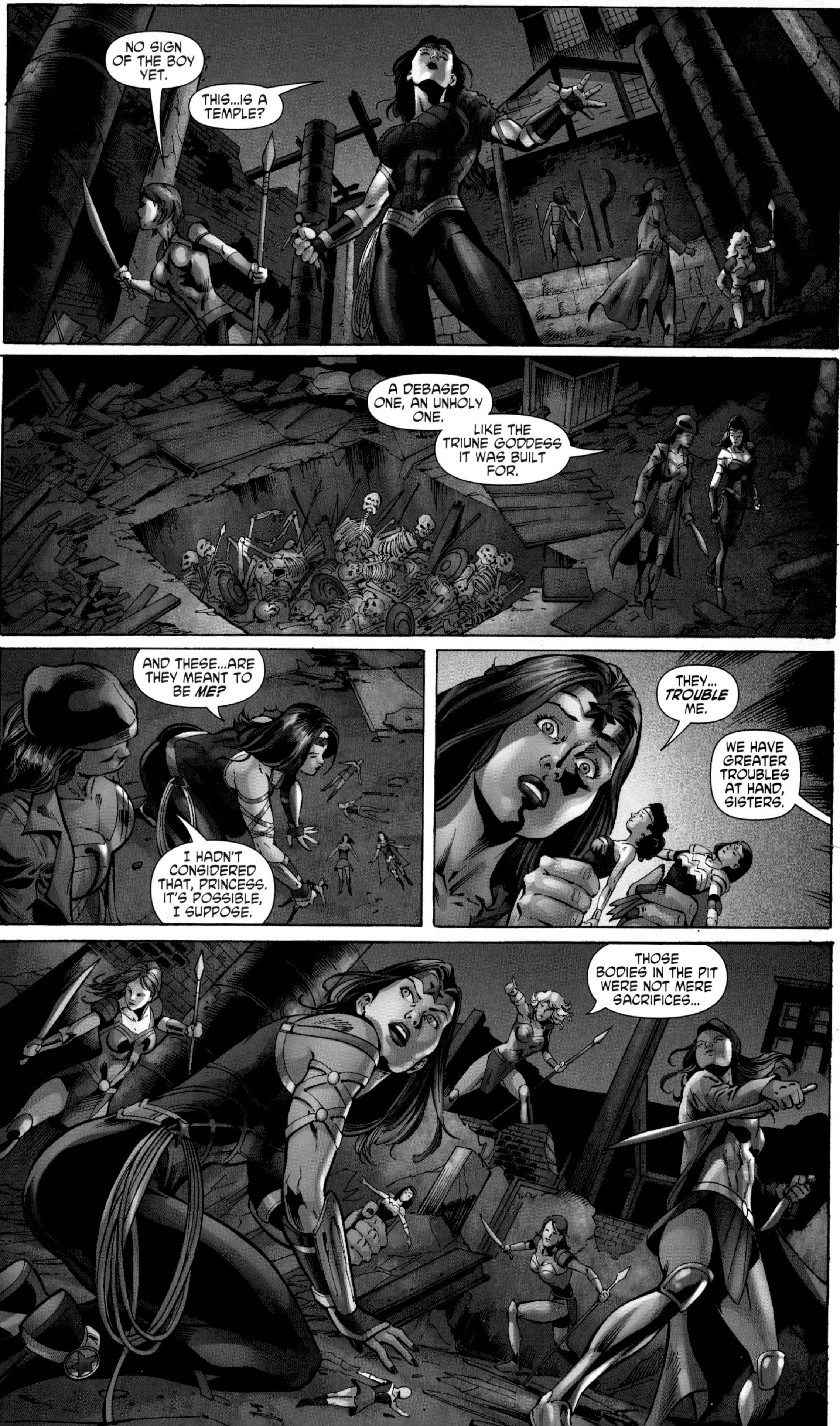
NO SIGN OF THE BOY YET.
THIS...IS A TEMPLE?
A DEBASED ONE, AN UNHOLY ONE.
LIKE THE TRIUNE GODDESS IT WAS BUILT FOR.
AND THESE...ARE THEY MEANT TO BE *ME?*
I HADN'T CONSIDERED THAT, PRINCESS. IT'S POSSIBLE, I SUPPOSE.
THEY... *TROUBLE* ME.
WE HAVE GREATER TROUBLES AT HAND, SISTERS.
THOSE BODIES IN THE PIT WERE NOT MERE SACRIFICES...

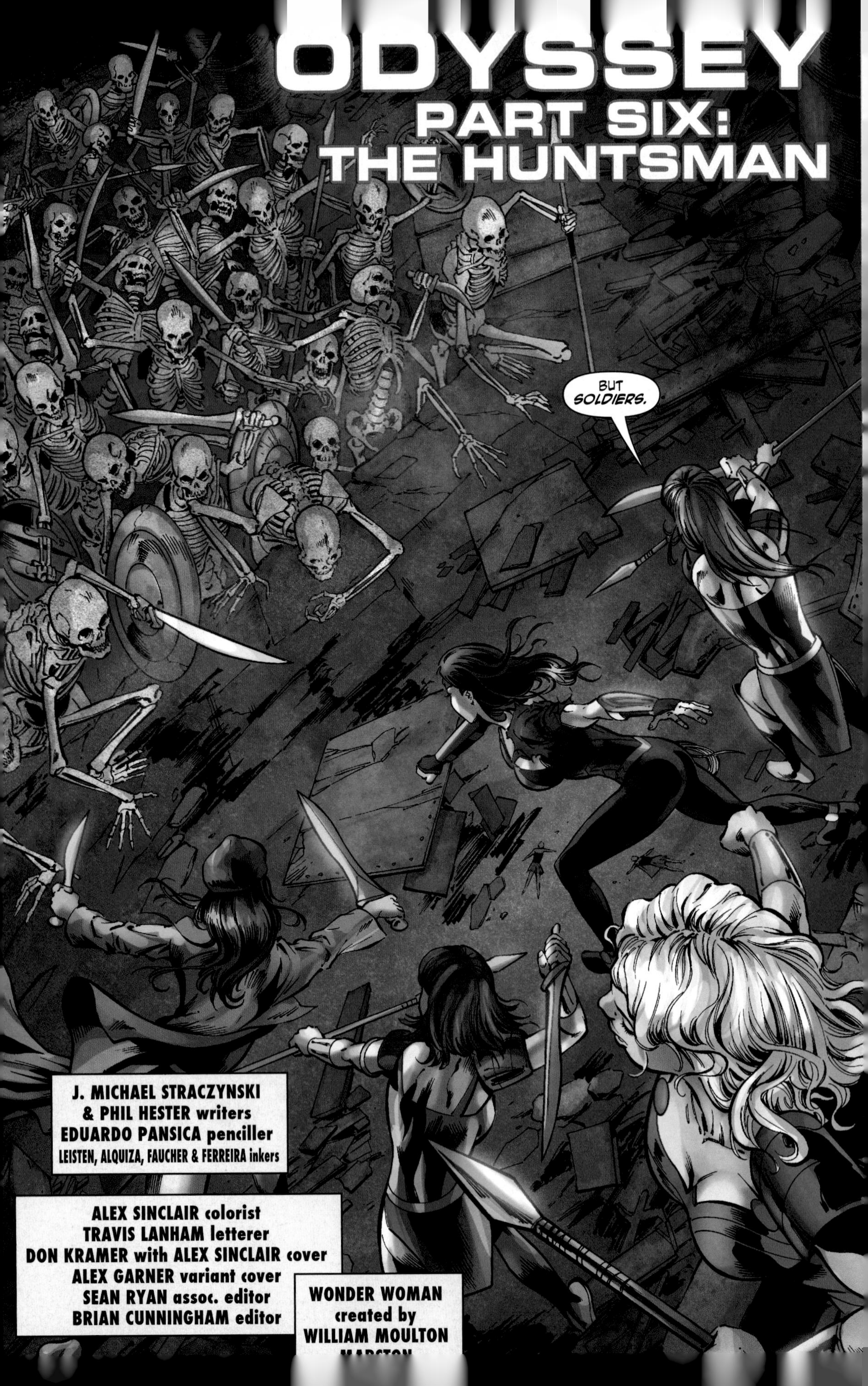
ODYSSEY
PART SIX:
THE HUNTSMAN
BUT SOLDIERS.
J. MICHAEL STRACZYNSKI
& PHIL HESTER writers
EDUARDO PANSICA penciller
LEISTEN, ALQUIZA, FAUCHER & FERREIRA inkers
ALEX SINCLAIR colorist
TRAVIS LANHAM letterer
DON KRAMER with ALEX SINCLAIR cover
ALEX GARNER variant cover
SEAN RYAN assoc. editor
BRIAN CUNNINGHAM editor
WONDER WOMAN
created by
WILLIAM MOULTON

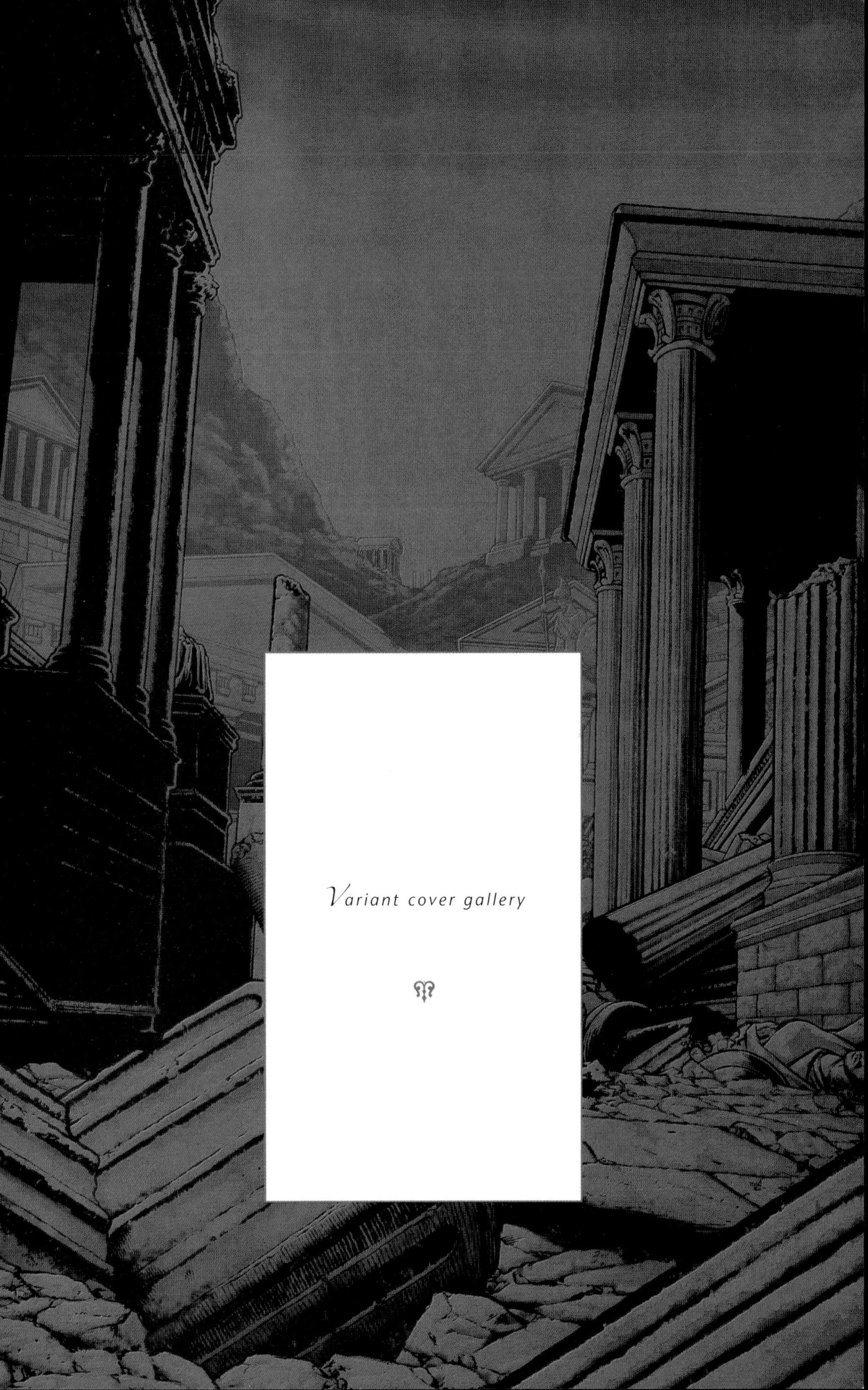

Variant cover gallery

Cover art by Alex Garner

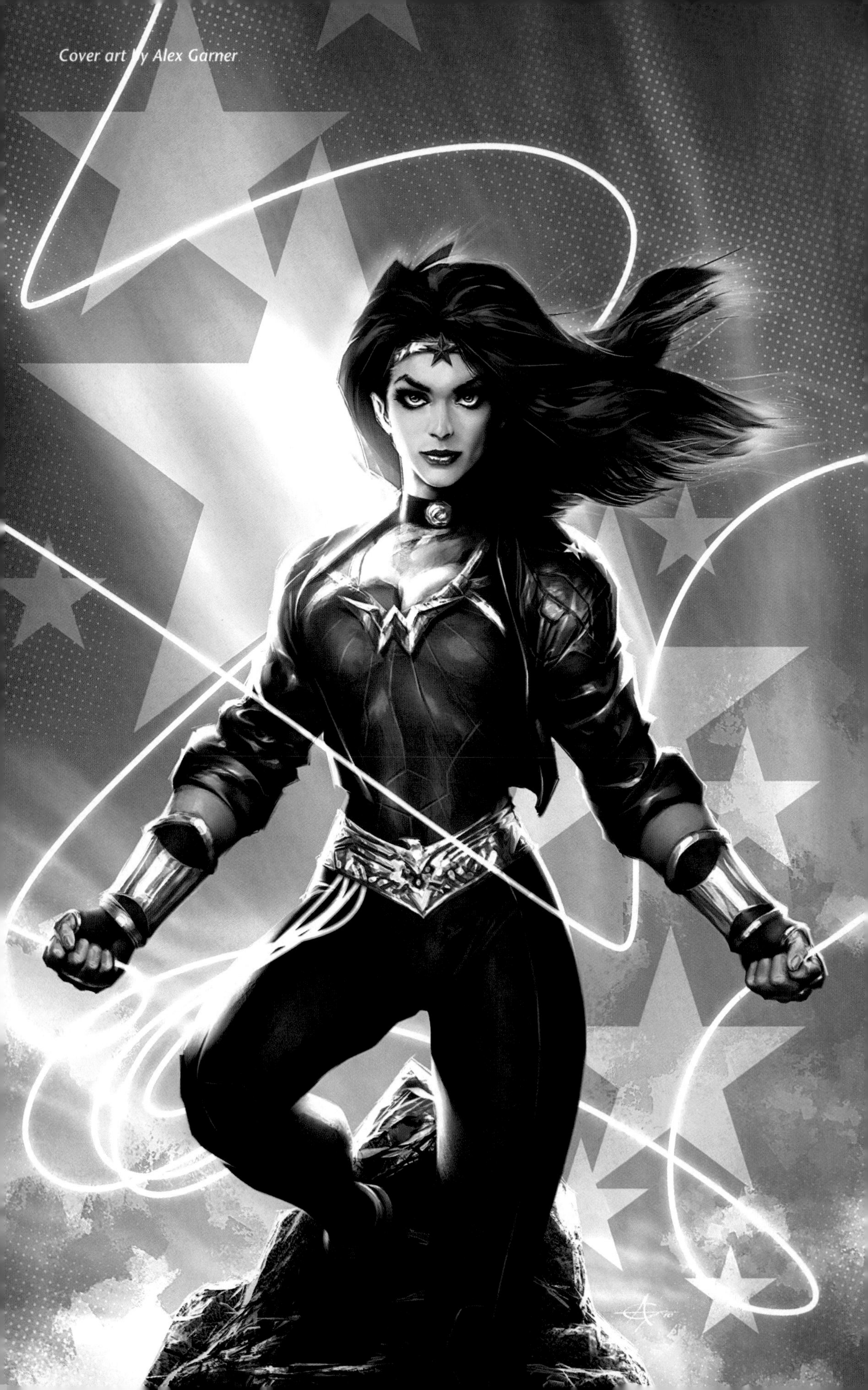

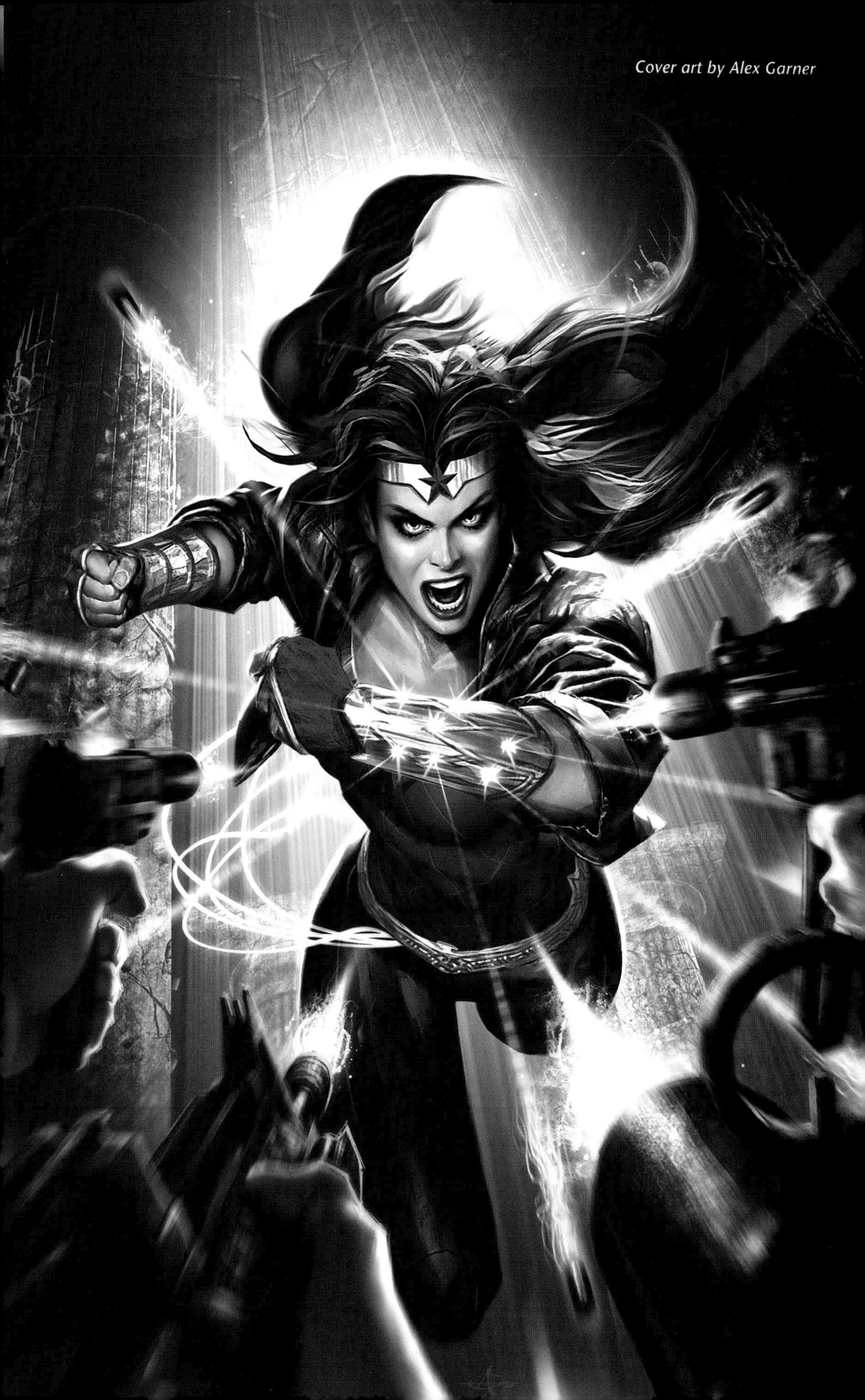

Cover art by Alex Garner

Cover art by J.H. Williams III after H.G. Peter. Cover color by Dave Stewart.

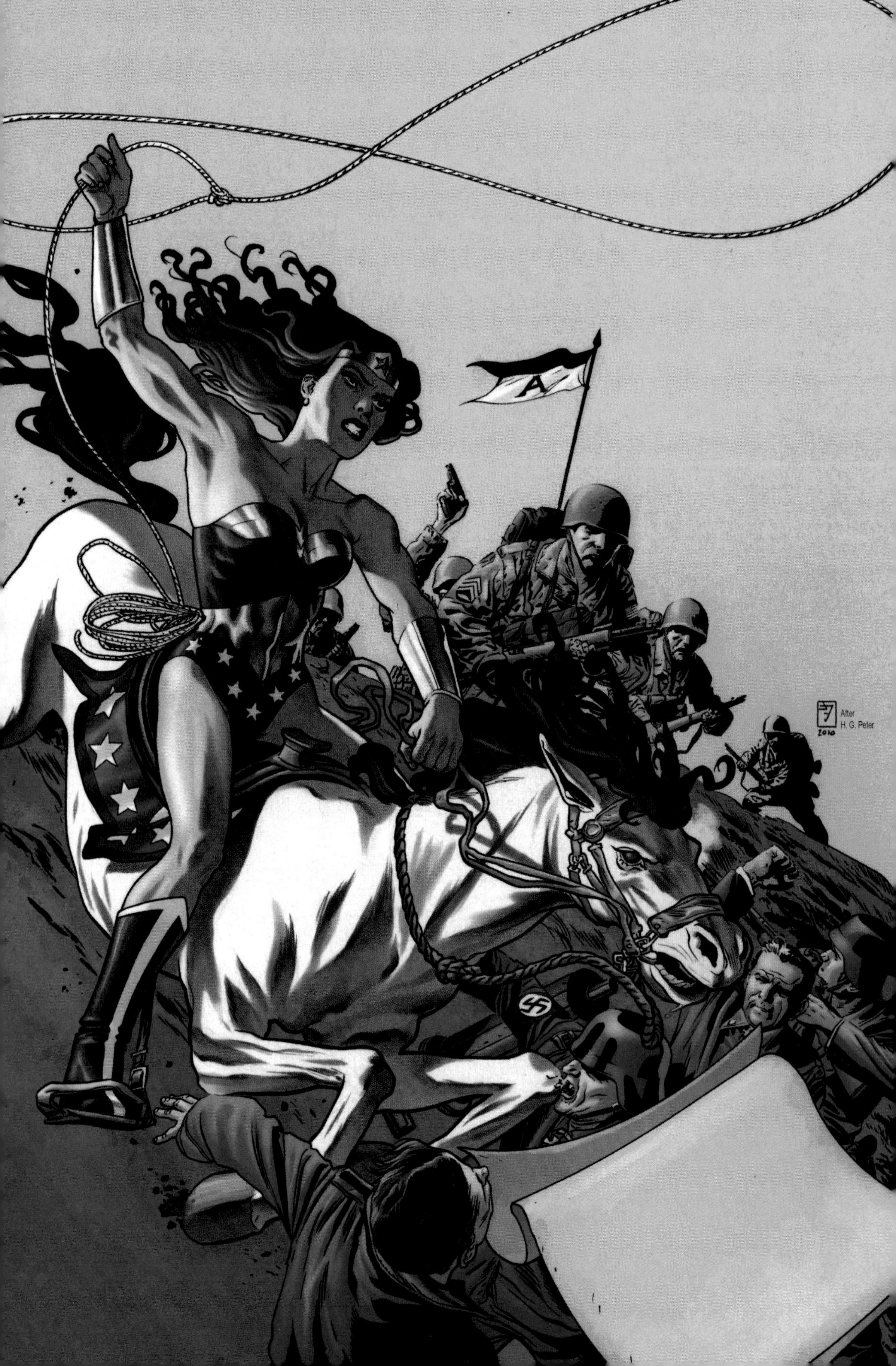
A
After
H. G. Peter
2010

the DC Universe, have undergone substantial changes over the years, Wonder Woman has remained pretty much the same in appearance. (With the exception of a mod look used briefly in the 1960s…about which the less said, the better.) What woman only wears one outfit for 70 years? What woman doesn't accessorize? And more to the point, as many women have lamented over the years…how does she fight in that thing?

"So my mission statement going into Wonder Woman was real simple: If we were to design her today, without any prior history…what would she look like?

"This is a character that is interesting enough and compelling enough to merit being in the top twenty books at minimum…so why was she languishing? The reason, I felt, was that she'd concretized over the years, had turned into this really cool Porsche that people kept in the garage because they were afraid of denting it rather than going flat-out on the open road. She had become, for lack of a better word, stuffy. She became the mom of the girl next door you wanted to date.

"This was really underscored to me when I used Wonder Woman in Brave and the Bold #33, and many were appalled that Wonder Woman told a joke…that she flirted…that she was relaxed and having fun. One podcaster said that Wonder Woman had become like his grandmother, and he didn't like to see his grandmother being flirty.

"It seemed to me that the only way to address the situation and turn the character around was to go in prepared to make massive changes in how we think about Wonder Woman. It wasn't going to work with half-measures. We had to be willing to go the extra mile. We had to be bold.

"So we came at this from a 21st century perspective. Visually, I wanted her to look strong and tough but still quite beautiful. Let's give her clothes that she can fight in, that add to her presence and her strength and her power. It took a while for us to get there, precisely because we've all become so locked-in to how we see her character, but in time we came to a final design.

"Rather than have the W symbol all over the place on her wardrobe, I wanted to highlight it in one area and make that our statement, letting everything else feel more youthful and street-wise. The exception would be the bracelets, which would be solid on the outer side, with a stylized, almost handwritten W symbol there so that when she crosses her arms you get the full effect. And if she hits you with it, it leaves a W mark. She signs her work.

"None of this would work, however, without a strong character behind it. I wanted to free her up from the weight of a lot of her supporting universe so that we could see who she was. Guys tend to see women in terms of what role they play—mother, girlfriend, wife—instead of who they are on their own terms. But I didn't simply want to eradicate all of it and destroy the work of those who came before me.

"So the solution was to tweak time: at some point about 20 years ago or so, the time stream was changed.

Paradise Island was destroyed, and Diana as an infant was smuggled out before her mother was killed along with most of the others. She was raised by guardians sent with her, and some surviving Amazons, so she has a foot in two worlds, the urban world and the world of her people, which still exists in the shadows, underground. So we keep what makes her an Amazon but mix it up with a more modern perspective.

"Those who can see those two worlds know that something has changed, and they try to get Diana to see that, but she only knows what she's seen and experienced.

"To solve the problem before them she must a) find out who attacked Paradise Island and why, b) stop those who are trying to kill the remaining Amazons now, c) rescue any more surviving Amazons, and d) find some way to straighten out the timeline and reconcile what was to what is. So we continue to get glimpses of Wonder Woman as she was juxtaposed against Diana as she is.

"The result—storywise and visually—is a character who is fiery, dynamic, a bit more vulnerable (she's still working her way up to her full set of powers), tough, determined and smart and, due to her background, tragic. She keeps her roots in the Amazonian universe while growing up in a more modern setting. The result will, we hope, be a redesign that is as current with the zeitgeist of the 21st century as the original was with 1941."